Legal Systems in Conflict

Legal History of North America

Legal Systems in Conflict

PROPERTY AND SOVEREIGNTY IN MISSOURI, 1750–1860

Stuart Banner

University of Oklahoma Press : Norman

Also by Stuart Banner

Anglo-American Securities Regulation: Cultural and Political Roots, 1690–1860 (Cambridge and New York, 1998)

Library of Congress Cataloging-in-Publication Data

Banner, Stuart, 1963–
Legal system in conflict: property and sovereignty in Missouri, 1750–1860 / by Stuart Banner.
p. cm. — (Legal history of North America; v. 7)
Includes bibliographical references and index.
ISBN 0–8061–3182–9 (cloth: alk. paper)
1. Law—Missouri—History. 2. Real property—Missouri—History.
I. Title. II. Series.
KFM7878.B36 2000
346.77804′2—dc21 99-36236
CIP

Legal Systems in Conflict: Property and Sovereignty in Missouri, 1750–1860 is Volume 7 in the Legal History of North America series.

Text design by Gail Carter.

The paper in this book meets the guidelines for permanence and durability of the Committee on Production Guidelines for Book Longevity of the Council on Library Resources, Inc. ∞

1 2 3 4 5 6 7 8 9 10

FOR JILLIAN AND HARRISON,
TWO NATIVES

Contents

Maps

Acknowledgments

For useful advice on the entire manuscript, I would like to thank Gordon Bakken, Charles Cutter, Tom Green, and especially David Langum, who offered suggestions on several occasions. Many more people helped on individual chapters, including Susan Appleton, Morris Arnold, Tamara Detloff, Robert Ellickson, Richard Epstein, Kathy Goldwasser, Michael Grossberg, Richard Helmholz, Bill Jones, Dan Keating, David Konig, Stan Krauss, Richard Lazarus, Steve Legomsky, Lynn LoPucki, Bruce Mann, Ronald Mann, Curtis Milhaupt, Andy Rutten, Bob Thompson, and participants in workshops in the law school and the economics department at Washington University. As the bibliography demonstrates, I owe an enormous debt to the archivists at the Missouri Historical Society. Thanks are also due the archivists at the University of Missouri's Western Historical Manuscripts Collection, the Missouri State Archives, the New-York Historical Society, and the New York office of the National Archives, and to the law librarians at Washington University. For extraordinary research assistance, I thank Joe Fiorill, James McElveen, and Shawn Van Asdale. Portions of this book have previously been published as "Written Law and Unwritten Norms in Colonial St. Louis," *Law and History Review* 14 (1996): 33–80, and "The Political Function of the Commons: Changing Conceptions of Property and Sovereignty in Missouri, 1750–1850," *American Journal of Legal History* 41 (1997): 61–93, and I thank the editors of those two journals for permission to reproduce this material here.

Note on Sources and Translations

Most of the documents cited in the first half of this book are translated from French or Spanish. These documents exhibit a wide range of literacy; many contain phonetic spellings and unusual syntax. The flavor of these documents proved difficult to convey when translating them into English. An initial effort to convert nonstandard eighteenth-century French or Spanish into nonstandard twentieth-century English required making dubious cross-cultural analogies and impossible judgments about levels of education and socioeconomic status. As a result, French and Spanish documents have been translated into standard English, which has the unfortunate effect of obliterating gradations of literacy among French and Spanish speakers, and which sometimes makes the English speakers, whose nonstandard usages have not been corrected or marked with "[sic]," seem less literate than the French and Spanish. An indispensable resource in translating from French has been *A Glossary of Mississippi Valley French, 1673–1850* by John Francis McDermott.

Many of the documents located at the Missouri Historical Society bear no titles, numbers, or other identifying features. In such cases, I have tried to give enough information to enable someone to locate the document in question. This often required assigning a title. The abbreviation AGI refers to the Historical Society's collection of microfilmed records from the Archivo General de Indias in Seville, Spain. All citations are from the section of the AGI called "Papeles Procedentes de Cuba," which includes most of the surviving records taken out of Louisiana by Spanish officials after the Louisiana Purchase. These are further divided into *legajos* (bundles), which are cited as "leg." in the notes.

Legal Systems in Conflict

Introduction

"We are endeavouring to establish the empire of the laws; and to substitute those laws in the place of the arbitrary Rescripts of proconsular Agents."[1]

This would be a remarkable assertion in any context—one could hardly find a more emphatic or optimistic justification of imperial expansion—but it is all the more worth considering given the time and place in which it was made. The location of the "empire" was present-day Missouri. The would-be empire builder was a minor American government official named Frederick Bates, who correctly understood himself by that initial "we" to be expressing the aims of the government of the United States. The year was 1807, four years after the Louisiana Purchase transferred the area to American control. The arbitrary "proconsular Agents" were the Spanish colonial officials who had governed the area for most of the preceding four decades.

This book is, in a sense, an exploration of what Bates meant. It is about the two legal systems in the area during the decades surrounding the Louisiana Purchase, the Spanish colonial legal system of the second half of the eighteenth century and the American legal system, colonial in its own way, of the first half of the nineteenth century. The Americans who poured into Missouri in the early nineteenth century brought with them notions of *property*, how land was to be owned, and *sovereignty*, how law was to be found, quite different from those dominant in the area in the late eighteenth century. These Americans, a great many of whom were lawyers, transformed the area's legal institutions. The story, like much of American history, especially west of the Atlantic seaboard, is thus one of serial colonization, in which the people overwhelmed by the incoming Anglo-Americans included earlier colonizers from continental Europe as well as Indians.

The book focuses on two basic differences between the area's pre- and post-Purchase legal systems. First, although both systems were composed in principle of a hierarchical structure of written law generated by government officials, the American legal system approximated that ideal in practice much more closely than did the Spanish. In rough outline, law under the Spanish colonial government tended to bubble up from the bottom, as informal unwritten norms tended to constitute rules of decision in contested cases, while law under American rule tended to flow down from the top, in the form of written rules promulgated by authorized government officials. The contrast gave rise to some fierce criticism by both sides.

The second major difference between the Spanish and the American legal systems in Missouri concerned the allocation of property rights in land. From the middle of the eighteenth century to the early nineteenth century, the residents of Missouri farmed, grazed their animals, and gathered wood in common fields. These commons were converted into private landholdings shortly after the Louisiana Purchase.

The book pays particular attention to the clash between these two very different legal cultures occasioned by the Louisiana Purchase, and to the resulting tensions and compromises that became manifest during the period of transition. There is no better way to understand the tacit suppositions of a legal culture than to watch it being imposed upon people unaccustomed to it, and to listen closely to what they have to say about it. And the legal culture of the early-nineteenth-century United States was, in the two respects emphasized here, not too dissimilar from our own legal culture today. There is some value, I think, in telling a story that emphasizes the novelty of features of the American legal system that most Americans normally take for granted because the system is so familiar. Two centuries of accumulated ordinariness can conceal aspects of our lives that would be quite noticeable if seen for the first time. Because of the course colonization took in most parts of the world, most of the stories of this kind that could be told would involve the encounter of a people with writing and a people without writing, a circumstance that would so skew the documentary record as to produce a one-sided account, regardless of the intentions of the author. One advantage of studying a case of serial colonization is that both sides created written records. The opinions of both sides are accessible. Many voices are still not heard—in this book the Indians are almost entirely absent, as indeed are all those who could not write, including many of the area's white residents—but two sides are at least better than one.

The subject is, I hope, interesting enough in its own right to justify this very short book. The book will also fill five historiographical gaps.

None is particularly large or troubling, but cumulatively they warrant some attention.

First, there is a gap in local history. With one stellar recent exception, descriptions of the legal system of eighteenth-century Missouri have been so colored by anti-Spanish bias and condescension to the area's predominantly French residents as to be misleading or downright false.[2] The earliest history of St. Louis describes a world where "[n]otaries public, lawyers, judges, and tribunals were unknown. . . . there was not a solitary instance of civil delinquency, or of crime. Bargains were sealed by a grasp of the hand."[3] Subsequent works recall "easily contented" Creoles who did not mind "an offensively paternal system of law," and "a frank open-hearted joyous people . . . almost entirely devoid of ambition . . . and careless about the acquisition of property."[4] Even the most recent and professional history of St. Louis asserts again "the Creole tendency to accept designated authority without question."[5] This view, as I will show, echoes the disparaging comments of the earliest American lawyers and government officials to arrive after the Louisiana Purchase, but bears little correspondence to the pre-Purchase legal system as it actually operated. The residents of late-eighteenth-century St. Louis and the surrounding towns often litigated against one another, according to consistent and well-established procedures, in government-operated courts. They were constantly acquiring and exchanging property, in carefully documented transactions, by techniques that could be quite complex. This book will, I hope, put to rest the enduring myth of the carefree, unambitious, unlitigious Creole.

The second gap is in colonial history. Colonial legal history once focused almost entirely on the English colonies along the Atlantic. While scattered articles discussed the legal systems of the non-English colonies to the west, particularly that of Louisiana (which still retains traces of its pre-English legal history), these were rarities. Legal history finally reached French and Spanish colonial Arkansas with Morris Arnold's *Unequal Laws unto a Savage Race* (1985) and Mexican colonial California with David Langum's *Law and Community on the Mexican California Frontier* (1987).[6] As historians generally have come to take more of an interest in nonmajority cultures, these books have been joined by others on the legal systems of Spanish Louisiana and Spanish Texas and New Mexico.[7] This book is the first on the legal system of Missouri before the Louisiana Purchase, and the first to examine the transition from Spanish to American law.

Third is a gap in western history. Much has been written recently about lawyers in the American West.[8] Here I focus on one of the earliest groups of lawyers to emigrate west, those who headed out to Missouri in the years after the Louisiana Purchase, men about whom very little has been written apart from the hagiographic capsule biographies that make up so many awful late-nineteenth-century "Bench and Bar of X County" collections. I am interested primarily in two questions. Why were lawyers so eager to move to the western territories? What role did they play in the economic development of the territories? In these respects, Missouri did not differ significantly from other parts of the West, so the conclusions drawn here should be useful in understanding the development of the West generally.

Fourth, a gap exists in economic history. There is an enormous recent economics literature on the allocation of property rights. That literature has sparked renewed attention to the enclosure of European open fields, a centuries-long process that included, among other things, a massive reallocation of rights to use land. Missouri experienced this process in miniature. French colonists established open fields in the eighteenth century; French and American colonists reallocated property rights in the fields in the early nineteenth century, to create the pattern of private landholdings that has been in place ever since. This book is the first to take a close look at open field farming and enclosure in the United States.[9] In so doing, it relates methods of property ownership to issues of local governance, to suggest that there may have been noneconomic reasons for owning productive land in common, reasons that largely evaporated with the transition from Spanish to American colonial rule.

Finally, there is a gap in legal history. Looming behind any work of legal history is a question that is not often addressed explicitly: What causes the law to change? The transition marked by the Louisiana Purchase can help us answer this question, because it serves almost as a natural experiment, in which some characteristics that might plausibly be expected to have influenced the law changed dramatically, while others barely changed at all. I will conclude that the area's legal changes of the early nineteenth century were primarily *culturally* driven; that is, that they were caused much less by the physical surroundings or by economic arrangements than by the ideas of the people who shaped the legal system.

It is a common rhetorical technique to begin a history book by criticizing historians for ignoring the people and events the book discusses, but, despite the lack of much previous attention to the subjects of this book, the criticism would not be warranted here. The characters who populate this story are largely obscure, and for good reason. To the extent any of them are well known, it is for parts of their lives different from the ones studied here. Meriwether Lewis, for example, is mentioned as a territorial official rather than an explorer. James Madison makes an appearance, but only as secretary of state during the Jefferson administration, and only to be badgered by lawyers seeking jobs in the territory newly acquired by the Louisiana Purchase. For the later eighteenth century, the first half of the period covered by this book, Missouri was a remote Spanish colonial outpost. Nothing discussed here had much significance within the larger context of the Spanish empire. In the early nineteenth century, Missouri would become a populous American state, and of course the focus of intense sectional controversy, but larger political issues figure only tangentially in this story. In terms of its legal system, Missouri was significant on a national scale, if at all, only in its representativeness; whatever happened elsewhere in the United States happened in Missouri, too. One cannot make any grand claims as to the importance, then or now, of the particular individuals whose lives make up this book. The value of attending to the details of what they thought and did lies only in the capacity of those details to illuminate aspects of the legal cultures in which they participated, a capacity that exists only because the Louisiana Purchase caused, for a brief period, two very different ways of thinking about law to be present at the same time in the same place.

There are a few issues of terminology that recur throughout the book that are best addressed at the beginning.

First, both the name and the effective geographical boundaries of the place in which these events occurred changed during the period covered by the book. As I will discuss in more detail in chapter 1, the area was generally referred to as "Upper Louisiana" or "western Illinois" (or sometimes just "Illinois") during the years before the Louisiana Purchase. Even afterward, the area was still called "Louisiana" or "Upper Louisiana" for many years. Until a decade or so after the Louisiana Purchase, the name Missouri referred to a local indigenous tribe and to a river, but not to any geographical area. Only in 1812, when the name Louisiana was given to the state that still bears it, did Missouri become the name of the territory in question. The title of the book is thus a bit anachronistic, but the possible alternatives would have required using "Illinois" or "Louisiana" to designate the area, which would have been even more confusing to readers accustomed to the present-day names of the states.

These names were sometimes used to designate a large zone theoretically under the sovereignty of Spain, France, or the United States, but they were also sometimes used to refer more narrowly to that part of the zone actually inhabited by white people. Divergence between these two usages grew smaller over time as white settlement expanded. Because I will be concerned primarily with the way the legal system actually operated, and because it operated only where whites lived, I will necessarily be using geographical terms in the narrower sense. In 1750, "western Illinois" was a tiny physical space, consisting of a handful of French-speaking people living in Ste. Geneviève. By 1860, "Missouri" occupied nearly seventy thousand square miles, and was home to well over a million people.

Second, many of the names used by the various groups in the region in the late eighteenth and early nineteenth centuries are not the names that would likely be chosen by those groups today. It is no longer in fashion, for instance, to limit the term "American" to English-speaking people from the United States—and there were at that time a few groups in the area who might have had equally plausible claims to the name—but that was contemporary usage. The French-speaking majority tended to call themselves (and were called) "French," even though many had lived in North America their entire lives. French people born in North America also sometimes called themselves "Creole," a term used throughout the Caribbean and Latin America to refer to native-born people of European descent.[10] The Spanish speakers, mostly government officials and soldiers, called themselves (and were called) "Spanish," whether or not they were personally from Spain. English-speaking emigrants from the United States called themselves (and were called) "Americans." The members of the various indigenous tribes in the area tended to use their tribal affiliations to describe themselves. Tribal names were also used by the French, Spanish, and Americans who dealt regularly with tribe members. As the general descriptive term, Americans used the word "Indian," the Spanish *indio*, and the French *sauvage*. The French and Spanish also had a common expression for the many residents of the area whose ancestry was part European and part Indian—*métis* in French and *mestizo* in Spanish. There is no good English equivalent. To avoid anachronism and complexity, I will use the same terms people used at the time, despite the possible discordance for modern readers.

Third, I will be speaking much of the "effect" of particular legal rules, and of the extent to which those rules actually "governed" the community or were "followed" by residents. I should make clear at the start what I mean by these words, because each can have at least two different meanings. A written law can lack practical effect for two reasons, which differ only in the subjective experience of the individuals concerned. In the first, the law lacks effect because members of a community do not experience that law as part of the body of rules acknowledged to regulate the community. They may not know of it, or if they do they may not accept the authority of the lawgiver. They do not experience the law as a law. They may act in a way thoroughly consistent with the law but do not understand themselves to be following the law. I may conduct myself in the precise manner prescribed by the law of Japan, for example, but that is not because I experience myself as a member of a community regulated by it. In the second sense, the members of a community *do* understand the law to be regulating them—they *do* experience the law as a law—but they violate it. In either case, one might say that the law lacks effect, or that community members are not following the law, but one would be describing two very different phenomena.

In contemporary American legal culture, the second category is a familiar one. Everyone has examples of laws that lack much of their theoretical effect because they are frequently violated by people who, if candid, would acknowledge that they experience themselves as members of a community governed by the laws in question. This category includes the laws establishing speed limits, the laws prescribing how one calculates income for tax purposes, the laws prohibiting drug use, and so on.

I am primarily concerned here, however, with the first category. When I say that a particular written law had no "effect," I will generally mean to say that the people of whom I am speaking did not experience that law as having any bearing on their lives. The reasons for this conclusion will vary, and will be discussed in subsequent chapters with reference to particular written laws. There was, of course, written law of the second category as well, acknowledged as law but frequently violated. When I intend to refer to that sort of lack of effect, I will be explicit about it.

The realization that written law and actual practice can coincide without any causal connection—that people might be acting exactly as written law says they should without experiencing themselves as following the law, and indeed without any awareness that the law even exists—leads to an evidentiary dilemma. In the absence of a subject's explicit statement that he is following a particular written law, when can his conduct be attributed to the law? In the absence of an explicit rejection of written law or behavior patently at odds with written law, when can one conclude that the subject does not experience himself as following the law? The relationship between law and action in any particular case becomes much more difficult to infer once one abandons the unjustified assumption that action in line with law means action *caused* by law. In the face of this uncertainty, the only way to make do is to pay close attention to the legal texts that exist in a place at any given time, and to accumulate examples of decisions actually being made, to see if any suggestive patterns emerge. This is the strategy I will pursue, for want of any better alternative, throughout the book.

Fourth, and finally, I will often contrast "written law" with "unwritten norms" or "customs." Because these terms have been used in widely different contexts for a long time, they can mean different things to different people. I should clarify how I am using them here. By "written law" I mean any written text issued by an authorized agent of the sovereign. This includes statutes, of course, but it also includes court opinions, which, once written, are commands of the sovereign as much as statutes are. Whether or not the common law was originally formed through the assimilation of unwritten practices, by the nineteenth century it had become an enormous body of written texts, the authority of which derived from their status as texts written by judges rather than as accurate reflections of long-forgotten custom. I emphasize this only because the longstanding Anglo-American tradition of thinking of the common law as *lex non scripta*, and of judicial decisions as attempts to discern the common law rather than pronouncements of it, might cause some readers erroneously to assume that a reference to written law is meant to exclude court opinions. By "unwritten norm" or "custom" I mean any rule that plays a part in governing conduct and that comes from a source other than written law. The word "custom" has a technical legal meaning, which I do not mean to imply here. Nor do I mean, by using either "norm" or "custom," to suggest that there is something organic or primitive or locally generated about the rules at issue here, in contrast to something artificial or advanced or foreign about written law. As will be shown, many of the relevant norms among the pre–Louisiana Purchase residents were most likely the remembered remnants of written law or unwritten practice in the places from which the residents had come, and some were as complex as any written law on the same subject could be.

PART I

France and Spain, 1750–1803

CHAPTER 1

Upper Louisiana

A legal system is both inhabited by and constituted by a particular set of people in a particular place. This chapter will accordingly provide a brief introduction to the residents of Upper Louisiana in the second half of the eighteenth century and to their legal system.

THE RESIDENTS

The earliest legal systems in present-day Missouri belonged to the various indigenous tribes who lived in the area for more than twelve thousand years before Europeans arrived. In the years immediately before white settlement, the largest of these tribes was the Osage, who were most numerous in what is now the southwestern part of the state. The eastern part of the state was inhabited by the Missouri and sometimes by the Illinois.[1] As St. Louis grew into a significant trading post in the later eighteenth century, many other tribes moved toward the surrounding area.[2] Because the governance structures of these tribes were altered when tribe members were forced out of Missouri into the Indian Territory in the early nineteenth century, the only evidence of local indigenous legal practices comes from the writings of the earliest Europeans who came into contact with the Osage. These early accounts suggest that the Osage were governed by hereditary leaders who resolved disputes primarily through mediation, but who could also impose sanctions of banishment or execution in extreme cases.[3] Whatever the nature of pre-European law in the area, all traces of it would effectively vanish in any area controlled by white settlers.

French Canadian fur traders began arriving in Illinois in the late seventeenth and early eighteenth centuries. These initial visits eventually turned into permanent French settlements in what is now southern Illinois, communities that grew steadily over the first half of the eighteenth century.[4] The first permanent European settlement in present-day Missouri was founded in 1750 at Ste. Geneviève by a small group of French families who crossed the Mississippi River from Illinois.[5] The first local census, conducted two years later, found eight households, all with French surnames, comprising seven men, four women, seven children, two "volunteers" (white laborers), and three slaves, all outnumbered by 185 pigs.[6] St. Louis was founded in 1763, approximately at the junction of the Mississippi and Missouri Rivers, by thirty French employees of a New Orleans trading company.[7] As time went on, the area's population increased, unevenly in the early years but steadily thereafter. By 1791 there were over 2,500 people living in six towns, and by 1800 there were over 7,200 people in fifteen towns, spread along a roughly two-hundred-mile north-south stretch of the Mississippi River and a much shorter east-west stretch of the Missouri River.[8] (These population figures include slaves and free blacks, but not Indians.) By 1804, when the first American government official arrived in St. Louis, he reported that "upper Louisiana contains 7876 whites and 1497 Blacks—in all 9373."[9]

These towns occupied an area the residents called either "Illinois" (sometimes "western Illinois") or "Upper Louisiana." The first name reflected social and cultural realities, while the second acknowledged the location of political authority. Throughout the second half of the eighteenth century, the people on both sides of the Mississippi, in what is now eastern Missouri and southern Illinois, formed a single French culture. Movement back and forth across the river was common. One visitor, for instance, remarked on how "short and easy" it was to get from Ste. Geneviève on the western side to Kaskaskia on the eastern; he described the location of St. Louis and Ste. Geneviève with reference to towns on the eastern side; and he identified a resident of Ste. Geneviève as "the richest inhabitant of the country of the Illinois," a locution that makes clear the absence of any cultural distinction between the two sides of the river.[10] This vaguely defined area, the Illinois country, was a long distance from anywhere with a substantial white population. In the days before the steamboat, the trip from New Orleans, for example, usually took eight to ten weeks.[11]

The cultural unity of the Illinois country slowly decomposed over the later eighteenth century, as both sides of the river underwent changes in sovereignty. The east side went to England at the close of the French and Indian War, then to Virginia during the American Revolution, and finally

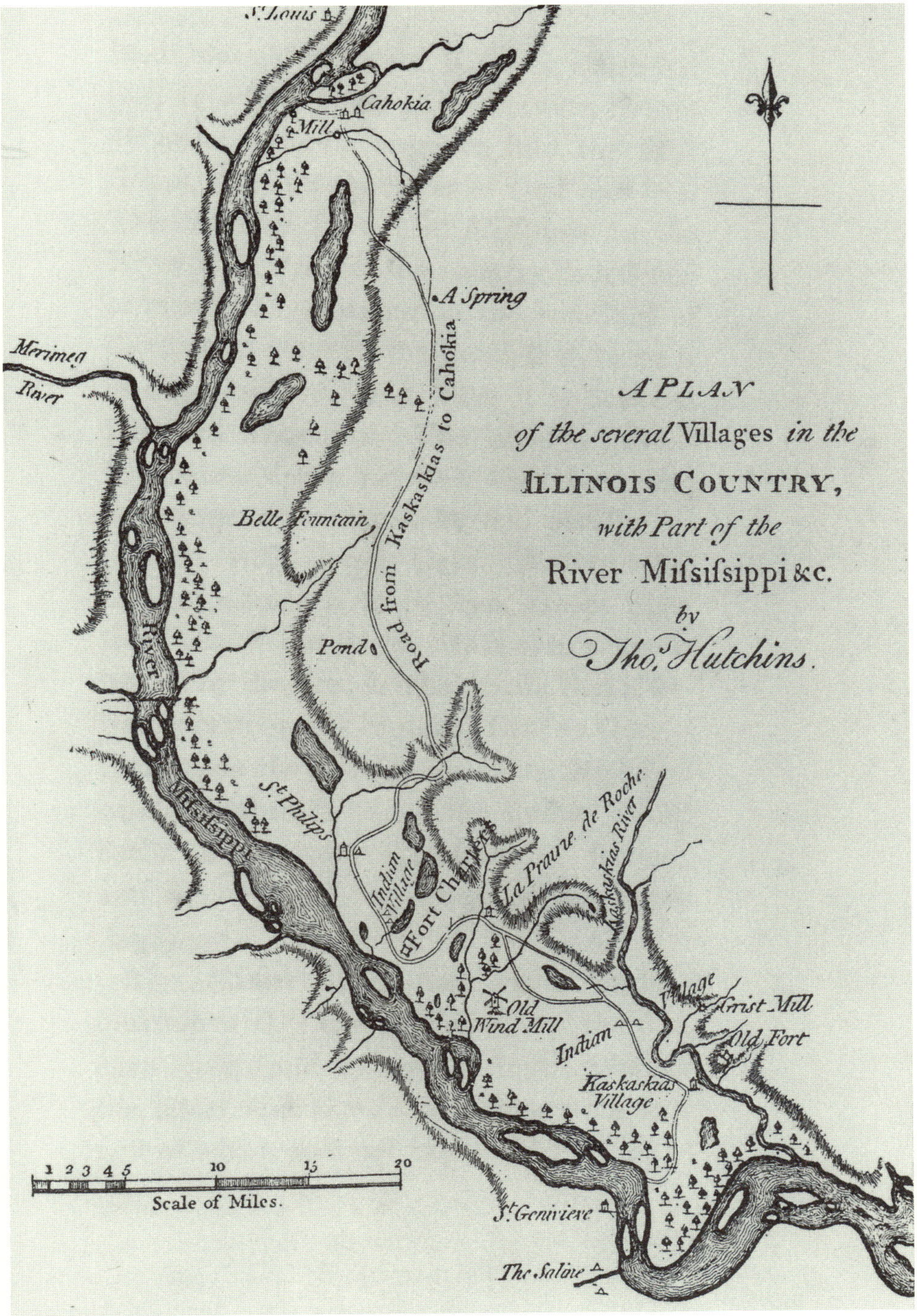

Map 1. Thomas Hutchins's map of the Illinois Country, 1778. There are at this point only two towns west of the Mississippi River, St. Louis (at the top of the map) and Ste. Geneviève (at the bottom), across the river from the older French towns of Cahokia and Kaskaskia. Although the two sides of the river were nominally governed by different sovereigns, the residents formed a single French-speaking culture. (Courtesy of the Missouri Historical Society, St. Louis.)

to the United States when Virginia ceded what became the Northwest Territory. The west side went to Spain after the French and Indian War, and remained under Spanish sovereignty until shortly before the Louisiana Purchase, when Spain ceded it back to France.[12] Except for the earliest years when it was the most thinly populated, therefore, the area was nominally governed by Spain from the beginning of white settlement up through the Louisiana Purchase. Despite the increasing heterogeneity between the two sides of the river, however, there remained a great deal of cross-river contact, among ordinary individuals and between governments. Even at the turn of the century, for instance, the most common route upriver from Ste. Geneviève to St. Louis was on the American side; it required a ferry across, a walk north, and a ferry back.[13]

If the area was western Illinois in a cultural sense, it was Upper Louisiana in a political sense. It lay at the northern edge of the immense Spanish empire. Upper Louisiana was formally governed by a lieutenant governor resident in St. Louis, who oversaw commandants posted in each of the surrounding towns, and who was supported by a small military garrison. This effective merger of military and civil authority was common in Spanish communities in North America. The lieutenant governor was supervised by the governor of Louisiana, located in New Orleans, who in turn reported to Spain. While New Orleans housed the full apparatus of a municipal government, including a *cabildo* (roughly equivalent to a city council) and a local judiciary, there were no comparable official institutions in Upper Louisiana.[14] The lieutenant governor and local commandants exercised all formal government authority.

Despite the formal supervision from New Orleans and Spain, Upper Louisiana enjoyed a large amount of autonomy, for a few reasons. Most obviously, the distance between St. Louis and New Orleans, and the much greater distance between Louisiana and Spain—approximately a two-month voyage each way—made close supervision difficult.[15] But just as important, Upper Louisiana was of little significance to the Spanish government. Its population was minuscule within the context of Spain's colonies as a whole, an empire of several million inhabitants. Upper Louisiana was never profitable, while other colonies were. If the area had any strategic value to Spain, it was as a buffer between the Anglo-Americans east of the Mississippi and the more valuable Spanish possessions in what is now Mexico and the southwest United States.[16] In addition, although in theory a Spanish possession, Upper Louisiana barely contained any Spanish or even Spanish-speaking people apart from the commandants and soldiers. Government business was often conducted in

French rather than Spanish, because, as Lt. Gov. Fernando de Leyba complained, "[t]here is not at this post anyone who can write Spanish even moderately well, unless it be a soldier, of whose services I have not availed myself because of the many errors which he makes."[17] Spanish soldiers were never numerous in the area, to the continuous dismay of the lieutenant governors. "Ylinueses [Illinois] has always been given little attention," one wrote in disgust. "It is without sufficient forces to defend itself, as only forty soldiers, including two sergeants and one drummer, at the present time are its total garrison."[18] These factors combined to limit the effectiveness of the political authority theoretically possessed by Spanish government officials outside the region.

A relatively small number of Spanish officials and soldiers thus found themselves largely on their own, governing several thousand people, most of whom spoke French and identified themselves as French. Anglo-Americans, a tiny minority at first but a significant part of the population toward the end of the eighteenth century, identified themselves as Americans. Spanish officials were painfully aware of how few of the residents felt any loyalty to the government that had power over them. One reported in 1792 that if war ever occurred in the area, the "Anglo-Americans . . . would take the part of the United States," and the French would side with France.[19] To govern at all in the early years, the Spanish delegated formal authority to local French leaders.[20] In later years, they appointed French-speaking lieutenant governors with French surnames, who could govern more as members of the community than as outsiders.[21]

Spanish officials responded to this gap between their theoretical and actual power by allowing the French residents of Upper Louisiana to retain the institutions of self-government they possessed before they lived under Spanish sovereignty. In the Illinois country east of the Mississippi River in the first half of the eighteenth century, villages had elected "syndics," local officials with authority over matters of what would today be called city planning—issues concerning roads, bridges, fences, and so on. The practice of electing syndics appears to have come from northern France.[22] West of the river, the villages under Spanish control in the second half of the century continued to elect syndics, who continued to exercise the same authority they had exercised earlier. In 1784, for example, "[b]y virtue of the authority given us by the people, by whom we are elected for this purpose," the eight syndics of St. Louis established "fixed and inalterable rules for the construction and maintenance of streets, bridges and canals of the village."[23] Syndics also inspected the fences surrounding the common fields, and imposed fines on residents whose sections of the fence were inadequate.[24] It was apparently not until 1792, and then again in 1795—after three decades of tolerating their authority—that the governor in New Orleans formally ratified the existence of the syndics.[25]

Local Spanish officials also left in place the old Illinois practice, also traceable back to France, of decision making by local assemblies.[26] These regular gatherings of the adult men of a village typically voted on agricultural matters—how the fences around the common fields should be fixed, whether to enlarge a common field, and so on. Such meetings could also be occasions for drawing up petitions urging government officials toward some course of action.[27] Again, this degree of direct democracy was not the product of any Spanish government planning; it was an accommodation made by understaffed officials in Upper Louisiana who otherwise might have faced difficulty in governing effectively.

Not much is known about most of the residents of Upper Louisiana. Most have left no written traces. Excluding Indians, roughly a quarter were black slaves; they appear now only in contracts as property bought and sold, and occasionally in court records when they were killed, but again only as property lost.[28] Approximately 6 percent were free blacks, some of whom were able to accumulate surprisingly large property holdings. The 1803 estate auction of "negra livre" Juaneta Forchet, for example, included a plot of land and enough property to occupy a five-page list. A former slave named Esther owned numerous tracts in St. Louis.[29] The majority of free blacks who were not property owners, however, are almost completely invisible now. White women made up nearly 30 percent of the population. They show up today primarily as parties to litigation and contracts, especially marriage contracts, in both respects in numbers large enough to suggest that they were able to exert control over the disposition of a significant fraction of the region's property.[30] Such power was especially likely to be wielded by the wives of the wealthiest local merchants, men whose livelihood required frequent absences from home for long-distance travel.[31]

The remaining 40 percent were white men. Most were illiterate or nearly so; their names survive today only next to their marks, beneath contracts or depositions drawn up by other people. These men were mostly small-time Indian traders, lead miners, and farmers. Spanish officials were constantly searching for ways to encourage more residents to take up farming. Even grants of large blocks of free land often could not accomplish this goal, because, as one lieutenant governor pointed out, "[t]hese people are interested in commerce and not in farming because the latter gives them little or no gain, while the former supports them and makes them rich." As a result, he complained, "1. There is always a scarcity of food at this post. 2. The classes of people are so mixed up that one cannot tell who is a farmer and who is a merchant."[32]

Censuses did not include Indians, and so there is no reliable information about the number of Indians in colonial Upper Louisiana. Some lived in the towns, while many more lived close enough to trade regularly in the towns. Many of the area's residents counted as "white" or "black" in the censuses were of partial Indian ancestry as well, particularly in the later years.[33] A substantial number of the Indians in Upper Louisiana were slaves. Although Indian slavery was prohibited by the Spanish government in 1769, it nevertheless remained common, in large part because people who already owned Indian slaves in 1769 were allowed to retain them, and many of these slaves were young children at the time. Censuses conducted in 1770 for the purpose of determining who would remain in slave status revealed the presence of ninety-six Indian slaves in St. Louis and Ste. Geneviève, at a time when the combined white population of the two towns was only around a thousand.[34] Although transactions involving Indian slaves were illegal after 1769, there is evidence of many sales after that date.[35] Free Indians, in turn, owned black slaves on occasion. In 1800, for example, Piwolene, a member of the Chavanon nation, sold a sixteen-year-old black woman to Jacques Cottu for five hundred piastres; there is no indication that anyone found any anomaly in the sale.[36] Apart from such transactions, the Indians of Upper Louisiana left little written evidence.

Some of the area's residents, however, left a large written record. Upper Louisiana was socially and economically dominated by a small and tightly connected merchant elite, a group of intermarried French families whose cultural and financial sophistication was utterly at odds with the popular conception of frontier life.[37] Their business consisted primarily of importing manufactured goods through New Orleans and the Great Lakes, exchanging the goods with Indians for animal skins and furs, and then exporting the animal products for eventual sale on the east coast and in Europe. But this was just one part of a much wider role. Because they regularly imported manufactures, these men were also provisioners to the area's white population. The estate of Pierre Laclède, one of the founders of St. Louis, included 781 pounds of coffee, eight gross of awls, three dozen "common hats," and a wide variety of styles of handkerchiefs. He may have intended to use some of this himself, and some was destined for the Indians, but some, especially the coffee, must have been intended for sale to whites, nearly all of whom were coffee drinkers.[38] These merchants were also the only sources of credit in the area. In a local economy chronically short of specie and lacking any financial institutions, the promissory notes accepted by the merchants in payment for goods served as currency. The papers of Auguste Chouteau, the most successful of the merchants, are full of promissory notes from various people, including many of Chouteau's own employees.[39] This reliance on promissory notes resulted in some spectacularly complex networks of credit, in which debts were usually denominated in units of peltries.[40]

The merchants of Upper Louisiana were simultaneously guardians of highbrow French culture. Some of these men had remarkable libraries, considering the geographical conditions.[41] In colonial St. Louis, as Jay Gitlin has observed, "French merchants were reading Voltaire while, far to the east, Daniel Boone was 'trailblazing' in the supposedly unmarked wilderness."[42] Elite merchants corresponded with trading partners all over North America and Europe, and often traveled as well. As a result, they were the area's primary sources of national and international news, and in effect became Upper Louisiana's unofficial emissaries to the variety of peoples outside the region, including Spanish officials in New Orleans, the surrounding Indian nations, the English in Canada, and the Americans across the river.

CIVIL DISPUTES

The earliest French residents of Upper Louisiana brought with them a simple pair of procedures for resolving civil disputes. Throughout French North America in the decades preceding the colonization of Upper Louisiana, most civil litigation had been resolved through a summary process, in which the parties would state their differences to a judge who would reach an oral decision immediately. In more complex cases, the person seeking relief submitted a written complaint to the judge, along with supporting documents. His or her opponent could then do the same, after which the parties and any necessary witnesses would appear in court for questioning by the judge. This pair of procedures was followed in Canada, and was most likely followed in the early eighteenth century in New Orleans and the Illinois country as well. Arbitration—an informal proceeding in which the parties would submit a dispute to a panel of their neighbors chosen by them to adjudicate the particular case, rather than to a government official—was also a common practice in French Illinois, and probably in other parts of French North America.[43]

The surviving evidence of litigation practices in Upper Louisiana before the arrival of the Spanish is slight, but it suggests that the French residents duplicated these procedures after arriving in the area. In January 1769, for instance, one Dame Gadobert submitted a petition to the commandant in Ste. Geneviève, "saying that she is owed by the man called Catalan a sum of 1652 livres 15 sols," and expressing her "fear that Catalan might be obliged to contract some other engagement which would put her in the position to lose such a legitimate debt." Dame Gadobert accordingly asked to have Catalan's property seized and given to her to satisfy the debt. In a short written order, the commandant appears to have granted her request.[44] Other contemporary evidence from Ste. Geneviève suggests the use of a similar process, which corresponds well with what is known of earlier French colonial procedure in more complex cases.[45] (The summary oral procedure for simpler cases would have been unlikely to leave a written record.) There is also evidence of an instance of arbitration in Ste. Geneviève from the same period.[46] The earliest French residents of Upper Louisiana thus appear, unsurprisingly, to have recreated methods of resolving civil disputes that were familiar to them from other parts of North America.

In late 1769, after subduing an attempted uprising by the French residents of New Orleans, Gov. Alexander O'Reilly issued a set of "Instructions upon the manner of instituting suits, civil and criminal" in Louisiana.[47] Section 1 of these instructions, titled "Of Civil Judgments in General," set forth the procedures that were thenceforth to be followed in resolving civil disputes.

These new procedures were quite similar to those that were already being followed in Upper Louisiana. In cases worth more than one hundred livres, the petitioner was to submit a written statement of his or her claim to the judge. The defendant was then to file a counterstatement, giving the opposing view of the case. After opportunities for a reply and a rejoinder, the judge was to decide the case if possible; otherwise, he was to examine witnesses. This examination was to be conducted outside the presence of either party, but the witnesses' testimony was to be transcribed and made available to the parties if they wished, before the judge reached a decision. The judge was then to "attentively examine" any documents submitted by the parties, "and determine the suit by condemning the debtor to payment, or discharging him from the demand, according to the merits of the case." O'Reilly's instructions provided no guidance in cases worth less than one hundred livres. Judges were left free to resolve such minor disputes without resort to formal procedures. This distinction between major and minor cases, and the respective procedures available for each, had been a feature of Spanish law since at least the middle of the sixteenth century, and had already been employed in Spain's other North American colonies.[48] Because the distinction also mirrored earlier French colonial practice, and was accordingly already familiar to the French residents of Upper Louisiana, O'Reilly's instructions could not have met with much local opposition.

The 1769 order also took the first step in inserting the Louisiana courts into the Spanish colonial court hierarchy. In ordinary cases, an appeal could be taken to the New Orleans cabildo. In cases where the sum at issue was exceptionally large, the appeal would be taken to some other tribunal, as yet undetermined. This gap was filled two years later, when the Spanish government created a special tribunal in Havana to adjudicate appeals from Louisiana. This new court was in turn supervised by the *audiencia* of Santo Domingo.[49]

In early 1770, O'Reilly issued a second order on the subject, which adapted the 1769 instructions to conditions in Upper Louisiana, where there were no lawyers, no notaries, and no government officials able to serve as judges other than the lieutenant governor and the local commandants.[50] "The Lieutenant-Governors of Illinois and Natchitoches not having an adviser with whom they can consult on judicial matters," O'Reilly explained, "they should only judge and determine suits whose judgments do not exceed the quantity of one hundred pesos." In suits for more than that amount, the lieutenant governor was to act as a judge right up until a decision was needed, at which point he was to "remit the court documents to the Governor-General [in New Orleans] for his decision." Because of the lack of notaries to ensure the authenticity of the witnesses' testimony, all interrogations of witnesses were to take place before two *testigos de assistencia*, observers unaffiliated with either party.

These two orders effectively constituted the civil procedure of Upper Louisiana from 1770 through 1804. Copies of the orders were present in St. Louis throughout the period, and were duly handed down from each lieutenant governor to his successor.[51] The second order modified earlier French practice in two ways. First, in the serious cases, judges were now in principle stripped of their decision-making power. This hundred-peso limit, however, was often not followed in practice. Lieutenant governors in St. Louis and the commandants in the satellite towns sometimes did refer cases to New Orleans for decision, but they also routinely decided cases involving amounts greater than a hundred pesos.[52] The great distance between St. Louis and New Orleans most likely caused litigants and government officials to prefer faster local decisions to strict compliance with O'Reilly's instructions. The second modification of earlier practice was the introduction of the testigos de assistencia, or, as the French in Upper Louisiana were more likely to refer to them, *témoins d'assistance*. Because no such role exists in Anglo-American law, there is no good English translation for this phrase. "Attending witnesses" would be a literal translation, but the témoins d'assistance were witnesses only to the testimony of others, not to the underlying events giving rise to litigation, and they had no role to play beyond passively listening to the testimony. Their use may have been welcomed by French litigants arguing before Spanish officials, because they facilitated community oversight of official inquiries. As the litigants were prohibited from being present during the questioning of witnesses, the témoins d'assistance were likely to be the only French people apart from the witnesses themselves capable of monitoring the progress of an interrogation. Because témoins d'assistance could be easily obtained locally, their use did not delay litigation or make it significantly more expensive, and so they became the norm in Upper Louisiana.

Apart from these two modifications, Spain's assumption of sovereignty over Upper Louisiana thus does not appear to have led to any significant change in the way government officials resolved civil disputes. One very simple 1800 case provides an example of how this process worked in practice. The dispute arose in New Madrid, the southernmost of the towns in the area, founded in 1789 by a group of Americans. (New Madrid is best known today for having been the epicenter of a series of severe earthquakes, probably the largest in recorded North American history, in late 1811 and early 1812.[53]) The case began with a written petition to commandant Henri Peyroux from Jacques Cottu, a trader in the town. Cottu alleged that while he was away on business, Adrien Langlois came to his house to collect some tobacco which Cottu owed Langlois's employer. According to Cottu's petition, his wife gave Langlois the key to the storehouse where the tobacco was located. Langlois took the tobacco,

> but instead of closing the door, it appears that he left it to a slave, who came to bring back the key to the petitioner's wife, who thought it closed. It was only the day before yesterday that [petitioner] heard, from Sr. Pasquin, who occupies the house in which his storehouse is, that not only was the door left open but that one of the hinges of the door had been broken. [Petitioner] went to inspect his storehouse and saw what he had expected, that someone had stolen from him.

Cottu asked that Langlois be ordered to compensate him for the stolen tobacco.

Peyroux read this petition and sent it to Langlois the same day. The following day, Langlois submitted his response. "Jacques Cottu that very day was under the influence of drink," Langlois contended, and "wanting perhaps to go himself to see his tobacco, may have left the door open." In light of the apparent delay of several days between Cottu's return to New Madrid and his discovery of the alleged theft, Langlois concluded, "all this seems strange." Later that day, Peyroux sent Langlois's response to Cottu, who submitted a reply the same day, reiterating his allegation that Langlois had exhibited "unpardonable negligence and carelessness" in failing to lock the door. Peyroux sent the reply to Langlois, who responded again the following day.

The very next day, Peyroux took the testimony of five witnesses, inspected the storehouse himself, and reached a decision. Peyroux concluded that regardless of whether any tobacco had ever been stolen, and regardless of who was at fault for leaving the door unlocked, the storehouse was in such bad condition that anyone could have entered without even going through the door. He accordingly denied Cottu's request for compensation.[54] The procedure used for deciding this case was typical of the means used by government officials to resolve civil disputes in Upper Louisiana. The entire litigation lasted only four days. It began with written arguments presented by the parties, continued with the commandant's interrogation of witnesses, and then concluded with a prompt decision.

Many civil disputes, especially the more difficult cases, were decided not by government officials but by arbitrators chosen by the litigants. Sometimes cases were difficult because the facts were not easily ascertained. In St. Louis in 1797, for example, Charles Sanguinet brought suit on behalf of Augustin Lapommeraye, against the estate of André Roy, to collect a debt Roy "was to pay to Lapommeraye after his voyage on the river des Moins where he died." Sanguinet supplemented his petition with a note bearing Roy's signature, and with the testimony of witnesses who had heard Roy speak of the debt while he was still alive. The representative of Roy's estate conceded that the note had been signed by Roy, but argued that Roy might already have paid it. Roy's representative explained that he had "no direct or indirect knowledge of the affairs of the late André Roy," and accordingly asked the lieutenant governor to refer the matter to arbitrators. The lieutenant governor did so. Each party chose one arbitrator. The two arbitrators examined the business records left by Roy, and agreed that because "a subsequent charge exists" against

Lapommeraye in Roy's records, "it would seem that this note must have been paid, and that it should be considered null and cancelled." The lieutenant governor approved the arbitrators' decision.[55]

One type of difficult factual question referred to arbitrators concerned the valuation of property. In 1796, for instance, an Indian slave named Joseph attempted to purchase the freedom of his daughter Victoria, who was owned by Gabriel Cerré. (Spanish law guaranteed slaves the right to purchase their own freedom. If a slave and a master could not agree on a price, the slave could ask a court to set a fair price.[56]) Joseph's petition explained that Cerré "demanded the sum of one thousand piastres, an exorbitant amount. The petitioner hopes you will take that into consideration, that you will be kind enough to order a just evaluation." Lt. Gov. Zenon Trudeau ordered Cerré to respond. Cerré argued that Joseph

> has never been in a position to make such an expenditure and the steps he takes today have been suggested to him by people whose only motive for making such a sacrifice is one of debauchery. I take the liberty of mentioning to you that I have already refused one thousand piastres for this woman for whom only the reasons of attachment both on my part and on the part of my wife made us decide not to part with her.

Trudeau promptly ordered each party to choose an arbitrator for the valuation of Victoria. Trudeau appointed a referee, in case the parties' arbitrators could not agree. Joseph's arbitrator estimated Victoria's worth at "six hundred piastres in currency of the country [i.e., peltries] or five hundred piastres in cash." Cerré's arbitrator came in with a figure of eight hundred piastres in cash. The referee also valued Victoria at eight hundred piastres, which then became the price adopted by Trudeau.[57]

Cases could also be difficult, and thus amenable to arbitration, when the operative rule of substantive law was not easily determined. In 1800, Jacques Clamorgan shipped something (most likely furs) to New Orleans on a boat owned by Charles Sanguinet. A dispute arose over whether, when Clamorgan reimbursed Sanguinet for the port fees in New Orleans, Clamorgan could pay in furs (as he wished) or whether he had to pay in cash (as Sanguinet wished). Arbitrators, one appointed by each party, determined that Clamorgan had to pay in cash.[58] Elizabet Vachard's 1785 suit on behalf of her son Jacques against Silvestre Labadie raised another issue typical of the sort decided by arbitrators. Jacques Vachard had sent Labadie a large amount of lead, in a boat driven by Vachard's brother Louis, to satisfy a debt Jacques owed Labadie. Labadie ordered Louis Vachard to tie the boat in front of Labadie's house, but that night, before the lead could be unloaded, the boat drifted away and the lead was lost. Who was to bear the loss, Labadie or the Vachards? The arbitrators "judged it fit that the boat and its cargo stay and remain entirely the responsibility of its guardian, because he failed to hand it over to Labadie the same evening." Although Labadie had ordered Vachard to tie up the boat, "appearances indicate that the guardian did not consider himself discharged of the boat, since he took precautions to watch over it and take care of it during the night."[59] Such cases were difficult, not because the facts were hard to gather, but because even after the facts were known the correct outcome was not apparent. Cases like this were often referred to arbitrators.

In the first couple of decades after Spain assumed sovereignty, arbitration was more of a practice held over from earlier years than an explicit preference of the Spanish government. Spanish officials in Upper Louisiana were most likely happy to delegate to arbitrators the responsibility for reaching difficult decisions, and arbitration provided another useful method of allowing the French community to continue to govern itself in a limited way. Arbitration had a long history in Spanish law, and so it would have been familiar to officials and their legal advisors.[60] In the late Spanish period, however, the preference for arbitration became official policy. By 1799, Gov. Manuel Gayoso de Lemos could advise Charles Dehault Delassus, the new lieutenant governor in St. Louis, that

> [i]n all disputes between interested parties or claims between residents, when they are not matters that might be injurious to the government or to the general public, it is best for the parties concerned to leave such cases to the decision of the arbitral judges or friendly arbitrators. All the judges must try to prevent the residents from becoming entangled in lawsuits.[61]

As a result, when Amos Stoddard arrived in St. Louis in 1804 to assume control of the area on behalf of the American government, he reported that "[i]t is customary here to have all matters settled by arbitration."[62]

Cases raising difficult legal questions were also often referred to New Orleans, to be resolved by the governor with the assistance of the *auditor de guerra*, the most prominent of his legal advisors.[63] Local officials in such cases would gather the evidence and send it to New Orleans; the litigants themselves did not normally make the trip. Even so, this procedure ensured that a dispute could not be resolved for at least several months, which prolonged litigation well beyond the short period it ordinarily lasted. The complex divorce litigation between Pierre DeVolsay and

Elizabet de Villiers, for instance, lasted at least two years. Neither was blameless. DeVolsay mistreated de Villiers during the marriage; she responded by selling all his assets while he was in New Orleans on business, taking the proceeds, and moving across the river to Cahokia to live with another man. After repeated petitions from both sides over a period of several months, each supported with affidavits from witnesses, an exasperated Lt. Gov. Fernando de Leyba noted:

> having carefully considered all this, and finding no person and no jurisconsult with whom we might confer regarding this affair in order to pass a judgment; we refer this affair, and the papers produced for us by Sr. Devolsey and the Dame his wife, to the tribunal of Monsieur the Governor general of Louisiana, that he may judge as he sees fit.

If the governor reached any decision, it has been lost. All that remains is a comment underneath Leyba's referral, signed by his successor, Pedro Piernas: "Sent to the Auditor de Guerra, so he can tell me what the law is."[64]

A similarly thorny question was raised by the inadvertent mortal shooting in 1785 of Baptiste, a black slave belonging to Marie Therèse Chouteau, while Baptiste was helping to capture runaway Indian slaves. Chouteau sued Joseph Marie Papin, the organizer of the capture (and Chouteau's son-in-law), to recover Baptiste's "entire value, which is at least a thousand piastres." She argued that "Papin acted inconsiderately, in his haste failing to recognize that he was risking the slave's life, either at the hands of the runaways or otherwise." Papin responded that he should not be held liable, because "my mother-in-law's slave was killed in a confrontation authorized by the government, . . . and initiated by the appearance of two dangerous runaway slaves." Faced with the difficult question of who should bear the loss, Lt. Gov. Francisco Cruzat sent the record of the case to Gov. Estevan Miró, who ordered that Chouteau's loss should not be paid by Papin, but by the owners of the runaway slaves.[65]

Many civil disputes in Upper Louisiana were thus resolved according to the procedures specified in O'Reilly's instructions of 1769 and 1770, procedures that did not differ significantly from those previously used by the French residents. Many other civil disputes were referred to arbitration, also a practice used earlier by the French. Some disputes raising particularly difficult legal questions were sent to New Orleans, to be decided with the assistance of legal advisors.

There is little in this process to suggest that the residents had a distaste for litigation, or that they had any greater of a preference for conciliation than Americans have today. In early-nineteenth-century Mexican California and New Mexico, by contrast, dispute resolution procedures were designed to encourage settlement.[66] The first step in civil litigation was a conciliation hearing before a judge. Each party was required to bring an hombre bueno, or "good man," whose task was solely to recommend to the judge a fair settlement. The témoins d'assistance of Upper Louisiana, like the hombres buenos, were selected by the parties and were not advocates, but the témoins d'assistance had no analogous role in promoting conciliation. There is no indication from the surviving records of litigation in Upper Louisiana that officials made as great an effort as did the judges of California and New Mexico to achieve a settlement. Nor is there any indication that the settlement rate in Upper Louisiana was anywhere close to what it was in California, a rate David Langum reports to have approached 90 percent. In its emphasis on decisions rather than settlements, the system of dispute resolution functioning in Upper Louisiana was quite different from the system present in the northern parts of Mexico.

Langum interprets the importance of conciliation in Mexican California as an indication of the primacy of community to the Californios, in contrast to the more individualistic Anglo-Americans, whose legal system was more likely to produce clear winners and losers.[67] The ambiguities lurking within the concepts of individualism and community have often been noted[68]—the words are slippery enough to have allowed historians to characterize nearly every period of American history as one marked by the breakdown of community—but I need not address that issue here. Under any definition, Upper Louisiana, a place dominated by entrepreneurial traders and their employees and families, was probably a less communal, more individualistic place than Mexican California. It is tempting to place Upper Louisiana on the other side of Langum's dichotomy. If individualism is associated with judicial procedures giving victory to one side or the other, and communalism with procedures facilitating settlement, one could draw a clean contrast between the two cultures. A preference for settlement, however, can be a product of several different causes, only one of which is the desire for harmonious relations among community members. In the United States today, nearly all disputes settle out of court. Many courts require parties to make efforts toward settlement before they are allowed to proceed with litigation. Many, in fact, require settlement conferences before a judge, just like in Mexican California. Individualism is not an easy thing to measure, but it is commonplace to observe that the late-twentieth-century United States is one of the most individualistic societies that has ever existed. Courts promote settlement not to achieve harmonious community relations, but primarily to save the taxpayers' money, through the reduction of court time. Parties normally settle largely to save their own money, which otherwise might go toward attorneys' fees, and to preserve the confidentiality of information they would otherwise have to make public in the course of litigation. It would almost certainly be wrong to interpret the high settlement rate today as an indication of the importance of community to Americans. Settlement is not necessarily a product of community.

Individualists, moreover, are not necessarily prone to litigation. Even a person concerned only with his own welfare, with no regard for the well-being of others except insofar as it affects his own, will expect repeated interactions with other people. Looking only to his own interests, he will perceive the need to maintain a good reputation and good relations with his neighbors. He will subscribe to whatever informal norms he hopes others will observe in their dealings with him. The commercial context may be the one most characterized by individualism, but firms that repeatedly deal with one another typically litigate only a very small fraction of their disputes and settle the rest, because, even apart from the simple cost of litigation, they recognize that a victory in the short run will be outweighed by the loss of business in the long run. It is not clear that individualism is inversely related with a desire for settlement.

Finally, while any individual litigated case obviously involves conflict between one party and another, one cannot necessarily make a parallel claim about whole societies. A society in which people litigate rather than settle their cases *might* be one in which community is less prized than a society in which people settle rather than litigate, but it might not. As David Konig has shown with respect to seventeenth-century Massachusetts, litigation itself can be a way of establishing standards of behavior and integrating individuals into the community, a way of constructing rather than destroying harmony.[69] Litigation need not be interpreted as pathological. Individual cases might generate winners and losers in equal numbers, but if participants in the legal system each tend to be involved in multiple cases and if they are generally satisfied with the system despite their losses in individual cases, the system as a whole can generate many more winners than losers. If cases are generally perceived to be concluded quickly, inexpensively, and fairly, a high litigation rate will not indicate the absence of community.

Mexican Californians may well have been community-minded people, and perhaps in that place and time one can find a link between community-mindedness and a propensity to settle disputes; but one ought not to expect the connection to hold generally. Individualists seem no less likely to settle their disputes than communalists. Indeed, one could plausibly expect precisely the opposite—that a communitarian society would devote a greater share of its public resources to dispute resolution, and could accordingly accommodate a greater proportion of disputes litigated to a close rather than settled at an early stage.

Instead of seeking an explanation for settlement rates in a society's communalism, it may be more useful to look at the cost of litigation to the parties. The more expensive it is to litigate, the greater incentive the parties will have to settle rather than pursue the case to a conclusion, and the greater the preference they will have for government-sponsored mediation. The less valuable a court judgment is, the less parties will spend to obtain one. Litigation in Mexican California appears to have been much more costly than in Upper Louisiana. Judgments in California were repeatedly modified after they were made, to suit the changing circumstances of the parties. A single case, although nominally concluded quickly, could thus last intermittently for several months. In Upper Louisiana, litigation was normally concluded within days. California lacked a mechanism for enforcing court judgments, which made a judgment less valuable than it was in Upper Louisiana, where judgments could be enforced by the seizure and sale of the loser's property.[70] Given these conditions, even the most individualistic Californios would have found it in their interest to reach a settlement. Residents of Upper Louisiana faced a very different set of incentives, and accordingly seem to have settled much fewer of their cases.

CRIMINAL PROSECUTIONS

Few records survive of criminal investigations or prosecutions in Upper Louisiana. Government officials nevertheless perceived crime as a persistent problem. "License, laxity of conduct, and vice," one early lieutenant governor lamented, "are the characteristics of [St. Louis's] inhabitants."[71] Another reported that "various settlers have complained to me that vegetables and fruits have been stolen from their gardens, cattle from their corrals, and boats from the banks of the river."[72] St. Charles, to the west of St. Louis, was thought by yet another lieutenant governor to be the "residence of the savages, mongrels, and worst scoundrels in Illinois."[73] Many of the area's criminals, it was believed, were Americans. American "rebels and bandits," Cruzat complained to American officials on the eastern side of the river, "are committing the most atrocious hostilities against the subjects of His Catholic Majesty in this colony."[74] While the Americans were fighting their revolution, Leyba bemoaned the presence of "fifty American deserters, turbulent and lawless fellows, who were in Ste. Geneviève, [and] were greatly troubling the town, eating without paying."[75]

In small communities surrounded by wilderness and bordering many foreign sovereignties (American and Indian), it was generally not difficult to ascertain the identity of a criminal, but it was often nearly impossible to catch him. A fugitive could move from town to town at least as fast as news about the crime could. Officials were reduced to spreading news and hoping that criminals would arrive in a place where they were already wanted. In 1792, for instance, Lt. Gov. Manuel Pérez wrote to François Vallé, commandant in Ste. Geneviève:

> Charles Peyroux wrote me regarding a considerable theft which was made from him & said that according to the rumors it was two Employees of Mr. John Laly who did it & that Madame Grenon can give news about this theft & in consequence you will inform yourself of this & arrest the two said Employees of Mr. Laly if you can find them.[76]

Vallé received a similar communication two years later, from Tomas Portell, the commandant in New Madrid.

> I send you attached the list of names of one employer and six employees who drove the carriage of Mr. Owen to the falls, and who assassinated him a little on this side of the mouth of the Wabash, and escaped with six thousand piastres of which he was charged, so that you may arrest them in case they come into your district.[77]

In neither of these cases is there any evidence that the culprits were ever found.

Further complicating the task of apprehending criminals was the ease with which fugitives could cross the river to the American side. When Thomas Allen, an American, fled Ste. Geneviève in 1800 after raping a twelve-year-old French girl named Marie, for example, there was little that Spanish officials could do beyond seizing the property he left behind.[78] Despite cooperation between Spanish and American officials (or at least the pretense of such cooperation, in the form of polite requests to send back criminals), there is no evidence that anyone who fled across the river was ever caught.[79]

When criminals were apprehended, they were tried according to procedures established in O'Reilly's instructions of late 1769 and early 1770, the same orders that established the modes of resolving civil disputes. The 1769 order applied throughout Louisiana. When a crime had been committed, the judge was to "order an inquiry to be made into the circumstances of the same." The suspect was to be taken into custody as soon as his identity was ascertained. The judge was then to examine the accused and any witnesses. As in civil cases, the interrogation was to be conducted in private, but the witnesses' testimony was to be made public shortly after the questioning. If the accused was convicted of the crime, "the judge shall pronounce sentence; and although in criminal causes an appeal should not be admitted, yet if the judge shall have doubts, or from some difficulties on the trial he shall think it advisable to submit the same to the examination of a superior, execution shall be suspended."

These instructions were modified by the 1770 order to meet the circumstances of remote areas such as Upper Louisiana. The lieutenant governor was directed to conduct proceedings in the manner detailed in the first order, but when the time came to pronounce sentence, he was to send the written record "to the Governor-General for his judgment, leaving the criminal or criminals in secure custody, until it should be provided what should be done with them." The commandant in Ste. Geneviève was instructed to let the lieutenant governor in St. Louis handle all serious crimes. All examinations of witnesses required the presence of two neutral témoins d'assistance, as in civil proceedings. Finally, local officials were delegated the discretion to dispose of minor criminal cases on their own, without any procedural formality: "if the cause is of such slight gravity, that it is not worthy of being converted to legal proceedings, . . . the said Lieutenant governor and local commandants in their respective towns may decide them verbally and without a judicial fuss."

The 1769 order also contained a section captioned "Of Punishments," which included a list of crimes. Many were crimes of violence—murder, rape, robbery, and so on. Others were crimes of morality, including blasphemy, adultery, fornication, and "el abominable crimen de Sodomia." Activities illegal in Louisiana were the same ones that were illegal elsewhere in North America in the late eighteenth century.

These orders established the criminal procedure that remained in effect until the Louisiana Purchase. The summary procedure for minor crimes would have left no written record, and government officials kept no relevant statistics, so it is impossible to know how often the summary procedure was invoked or how it operated in practice. If, as is the case today, minor crimes were much more common than serious crimes, the bulk of Upper Louisiana's criminal justice system would be invisible to scholars today. The more serious crimes, those justifying the formal procedure, can be divided into two classes. When crimes did not involve violence, lieutenant governors tended to sentence the criminals themselves rather than sending the record of the case down to New Orleans for sentencing. In cases of violence, however, lieutenant governors were more scrupulous in following O'Reilly's instructions.[80]

The mechanics of a typical prosecution can be seen in a 1779 case, in which two men named Buteau and Baribeau were caught illegally selling taffia on the Cuivre River. (Taffia, a kind of rum, was the liquor most prevalent in Upper Louisiana.) A group of trappers and soldiers arrested them, seized the taffia, and attempted to bring them back to St. Louis for trial. On the way, Buteau escaped by diving into the water at night and swimming away. But Baribeau was tried in St. Louis by Lt. Gov. Fernando de Leyba. In the presence of two témoins d'assistance, Leyba took the testimony of the four men who had captured Baribeau. He then went to the post's prison to interrogate Baribeau. The questioning did not take long.

> Asked his name, age, vocation, and what religion he professed.
>
> Responded that he was named Joseph Baribeau, 31 years old, a boatman by profession, and professed the Roman Apostolic Catholic religion.
>
> Asked for what reason he was being held in prison.
>
> Responded that it was because he was hired by the man called Buteau to go to the Mississippi; that this Buteau had entered the Cuivre River despite the testifier's protests; that once there, the testifier told him not to trade, that it was against the orders of the Spanish government; that he knew that this trade was prohibited, and that Sr. Blanchet, who was on the river, had even warned Buteau not to trade, and to leave the river; that despite all his protests and remonstrances, this Buteau traded about 3 bottles of eau-de-vie, which caused Sr. Blanchet to seize the boat; that he, the testifier, told Sr. Blanchet that although Buteau, his leader, wanted to put himself in a bad position by carrying on illegal commerce, he himself was innocent.

Evidently reluctant to proceed further without interrogating Buteau, Leyba suspended the trial for a month, and tried to secure Buteau's presence by having the bailiff summon him verbally every so often outside the church door at the end of mass. At the end of this period, Leyba auctioned off the seized taffia, sentenced the absent Buteau "to six months in prison, if he can be captured," and sentenced Baribeau to fifteen days in prison.[81]

When crimes involved violence, however, lieutenant governors did not sentence the criminals themselves. When one Spanish soldier assaulted another with an axe, for example, or when one slave murdered another, lieutenant governors gathered all the evidence and then referred the cases to New Orleans for disposition.[82]

In practice, the line between civil and criminal litigation could be unclear. The evidence-gathering procedures used in both types of cases were nearly identical: both involved the same kind of interrogation of witnesses in the presence of témoins d'assistance. Both types of cases were often initiated by the petition of a victim, and in both the relief sought could be characterized as either compensatory or punitive. In 1804, for instance, an inhabitant of New Madrid filed a petition that is interesting enough to quote at length.

> Benjamin Louis Venanburgh, resident of the little Prairie of this district, supplicates you humbly saying that Sunday the twelfth of last February, he had been invited to a dance being held at the village. . . . the supplicant was among the spectators and those not dancing at that moment, and was amusing himself by leaping and capering about (as happens often enough, ordinarily, at such dances, and particularly the day of Carnaval) in a corner of the room, without the least intention of insulting anyone of the company, when a certain Jean Ruddell, . . . who was dancing at the moment, turned toward said supplicant and began to insult him, saying that he was making fun of the aforementioned Jean Ruddell, and that the gestures he was making were in order to ridicule M. Ruddell's manner of dancing. . . . Ruddell punched the supplicant in the face so hard, that he knocked him over backward onto the ground and continued to intensify his blows so that the supplicant was so overcome by the blows that said J. Ruddell delivered, that not only did he not try to avenge himself, but he even lost consciousness, asking for grace and crying "enough," and he could not stave off any of the kicks, punches, and bites under which he was expiring. . . . Finally, it was only when the supplicant had regained lucidity that he realized that both his eyes were nearly out of his head, that his ear was half-eaten by this modern-day cannibal, and that he was in grave danger of losing his sight.

After this account of the beating, Venanburgh followed with a series of rhetorical questions that could be understood to ask for compensation, for the initiation of a criminal prosecution, or both:

> Did [Ruddell] have to succumb to the temptations of infernal vice which were able to lead him to commit such a criminal act? . . . can there exist a favorable compensation for an unfortunate who is deprived of light[?] . . . please condemn [Ruddell] to such a punishment as you deem fit, as well as to pay the expenses, damages, and fees that the present trial may necessitate.[83]

There is no record of any action taken upon this petition, so there is no way to know how it was understood by Jean Lavallée, the commandant to whom it was addressed. That it is a request for both punishment and compensation suggests that the division between civil and criminal litigation, which is unmistakable in O'Reilly's orders, could be blurred in practice.

Requests for government action to resolve other disputes suggest a similar blend of civil and criminal. When William Clark and Elizabeth Tigner accused Samuel Greffeth of kidnapping their sixteen-year-old daughter Nancy for the benefit of George Raimey (who had allegedly "developed a passion" for her), they asked as remedies "the punishment such a case merits, and further . . . all damages, fees and expenses."[84] When Gabriel Cerré was robbed by his own hired men in 1784, his petition requested the lieutenant governor to "sentence all of them to all expenses, damages, and interest toward the petitioner, ordering yourself what seems appropriate to you for the civil reparation."[85] Such cases were probably, in effect, civil and criminal at the same time. Because the procedures for adjudicating both types of cases were so similar, they could easily have been handled simultaneously.

Litigation in Upper Louisiana was thus conducted according to regular procedures. Some were established by the Spanish government soon after the transfer of sovereignty to Spain. These procedures were very similar, as far as one can tell, to those already used by the small French community in Upper Louisiana. The Spanish also permitted the French residents to continue to refer disputes to arbitrators of their own choosing. This too became a standard mode of decision making, and it was eventually officially ratified by the Spanish government. Despite its remoteness and the absence of legal professionals of any kind, Upper Louisiana exhibited a high degree of procedural regularity from the start, and maintained it throughout the second half of the eighteenth century.

CHAPTER 2

Sources of Written Law

As a Spanish colony inhabited largely by French people, Upper Louisiana was, in Hans Baade's useful phrase, a "dual state," one that was regulated in part by the rich legal traditions of both Spain and France. Much substantive written law was produced closer to home, in New Orleans and in Upper Louisiana itself.

SPAIN AND FRANCE

Governor O'Reilly's 1769 order, discussed in chapter 1, was prefaced with the explanation that it was intended to bring Louisiana law "in conformity to the laws of the Nueva Recopilacion de Castilla, and the Recopilacion de las Indias, . . . until a more general knowledge of the Spanish language, and more extensive information upon those laws may be acquired."[1] Contemporaries understood this order to mean that Spanish law was now to be in effect generally, even as to matters not explicitly governed by O'Reilly's instructions.[2] Informal approval from Spain came a few months later, in a letter objecting to only one provision of O'Reilly's order, a clause permitting husbands to kill adulterous wives.[3] Formal approval came from Spain in 1772.[4] For more than three decades thereafter, Upper Louisiana was in principle governed by the same body of Spanish colonial law as that which applied in Mexico or Peru.

This law, the subject of a centuries-old, learned tradition, came from a variety of sources. Its most important text was the *Recopilación de leyes de las Indias*, first published in 1681, a nine-volume arrangement of approximately 6,400 laws, compiled under royal authority from hundreds of thousands of earlier royal orders pertaining to Spain's colonies in the western hemisphere.[5] Most of these laws concerned the administration of colonial government; the *Recopilación de Indias* was not intended to be, and thus did not serve as, a comprehensive code regulating other aspects of colonial life.[6] In recognition of this limitation, the *Recopilación de Indias* itself stated that in cases where it lacked a provision, one should consider other royal orders concerning the Indies that had not been included within its pages. If guidance were still absent—and because of the limited scope of such orders guidance was likely to be absent—the laws of the Kingdom of Castile were to be consulted.[7]

Castilian law was itself a complex tradition, which had evolved over several centuries among a litigious people with a well-developed judicial system staffed by university-trained lawyers.[8] In the eighteenth century its primary text was the *Nueva Recopilación de todas las leyes de Castilla*, a compilation of over four thousand royal laws first published in 1569. But the written law of Castile also included many royal orders not compiled in the *Recopilación de Castilla*, as well as a maze of *fueros* (municipal charters) and other special privileges, all administered by a host of different types of courts with overlapping jurisdictions.[9] And at the base of Castilian law stood the *Siete Partidas*, the comprehensive thirteenth-century code that still retained vitality where subsequent law was not inconsistent.[10] These three major compilations—the *Recopilación de Indias*, the *Recopilación de Castilla*, and the *Siete Partidas*—thus formed the backbone of written Spanish colonial law. They were present in most of the major northern Spanish colonial settlements, often supplemented by works of commentary by jurists.[11] By formally establishing Spanish colonial law in Louisiana, the Spanish government almost certainly intended this body of rules to play an important role in governing the new colony.

Spanish law, including the law governing the colonies, also included norms derived from unwritten sources. Spanish jurists, working under the influence of Roman legal thought, distinguished *ley*, the written law, from *derecho*, a more general sense of justice. In doing justice to litigants, judges were expected to draw upon custom and a generally shared sense of fairness as well as the written law.[12] The importance of these unwritten sources was formalized in the *Siete Partidas*, which recognized that custom could serve as the basis for resolving disputes. This tradition was quite strong in Spain's North American colonies, even in places such as California and New Mexico, where law books were available but where custom and fairness—what David Langum calls "curbstone" law—were nevertheless often used to decide cases.[14] The tradition of unwritten law might reasonably be expected to have had a particularly strong effect in tempering the legal system's reliance on written sources of law in those parts of the Spanish empire where, for other reasons, the use of written Spanish legal authority would have been difficult.

Upper Louisiana was such a place. For three reasons, the extensive body of formal Spanish legal doctrine had much less practical effect in Upper Louisiana than in more populous parts of the empire.

First, there were never any trained lawyers in the area, either in or out of government, during the entire Spanish period. As in the other less populated parts of Spanish North America, the administration of justice was carried out by men with no education in the subject beyond what could be acquired on the job. Law on the frontier thus tended to be less formal than in Spain or even in the larger Spanish American cities such as Mexico City or Havana.[15] A learned tradition can fully survive only where there are people who possess the relevant learning. The absence of men trained in Spanish law would have made it very difficult, even in the best of circumstances, for Upper Louisiana to have been a place where written Spanish colonial law was a significant institution.

Second, there do not appear to have been any copies of either the *Recopilación de Indias* or the *Siete Partidas*, or any commentary thereon, present in Upper Louisiana during the Spanish period. At every change of lieutenant governor in St. Louis, and at every change of commandant in the satellite towns, Spanish officials compiled inventories of all the papers in the local archives that were being handed over.[16] Two sets of inventories were produced in St. Louis and each of the towns in 1804, one for the documents handed over to the Americans, and the other for the documents shipped to Havana.[17] These lists are quite extensive, including documents pertaining to the full range of government activity—"all the orders, published and established by order of Don Pedro Piernas, in this village of San Luis, during the time of his command"; an "index, containing 47 concessions of land for houses in the village [of New Madrid], of the year 1791"; "Information regarding the tribes with whom we generally trade in the dependency of the Misuri River, with a note of . . . the amount of merchandise which is sufficient for them."[18] None of these inventories mentions any Spanish codes or commentary in the possession of any government officials.

Nor do these books appear to have been in private hands during the period. The elite merchants owned a surprisingly large number of law books, mostly treatises by French authors. Louis St. Ange de Bellerive, for instance, had a copy of Briquet's *Code militaire ou compilation des ordonnances des Roys de France conçernant les gens de guerre* (1728). Pierre Laclède owned many such works, including Frain de Tromblay's *Essais sur l'idée du parfait magistrat* (1701) and P. J. Masson's *Instruction des négoçiants, tirée des ordonnances et des usages réçus* (1744). Auguste Chouteau even had the first French edition (1766) of Cesare Beccaria's *Traité des délits et des peines*. But no one appears to have owned a Spanish code. The only mention of a Spanish law book in estate records is that of "a volume of Spanish laws" belonging to Louis Lebaume, who arrived in St. Louis in 1792 and died in 1821. This volume might have been a part of one of the codes, but because it is not mentioned in any surviving correspondence or in the sampled portion of the surviving litigation records, it does not appear to have played a part in the resolution of many disputes.[19]

A sample of roughly half of the several hundred surviving litigated cases in Upper Louisiana likewise discloses no reference to the *Recopilación de Indias*, the *Siete Partidas*, or any Spanish legal commentary. The *Recopilación de Castilla* is mentioned only once. In 1777, Ste. Geneviève resident Joseph Tellier complained to the government in New Orleans about a decision rendered against him by François Vallé, the commandant of Ste. Geneviève. Gov. Bernardo de Gálvez responded by criticizing Vallé's order to seize and sell Tellier's slaves in order to pay off Tellier's creditors. This reproach prompted Vallé to explain the decision to Gálvez. Vallé noted that before ordering the seizure, he consulted "the Recopilation of the laws of Castile that Monsieur O'Reilly left in this Colony to guide the administration of justice," but that it offered no assistance.[20] This is the only surviving evidence that any of the three major Spanish compilations of law was present in Upper Louisiana in the second half of the eighteenth century. Even in this case, the role played by the *Recopilación de Castilla* is doubtful. Vallé was a French official trying to justify his conduct to a Spanish superior, which leads to the suspicion that he may have misrepresented the extent of his reliance on written Spanish law, and of course by his own admission the *Recopilación* did not provide any guidance.

The subsequent history of this copy of the *Recopilación de Castilla* is a bit of a mystery. It does not resurface in any of the later sampled cases, or in any correspondence to or from the government officials of Upper Louisiana. It does not appear in subsequent documentary inventories. By the nineteenth century the fact that a copy had ever been in the area had been forgotten, and a consensus seems to have formed among American lawyers that no Spanish law books of any kind had been present under the Spanish government. "We are informed," the Missouri Supreme Court would report in 1852, "that the first printed book brought into this State, containing any Spanish law, was the Partidas, and that event occurred later than the year 1820."[21] Someone may have removed Vallé's copy of the *Recopilación de Castilla* from Ste. Geneviève during the period, or it may simply have languished, unconsulted.

Other local legal documents that could have mentioned the Spanish codes do not. Some of the many surviving local ordinances might have been expected to refer to the codes as authority, but none does. The contracts entered into in Upper Louisiana during the period might have mentioned the codes, but with the exception of one category they do not. The exceptional category is that of marriage contracts. The French residents of Upper Louisiana, particularly the wealthy, traditionally signed marriage contracts providing for the transmission and distribution of wealth within newly formed families.[22] These contracts, like contracts today, typically included a boilerplate clause stating the law that would govern matters arising under the contract. In Upper Louisiana, such clauses sometimes referred to the *Recopilación de Castilla*.[23] In the absence of any evidence of actual resort to the *Recopilación*, however, this provides only a very weak inference that the *Recopilación* was physically present. Marriage contracts among the French in the Illinois country had traditionally included a similar boilerplate clause referring to the *Coutume de Paris*, in communities where the *Coutume* was clearly not present.[24] The French residents of Upper Louisiana may simply have converted the standard reference from a French to a Spanish code to acknowledge the sovereignty of Spain, without any real expectation that the code would play any role in determining the conditions of their marriages.

In short, therefore, two of the three major compilations of Spanish colonial law do not appear to have been present in Upper Louisiana during the second half of the eighteenth century, and the third registers only brief, and probably misleading, appearances. This provides a second reason for concluding that the complex edifice of Spanish colonial law theoretically in force in Upper Louisiana after 1769 did not have a great practical effect.

Third, despite the opportunity to appeal unfavorable local decisions to higher authorities in New Orleans, Havana, Santo Domingo, and ultimately Spain—a hierarchy in which each step would have brought litigants before decision makers more learned in Spanish law—there is no evidence to suggest that anyone in Upper Louisiana ever took even the first step. A trip from St. Louis to New Orleans and back for the purpose of litigation would have required several months of travel, as well as a period of residence in New Orleans, which rendered an appeal so costly and time-consuming that it would have been a pointless exercise, whatever the stakes. Subsequent stages of litigation would have only added to the expense. Residents of New Orleans, who avoided the initial expense of traveling to and from Upper Louisiana, appealed cases to Havana only rarely, and then to Santo Domingo even more rarely.[25] It would have been even more unlikely for residents of Upper Louisiana to have done so.

The Spanish legal tradition thus had little direct effect on the lives of the residents of Upper Louisiana. It did influence local practice indirectly, however, in a few different ways.

First, Upper Louisiana was governed in part by a stream of orders from New Orleans, written by officials advised by lawyers. The lawyers' knowledge of Spanish law almost certainly affected their advice in many cases. This influence was sometimes made explicit. In 1802, for instance, Intendant Juan Ventura Morales explained to Lt. Gov. Charles Delassus that no slaves could be imported into Upper Louisiana, because of "what is mandated in Law 18 to 26, book 9, of the Recopilación of these Kingdoms, which absolutely prohibits the admission of slaves."[26] Even when reliance on Spanish law was not explicit, the wording of some of these orders strongly suggests the hand of trained lawyers working within an educated tradition. In 1770, for example, when officials in Upper Louisiana were authorized to conduct informal criminal proceedings in minor cases, the Spanish phrase used to describe the means by which officials should proceed—"sin estrepito de juicio" (loosely, "without judicial fuss")—was strikingly similar to a formula used in canon law—"sine strepitu et figura iudicii"—since the early fourteenth century.[27]

Second, when disputes were sent from St. Louis to New Orleans for resolution, the same lawyers advised the officials making the decisions. The extent to which these lawyers relied on Spanish law for the content of their advice is again largely a matter of inference from their training, because communications from New Orleans to St. Louis generally did not include legal citations. The influence of a written legal tradition is nevertheless unmistakable from the tenor of some of those communications. Thus Governor Miró advised, after having consulted "my Auditor," that

> the rights the women have on the successions of their deceased husbands are first the right to claim her dowry which is that portion a woman brings to the marriage to sustain her expenses. The dowry has several names according to the persons who give it. The other right the women have is to claim the donation made to them by their husbands in consideration of the marriage. Said donation is called the marriage settlement.[28]

Advice like this can only have come from someone familiar with law books. When such advice influenced decisions made by officials in Upper Louisiana, the Spanish legal tradition was at work.

Third, the Spanish government consistently regulated international trade throughout the period, in ways that affected the lives of the more commercially inclined residents of Upper Louisiana. From Spain came orders setting and lifting tariffs, requiring the use of Spanish vessels and crews, prohibiting the importation of various products, and so on.[29] This was Spanish law in a different sense from that used above; these were shifting political decisions, not the manifestations of a learned tradition. But this *was* written law emanating from Spain, and indirectly influencing commercial activity in Upper Louisiana.

Formal Spanish law thus played some role in Upper Louisiana, but its influence was largely indirect. Because of the absence of lawyers and the near-absence of legal texts, Spanish law was not as important in Upper Louisiana as it was in the more densely populated parts of the Spanish colonies.

Because most of the inhabitants of Upper Louisiana were French, French law also played a role in governing the area. The law of eighteenth-century France was, like that of Spain, the subject of a long, learned tradition. The law in France varied from region to region, and sometimes from town to town. It was often embodied in *coutumes*, or collections of customary local practice. This law was administered by an assortment of different kinds of courts. As David Bell points out, "[m]anuals for aspiring barristers routinely warned that a basic mastery of French jurisprudence took *decades* of applied study."[30] The most important of the coutumes, and the only one with any significance in Louisiana, was the *Coutume de Paris*, first compiled in 1510 and then revised in 1580. The 1580 version comprised 372 articles governing a wide range of subjects, including property, marriage, and wills. The French charters authorizing the colonization of Louisiana in the early eighteenth century provided that the *Coutume de Paris* would be in effect in the colony.[31]

In principle, the *Coutume de Paris* lost its force after the Spanish assumed control. One continues to find references to it as governing law in Upper Louisiana marriage contracts throughout the period, although one must assume that most or all of these references were formulaic, with no real intention to consult the *Coutume* to resolve any disputes.[32] A copy of the *Coutume* must have been present in the area, however, and it must have continued to exert some normative influence, because in one 1800 case, a protracted dispute over who would inherit the estate of Geneviève

Charleville, the parties on both sides made repeated references to scattered sections of it.[33] Of the cases sampled, this is the only one to mention the *Coutume*, a circumstance that suggests that the *Coutume*'s role was very small. The fact that so many of the French mercantile elite owned copies of French legal commentary also weakly suggests the lingering influence of French law, although it is possible that these books had been acquired before 1770.

The only aspect of life that continued to be formally regulated by French law was slavery. The *Code Noir*, published in 1685 to govern slavery in the French colonies, was adapted to French Louisiana in 1724, and became the only French law expressly retained in Louisiana by the Spanish. Spanish officials in New Orleans, however, seem to have generally ignored the *Code Noir* in favor of Spanish slave law, which on certain points was more favorable to the slaves.[34] In Upper Louisiana, neither the French nor Spanish law of slavery appears to have had much of an impact. A copy of the *Code Noir* was probably present in Ste. Geneviève for at least part of the period, because in at least one case a commandant claimed to have consulted it.[35] But the surviving record of disputes involving slavery, like that of other disputes in the area, barely includes any mention of Spanish or French law of any kind.

The French legal tradition thus played an even smaller role than the Spanish in governing Upper Louisiana.

NEW ORLEANS

Much of the law governing Upper Louisiana came from New Orleans, in the form of orders from O'Reilly and his successors as governor. The transfer of property upon death, for instance, was regulated by O'Reilly's orders of 1769 and 1770, which included prerequisites for the legitimacy of a will and specified who would receive property in the absence of a will. As in other areas of law, the 1770 order was tailored to posts such as Upper Louisiana that lacked notaries; the order required three witnesses to a will in the absence of a notary. Wills generally complied with this requirement. The order's primary effect was to ratify preexisting practices, as the French residents of Upper Louisiana were following this procedure even before 1770.[36]

The 1770 order also provided procedures for the formalization of "proxies, deeds, and other necessary instruments." Because there were no notaries in Upper Louisiana, such documents were to be prepared by the lieutenant governor or one of the commandants, in the presence of two témoins d'assistance. Performing this service must have taken a large percentage of the time of local government officials. The archives of St. Louis and the surrounding towns are full of sale contracts, promissory notes, appointments of agents, and the like, all bearing the signatures of lieutenant governors or commandants.[37] In light of the number of residents who could not write (many of these documents bear marks rather than signatures), and considering the uniformity in the wording of many of the documents, it is likely that government officials played a large role in drafting them. Officials thus spent much of their time doing what is done today in the United States by lawyers, and what was done at the time throughout the borderlands (and often still today in civil law countries) by notaries.[38] The use of officials or notaries to draft contracts, and then the deposit of such contracts in government archives, served an evidentiary purpose; they would be accepted as genuine and as accurate reflections of the parties' intentions in the event of a subsequent dispute.[39]

Some people, especially the French merchant elite and the American immigrants from the United States, wrote at least some of their contracts themselves. The French were able to produce work as skilled as that of government officials, but Americans typically were not.[40] When two Americans wished to establish a salt-mining partnership in 1801, for instance, they agreed to the following:

> Articles of agreement Between Jessy Shelly and Thomas Gibson Conserning a Saleen [saline] of Thomas Gibson on the Masury the Sade Shelly Doth Autherise to furnish twenty fore Sault Cittles [kettles] on or before the furst of May at the Saleen on the Masasipy the Sade Gibson Doth autherise to Furnish Men Suffisiant to Carry on the Business to perfection and Likewise furnish provition for the Work hands the Sade Shelly Doth Gose Eaqul part in the Sade Salleen for the space of three years.[41]

But legal instruments prepared without the assistance of a government official were understood to be exceptions, not the norm. Such documents were often referred to with modifiers indicating their unusual status; they were not contracts but "secret contracts"; they were not agreements but "private agreements."[42]

Again, the order from New Orleans appears to have ratified preexisting practice. There was a notary living in Upper Louisiana until 1770, who wrote, witnessed (along with two témoins d'assistance), and archived the few contracts from that period that have survived. When François Cotin and Jean Ortès exchanged their St. Louis houses in 1768, they formalized their agreement before a notary and two witnesses.[43] When Simon Huberdeaux, a merchant in Ste. Geneviève, hired a "master carpenter" named Gerard Langlois to build his house in 1769, they followed the same procedure.[44] The continuity between pre- and post-1770 contracting practices is equally apparent in the formulaic wording of the contracts, which barely changed after the Spanish assumed sovereignty, apart from the fact that in the 1770s contracts began to be written in Spanish as well as French.[45] The manner in which the earliest French residents of Upper Louisiana produced their contracts was almost certainly drawn from their experiences in Illinois and New Orleans when those areas were under French sovereignty. New law in this area from the Spanish colonial government required almost no change in practice.

The allocation of land was another matter regulated by a series of orders from New Orleans. The first of these accompanied the initial Spanish expedition to the Illinois country in 1767. Each resident was to receive a square plot, ten quadras on each side; "endeavor shall be made to assign the land in perfect squares, which will avoid many suits at law and quarrels in the future." Between each pair of house lots there was to be a road.[46] The details of the land allocation system—lot sizes, requirements that land be developed within a certain time or else forfeited, restrictions on resale, and so on—were altered by subsequent governors to track the evolution of Spanish immigration policy. One substantive feature remained constant. Land was given away, never sold, primarily to subsidize the immigration of people considered useful by government officials in New Orleans, especially farmers.[47]

The formal procedure for allocating land remained constant as well. On paper, the power to grant land rested with the governor in New Orleans. He was to appoint a surveyor, who would ascertain the boundaries of the grant in the presence of the two adjoining settlers. Because the amount of allocable land relative to the population was practically infinite, however, the cost of surveying land and securing the governor's approval of a land grant nearly always exceeded the value of the land itself. The formal procedure was thus rarely, if ever, followed.[48] In its place was a procedure that had been established informally, before the Spanish assumed sovereignty.[49] As the last of the lieutenant governors recalled, "the regulations of O'Reil[l]y were so old, that they were not regarded.... [I] was likewise governed by the usage and customs of [my] predecessors."[50] Residents or immigrants who wished to acquire land would request land grants from the lieutenant governor, who would approve the grants, with the advice of the local commandant if the land requested was outside St. Louis, upon receiving an explanation of the land's intended use. This requirement does not appear to have been difficult to fulfill. Land was granted because, for instance, the applicant had already worked it, because the applicant desired to raise livestock, because the applicant wished to construct a gristmill, and because the applicant believed himself entitled to a reward for having discovered previously unknown Indian tribes.[51] Often land was granted to residents with no plans more specific than an intent to live "as a peaceful and submissive cultivator," as Daniel Boone described himself in his 1799 application for a grant along the Missouri River.[52]

Surveys were rarely made, especially in the early years. Record keeping was spotty, largely because remote land was so plentiful and easily available from the government that there was barely any private market in it, and so there was little incentive to record mortgages or other documents. (Land in town, in contrast, had already been allocated, existed in limited quantities, and had often been improved. As a result, there was an active market for such land. The seller would typically accept a promise of future payment, secured by the property. The colonial archives accordingly contain a great number of mortgages.) If a dispute ever arose over a grant from the government, it could be resolved simply by granting more land.[53] This discrepancy between written law and unwritten practice would later fuel much litigation in American courts, lasting much of the nineteenth century, devoted to determining the validity under Spanish law of claimed pre–Louisiana Purchase land grants.[54]

Orders from New Orleans covered a wide range of other matters. As in other parts of the borderlands, most such regulation involved issues of public law.[55] Perhaps the most frequent subject was relations with the Indians, a topic that embraced military policy, trade, the sale of alcohol, and a host of other concerns.[56] Slavery was another common subject.[57] Governors repeatedly sent instructions on "the treatment which the inhabitants must give to their Negroes so that they may get a suitable usefulness out of them without infringing with impunity the laws of humanity."[58] Instructions sometimes concerned the local economy. "Nothing requires greater attention from the government," one such order explained, "than the equitable regulation of the prices of food products."[59] Every so often, when an issue attained unusual local significance, the government in New Orleans would step in. Thus in 1793, as the news from France caused Spanish colonial officials to worry that the French residents of Louisiana might entertain dangerous ideas, the governor proclaimed, "It is absolutely prohibited to peruse or read aloud in public writings, printed matter or papers relating to the political affairs of France, whether pro or contra."[60]

Such orders seem to have been generally known in Upper Louisiana. They were preserved in St. Louis, and handed down at each succession of lieutenant governor.[61] In litigation involving matters addressed by instructions from New Orleans, parties were quick to mention the "public ordinances" in their favor.[62] However, these orders figure in only a tiny percentage of the litigated disputes of which records survive. There is almost no evidence indicating how orders from New Orleans were enforced, or indeed if they were ever enforced. Written law from New Orleans appears to have played very little role in regulating the ordinary, day-to-day interactions of the residents of Upper Louisiana, the standard stuff of lawsuits. From New Orleans came almost no private law: no commercial law to govern the countless transactions among the residents; no law to redress the various harms inflicted intentionally or inadvertently by one resident upon another; and no law to regulate the standard types of relationships in which the residents repeatedly found themselves, whether employer and employee, debtor and creditor, or neighbor and neighbor.

UPPER LOUISIANA

The final source of written law in Upper Louisiana was Upper Louisiana itself. Such law took two forms. First, lieutenant governors and local commandants issued orders relating to whatever problems seemed pressing at the time. Second, syndics and local assemblies voted on resolutions governing town planning and the common fields. Both sets of rules virtually always fell within the realm of public law; they almost never purported to regulate the interactions of private individuals.

Local orders were sometimes the products of instructions from New Orleans. "[B]y virtue of an order from Monsieur le Baron de Carondelet, governor general of the province," one lieutenant governor proclaimed in 1792, the Indian trade would henceforth be open "to all subjects of His Majesty" willing to pay for a license.[63] More often, however, local orders responded to local conditions. When some farmers of St. Ferdinand complained that people were sneaking onto their land and chopping down their trees, Lt. Gov. Zenon Trudeau issued an order imposing a fine on "those who touch another's wood."[64] When the popularity of horse-racing in the streets threatened the safety of pedestrians in St. Louis, Lt. Gov. Francisco Cruzat "very strictly" prohibited "every person, of whatever sex, occupation, rank, or condition, to go on horseback, or in a cart, sledge, or carriole, faster than a trot."[65] When Ste. Geneviève residents failed to dispose of their dead animals in sufficient number as to pose the risk of "epidemical maladies in this Post," Antonio de Oro, the local commandant, ordered anyone finding a dead animal to report it to him, "so that we may discover the owner of the animal and force him to throw said dead animal into the river."[66] Local officials were putting out fires, in the sense that such local regulation was reactive to isolated issues rather than comprehensive. In at least one order, in fact, an official was literally putting out fires: in 1785, Cruzat ordered a new collective procedure for responding to "[t]he fires, of which there has been no instance until the present time, and which are singularly making their appearance for some days past without our being able to discover the causes."[67]

Such orders were widely known even to the illiterate, as they were routinely "read, posted, and published in the customary places," typically outside the church door on Sundays.[68] Despite their nondemocratic form, they were sometimes the result of pressure from ordinary citizens, and were sometimes the subject of public deliberation before they were issued. In 1802, for instance, Henri Peyroux, the commandant in New Madrid, received a petition from two local residents, informing him that

> Pierre Dapron, M. Colar Dapron, and Jean-Baptiste Aimé were on the other side of the bayou Saturday, near Monsr. Joseph Vandenbemden, killing pigs, supposedly on the orders of Monsr. Joseph Michelet. The petitioners have been told that out of three pigs killed, two of them were not branded and they killed them as wild pigs.
>
> The petitioners pray you, Monsieur le commandant, to consider how outrageous is this pretext of non-branded pigs being called wild, when they are so close to the village, and how this can work in the favor of those with bad intentions.

The petitioners were probably not the owners of the dead pigs, as they did not seek damages or claim the pigs as their own. They were most likely the apprehensive owners of pigs still living. Whatever their motive, they viewed pig-killing as a fit subject for local regulation.

> For these reasons, in these circumstances, Mons. le commandant, the petitioners in the name of all honest residents pray you to create an order or a policy regulation forcing those who go kill animals outside the village to show these animals' brands to whatever person you wish to name in this capacity; with this person also it would be advisable that all residents register the brand of their animals. Further, said regulation

> should determine at what distance and under what circumstances animals can be called wild, and can be killed.

Peyroux agreed that regulation was necessary, but declined to issue an order by himself. He instead decreed

> that justice will be done in this matter, by way of a regulation which we will create as soon as we have the views of the notable residents of this post as to the distance necessary for pigs to be considered wild; to this end, they will be assembled at our house next Sunday.

The production of local law in this instance, as in others, was far more democratic than the simple procedure of issuing orders would suggest. The initial demand for regulation came from the people that would benefit from it. The regulation itself rested on two popular norms not previously backed by government sanction, that wild pigs can be captured and killed while pigs already owned cannot, and that pigs found far away from a settled area can be presumed wild while pigs found in a village should be presumed to be already owned. The actual content of the regulation was determined only after consultation with residents, although only the "notable." In all these senses, local officials of the Spanish government accommodated the views of the area's French residents.[69]

Self-government was clearer when the residents regulated matters themselves, either through elected syndics or in large meetings. The rules enacted by syndics typically concerned roads, bridges, and the like. The syndics of St. Louis, for instance, declared that "the streets in general will be repaired by the owners of the land facing the streets," and that "[a]ll inhabitants facing a street through which a brook is running, are under obligation to provide for the running water a bed that leads to the Mississippi River." Law created in town meetings typically pertained to the common fields. In 1793, for instance, the inhabitants of Ste. Geneviève assembled "to deliberate as to the manner most convenient to the interests of everyone with regard to the fixing of the fences of the fields." New regulations were enacted by a plurality.[70] In 1801, the residents of St. Charles gathered "to decide if the bottom end of the common would be enlarged or not." The vote was in favor of expansion.[71]

Such local regulation, like that from New Orleans, consisted largely of ad hoc responses to the perceived needs of the moment. It was not intended to be, nor did it serve as, a source of comprehensive rules governing the area.

Upper Louisiana was thus in principle governed by written law from Spain, France, and New Orleans, and by written law produced locally. Despite all the law nominally in effect in the area, Upper Louisiana in practice possessed no written law governing the kinds of issues that gave rise to ordinary, run-of-the-mill disputes—no written law governing relations among merchants, no written law regarding liability for injuries, and so on. For that, residents looked to another source.

CHAPTER 3

Unwritten Norms

"In all the new and small towns," Francisco Bouligny reported to Gov. Estevan Miró from the Natchez post in 1785, "there is much litigation." Because there was too much for the commandant at Natchez to handle, Bouligny recommended dividing the post into districts, appointing a resident of each district as captain, and authorizing the captains to adjudicate disputes. The primary advantage to this scheme, Bouligny reasoned, was that the captains,

> knowing the temperament and character of each one of the inhabitants of their respective jurisdictions, possessing their language, cognizant of the manners and customs prevailing in the district in regard to fences, animals, and above all, the sale and trading in horses which is generally the principal cause of their disputes, could easily settle their differences, and pass judgments on the disputes.[1]

Knowledge of the formal law was thus not an attribute necessary to be a good judge in Natchez. Much more important, at least to one midlevel official of the Spanish government, was familiarity with the local "manners and customs" regarding trade disputes and damage caused by animals.

Years later, Amos Stoddard, the American official charged with taking possession of Upper Louisiana, would recall that none of the Spanish codes ostensibly providing the rules governing disputes in St. Louis was ever actually present, "except one or two . . . and those disposed to consult them were obliged to examine a voluminous digest. This obstacle to legal information" required lieutenant governors and commandants "to decide according to their conceptions of equity." "No wonder," Stoddard concluded, "that the Spanish government in Louisiana was deemed arbitrary."[2]

But deemed arbitrary by whom? Evidently not the litigants themselves, who do not seem to have been concerned with the absence of written law. The residents of Upper Louisiana were quite willing to express their grievances about corruption on the part of individual government officials, but none of these complaints suggested that such dishonesty was a result of a lack of written law.[3] It is hard to see how such an argument would even have been plausible; corrupt judges are hardly unknown in even the most text-based legal systems. Indeed, the flurry of post–Louisiana Purchase complaints from St. Louis residents about the new American legal system (to be discussed in chapter 5) strongly suggests that, if given the choice, they would have preferred to retain the old one.

Remove Stoddard's tone of disapproval, and one can see that the "conceptions of equity" disparaged by Stoddard and the "morals and customs" favored by Bouligny are two different ways of describing the same thing. Litigation in Upper Louisiana was generally resolved with reference to norms that had received no written expression (except perhaps in resolving prior cases) before the dispute arose. Cases were decided according to an intuitive sense of justice shared by the community, or at least by a large enough fraction of the community to make the decision acceptable.

The Anglo-American legal vocabulary lacked, and still lacks, a word that accurately describes these norms. One can call them "customs," or "traditions," but because custom and tradition in our legal system are elevated to the status of "law" only in narrow, well-defined situations, those names do not adequately convey their role in Upper Louisiana.[4] One can follow Stoddard and call them principles of "equity," but equity is likewise a word that for Anglo-American lawyers already bears connotations misleading in this context.

Perhaps the best way to describe the use of these norms would be to imagine the existence of a court of table manners, or a court of fashion, or (maybe among adolescents) a court of coolness. Given a population that is not too diverse, public officials could use widely accepted unwritten conventions to adjudicate issues of good or bad table manners, fashionable or unfashionable clothing, cool or uncool behavior. To most members of the community, such decisions would appear reasonable most of the time. At the very least, there would be general agreement on which were the easy cases and which were the close cases. To outsiders with no interest in understanding the community, however, all decisions would appear equally arbitrary.

That is the way public officials resolved disputes in Upper Louisiana. Without ever explicitly saying they were doing so, and often without ever articulating the grounds for their decisions, public officials drew on the unwritten norms of the community to decide cases.

Anyone trying to discuss the unwritten conventions of people who are now dead faces an obvious practical problem. To the extent those conventions remained unwritten, there is no direct way of knowing what they were. To the extent they were embodied in written rules, however, they are no longer unwritten custom but, instead, written law. One can thus get at the norms of the past only indirectly, by trying to infer them from whatever written or physical evidence one has. The existing evidence is primarily the record of hundreds of litigated cases in Upper Louisiana. Most of these cases appear to modern readers as black boxes; facts go in and a decision comes out, but the reasoning process behind the decision remains invisible. Like students of fashion or table manners, we have to try to back out the norms from an observation of repeated instances of conduct. As Morris Arnold has suggested with reference to fourteenth-century England, where the case reports are similarly opaque, this way of reading cases may yield an understanding of

> commonly held social assumptions about the way a moral world is ordered, founded on logic and experience, that people accept in their dealings with each other, and this entirely apart from whether there are places to resort to for their systematic and dependable vindication. This natural law, as we may call it, counts, it seems to me and despite Austin, as much for law as the product of the most sovereign decree ever could. Others will not see it that way, but if for our black box we are able to substitute not only a sentient but as well an intelligent trial device capable of appreciating, responding to, transmitting, and applying these social norms, then it seems to me that we have law in its fullest and most modern sense: Rules to which resort is consistently had for the settlement of disputes.[5]

In discussing these unwritten norms, it will be convenient to divide the cases in two groups and consider each separately. Some were easy cases; in these, there could be no serious dispute as to the governing principles. Others were hard cases; in these, the relevant norm was not so easy to find. The decision procedure tended to differ depending on the difficulty of the case. But first it may be useful to discuss briefly the quantity of litigation in Upper Louisiana, as well as the subject matter of the cases.

RATES AND SUBJECTS

The uneven condition of the surviving litigation records in Spanish government archives makes it difficult to estimate the frequency of litigation in colonial St. Louis and the surrounding towns. Even in Ste. Geneviève, where the records are the most complete, there are peaks and valleys in the yearly count of litigated disputes so large and so inexplicable as to prevent one from having any confidence that all the records have survived.

There is no particular reason why the residents of Ste. Geneviève should have been ten times more litigious in 1771 than in 1772 and three times more than in 1770, or why litigation rates should have dwindled to zero in four of six years in the early 1780s. These disparities more likely indicate the state of the preservation of the records than actual litigation rates. Allowing for the loss of records over the past two hundred years, it seems fair to take the higher numbers as closer approximations of the true frequency of litigation in Ste. Geneviève.

Table 1

SURVIVING STE. GENEVIÈVE LITIGATION RECORDS, 1766–1804

Year	*Cases*	*Year*	*Cases*	*Year*	*Cases*
1766	4	1779	4	1792	2
1767	1	1780	—	1793	5
1768	2	1781	—	1794	2
1769	2	1782	3	1795	4
1770	12	1783	—	1796	7
1771	30	1784	5	1797	9
1772	3	1785	—	1798	23
1773	3	1786	1	1799	24
1774	2	1787	2	1800	26
1775	6	1788	11	1801	13
1776	11	1789	10	1802	8
1777	6	1790	3	1803	23
1778	9	1791	1	1804	6

The St. Louis records are even spottier. There are no surviving records of any litigated disputes in the period from 1764 to 1778. There are many cases from 1779 and then no cases in 1780, 1781, or 1782. This pattern repeats itself: a few cases each year in 1783, 1784, and 1785, followed by another litigation explosion in 1786, followed by no cases at all in 1787, 1788, and 1789. The subsequent record is even more erratic: a few cases in 1790, then no cases for an entire decade until a few in 1800, another spike in 1801, and then a few more in each of 1802, 1803, and 1804. As in Ste. Geneviève, this pattern must be more a testament to the state of record keeping than an accurate account of the litigation rate. There is no reason why St. Louis should have seen bursts of litigation in 1779, 1786, and 1801 and no litigation at all through most of the 1770s and 1790s. Litigation rates show similar unevenness in the smaller surrounding towns, where the problem is, if anything, exacerbated by their late establishment and small populations throughout this period.[6]

Confidence in these rates is further undermined by the fact that over the last two hundred years many litigation records have slipped out of the government archives and into private hands. (This is true of all the documents cited in the notes that are held in collections bearing personal names rather than names of towns.) There is no way to know how often documents have migrated in this way. The records that have remained, moreover, are obviously incomplete in many cases; one often finds a response but no original petition, or a written decision without any written submissions by the parties. Again, there is no way to assess how many records have been lost. For these reasons, a statistical analysis of the cases would be pointless.

All that said, if one takes 1771 and Ste. Geneviève as the time and place for which the greatest percentage of records has survived, and thus the best choice for a representative year, the residents of Upper Louisiana were frequent litigators. That year, when there were thirty litigated disputes, the white male population of Ste. Geneviève was only 212.[7] Since each case requires at least two parties, every white man stood a two in seven chance of being a party to litigation that year. When one adds the possibility that a case might include more than two parties, and when one considers the need for witnesses in many cases, the chances of being involved somehow in litigation in Ste. Geneviève in 1771 must have been much higher even than that. This is a litigation rate much higher than exists in the late-twentieth-century United States, where litigation is an unusual occurrence for the overwhelming majority of the population, although it may be in line with the higher litigation rate typical of frontier communities.[8]

If one assumes that the subject matter of the surviving cases is similar to what has been lost, one can get a sense of what all this litigation was about. As in Mexican California (and most other places and times), the great majority of these suits were to recover voluntarily contracted debts.[9] The remainder divide into many categories, none constituting a significant percentage of the total. There were some disputes over who would inherit an estate; some suits for damage caused to one's slaves; some allegations of libel; some claims for damage caused by animals; and a variety of suits claiming injury as a result of what an Anglo-American lawyer would today characterize as negligence. None of these areas was the subject of any written law understood to govern disputes. These cases were decided with reference only to the unwritten norms of the community.

EASY CASES

Most litigated disputes in Upper Louisiana, like most in the United States today, raised no serious question as to what law should apply. The most common sort of case, a simple suit to collect a debt, was easily decided with reference to nothing beyond the generally accepted norm requiring debtors to pay their debts. Thus when Joseph Story (no apparent relation to the nineteenth-century justice) filed a petition seeking to be placed in possession of William Gibson's land because Gibson had failed to pay a debt of 134 piastres, and when Story submitted a copy of his mortgage on Gibson's land, commandant Henri Peyroux needed to consult no written law before awarding him the land.[10] Everyone knew that debts should be paid and that contracts would be enforced; the law was simply not a field for argument.

Suits to recover debts could, of course, be more complicated than this, but most were still easily resolved without much dispute over what the law should be. Perhaps the most common complication involved issues of fact; in small towns where currency existed more as an accounting fiction than an actual substance, the credit relationships among residents often grew so intricate that their unraveling took some time. For the entire summer of 1794, for instance, Augustin Bertau and Jean Baptiste Bequet petitioned and counterpetitioned over who owed whom how much. Bertau began by complaining to commandant François Vallé that Bequet was harassing him about a nonexistent debt. Bequet responded that Bertau was indebted to him for his share of the cost of constructing Ste. Geneviève's new church, and that he was holding some of Bertau's possessions in his house as security. Bertau then claimed that Bequet was wrongfully detaining both his land and his personal property; Bequet replied that Bertau had left the land in his care when Bertau had left the country, and that he had actually performed a service for Bertau by preserving the land's value. Many more rounds followed, each adding a layer of complexity to the financial relationship between the two men, while each document pointed out the "malice" and the "chicanery" of the opponent's previous submission. Vallé eventually referred the case up to Lt. Gov. Zenon Trudeau in St. Louis, who sorted everything out by restoring Bertau to his land and his possessions, and by concluding that neither party had sufficiently proven that the other owed him anything.[11] Again, once the facts had been straightened out, the case was reduced to cross-claims for debt; no law was needed other than the uncontested principle that legitimate debts should be paid.

When a suit to recover a debt involved some legal complication, the governing rule could often be discerned by local government officials simply by reference to standard business practices. In 1799, for example, Robert Rogers sued Jacob Bogard to recover sixty piastres on a note, but explained that "he was unfortunate enough to lose the note in question." Should a creditor be able to recover on a lost note? Rogers argued that he should; in his petition, he offered Bogard "all possible securities, in case the note is presented afterwards." Bogard did not contest the existence of the debt. He responded instead with a short lecture on contemporary commercial practices:

> Mr. Rogers understands very poorly the force of a note, if he thinks that a receipt and a guarantee would keep me from paying, were it presented to me at Philadelphia or in any other place. . . . Mr. Rogers will say, "Take recourse in the guarantee, and you will be compensated." I respond to him that the guarantee is good today, but it may not be so in ten years, and that if my affairs take me to Russia, it would be very difficult for me to come and be reimbursed here, should the note in question be presented to me in that country.

Commandant Charles Delassus was persuaded by the "well-founded reasons produced by Sr. Bogard." It was this appeal to the practices of merchants, understood as the foundation of (and synonymous with) the law governing notes, that persuaded Delassus to rule in Bogard's favor.[12] This example should dispel any notion that unwritten norms are necessarily simpler or more homespun than official written law. The merchants of New Madrid evidently knew a great deal of what lawyers would call the law of negotiable instruments. The point here is that they understood this law to derive from the practices of merchants like themselves, not from the command of any official of the Spanish government.

Another sort of debt-related issue of law arose when Moses Austin requested the seizure and judicial sale of a black slave belonging to Robert Greer, to satisfy a debt Greer owed to Austin. As the auction was about to begin, the slave (who remains unnamed in the litigation records) pointed out that Greer had promised to free him at the end of seven years. Delassus immediately halted the sale, so that Austin could determine if this was true; all proceeded on the tacit assumption that if Greer had made such a promise, the slave would soon be free, which would drastically reduce the price the slave could command at a sale. Two days later, Austin reported that Greer had in fact promised the slave freedom, but that Greer himself had not yet fully paid for the slave, who remained mortgaged for more than half of his original sale price. Could the owner of a partially mortgaged slave grant the slave freedom? Delassus reasoned that he could not, because such a grant would "diminish his value to the detriment of his creditors." Again, an issue of commercial law was resolved with reference to generally accepted unwritten mercantile norms; no law derived from any other source was necessary.[13]

Noncommercial cases also could often be resolved with reference to nothing more than the unstated norms of the community. In 1804, for example, John Butler complained that Jesse Demint and Andrew Simison were spreading "scandalous gossip" about his wife and his daughter Rebecca. Butler accused both of claiming that "the said Jesse Demint had laid with the petitioner's daughter in the same bed where her mother was, the petitioner's wife, and that lying between the one and the other, he had done with the daughter what he wanted to do." Butler asked the commandant, Pierre Antoine Laforge, to "condemn them to such penalty as your wisdom will find appropriate and which is prescribed by the law." The day Butler submitted his petition, Laforge ordered everyone mentioned in it to appear before him to testify.

The first witness was Demint himself, who claimed to be a victim of the gossip as well:

> We asked him what sort of scandalous and dishonorable discourse was spread about the Dlle. Rebecca. He responded that Simison told him that he learned from Joseph Dumay that one day he heard that the declarant [Demint] found himself in the house of M. John Butler with his wife and his daughter the husband being absent, he stayed at first with them around the fire and that the bad weather continuing he asked

> to spend the night in the house, which the Dlle. Butler refused at first, but then the Dlle. Butler permitted him to stay and that he then lay between the mother and the daughter, and that fearing by his movements to wake the mother of the Dlle. Rebecca, the latter placed herself on the declarant to consummate what was their design to do.

Demint testified that the gossip "against the reputation of Dlle Rebecca daughter of John Butler was absolutely false that he had never taken any liberties neither with the daughter nor with the mother, and that he had never told anyone that he had obtained any favors."

Laforge then took the testimony of everyone—and there were many—who had heard Demint and Simison tell stories about Rebecca Butler. He interrogated each witness in the presence only of a bailiff, an interpreter if needed (the parties and many of the witnesses were Americans who had recently crossed the Mississippi and did not speak French), and two témoins d'assistance. The witnesses described increasingly lurid versions of the gossip they had heard from Demint and Simison. Joseph Dumay had heard from Simison that Demint "lay down between the mother and the girl Rebecca, that he didn't dare move, but that the girl being passionate placed herself on Jesse Deminte to accomplish what she desired." Etienne Dumay, a miller, recalled that Simison had come to his mill to tell him that he had "slept between the mother and the daughter and that he had enjoyed the daughter but that the mother had awoken." David Winzelle also recalled that Simison claimed to have been the one involved. Simison blamed the gossip on Demint; he testified that Demint had told him that Rebecca Butler had "put her hand in the pants of the said Jesse Deminte." Robert Caldwell had heard from Demint that Demint

> was on good terms with the Dlle Butler and that he was in the position of obtaining from her all that one can desire from a girl that he added that he often went there to stay up late and that there under cover of darkness he had the liberty of putting his hands everywhere he wanted on the person of the said Dlle Butler.

This version was topped by John Lamb, who had heard, originating from Demint, an even more scandalous story about Rebecca Butler.

> there was in the field a young girl who let young men take all sorts of liberties with her and who also took them with young men . . . one

> young man after having run his hand where he wanted on the Demoiselle, she in turn caressed him, had put her hand in the pants of the young man and after having unbuttoned him had pulled which gave him such pleasure, and the young man while lying down asked if she found that nice to which she responded yes and that it was very nice.

Before calling the next witness, Laforge noted his displeasure with the "notorious contradictions" in the testimony so far. He then recalled Joseph Westbrook, who, despite having been mentioned as a gossip recipient by others, had earlier claimed not to have heard anything. Westbrook then changed his testimony. He now recalled Demint speaking of "certain girls," such as Rebecca Butler, who were

> so free with the goods that there was one with whom he did what he wanted and ran his hand freely on her where it seemed good to him and that the girl on her part gave him caresses, that one day his pants having been unbuttoned the girl grabbed and caressed his virile parts that he on his part caressed her at the same time and that he asked her if she found that nice to which she responded while still caressing him and running her hand on what accompanied, that she had never seen one before.

Rhen Shelby then also recanted his earlier claim not to have heard any gossip, and told the same story, almost word for word.

After three full days of this testimony, probably recognizing the inevitable, Demint asked Laforge to "stop the course of the present investigation" in order to pursue settlement negotiations with Butler. The following day, Demint and Butler appeared before Laforge and

> told us that after having conferred between them and that as the greatest desire of John Butler is that there be no doubt in the public mind about the virtue of his daughter's morals, they reached agreement as to what follows: . . . that Jesse Deminte acknowledge before four notable persons of this post in our presence . . . that indiscreetly, he held various conversations which against his will compromised the reputation of the Dlle Rebecca Butler who he has never ceased to respect.

Demint made this declaration the same day; somewhat unconvincingly, he explained that "he is very sorry to have held such discourse, but that his intention never was to make people believe that he took any liberties with the said Demoiselle."

The case proceeded against Simison, but the outcome was no longer in doubt. Laforge announced his judgment later that day:

> We declare him, said Andrew Simison, to be convicted of having wounded the reputation of the Dlle Rebecca Butler by slandering her morals; and as such, we denounce him to the fathers and mothers of families, as a slanderous man, and a man dangerous in his discourse against women. . . . We ordain that this present judgment shall be posted in public, to the number of twelve copies, six in French and six in English, the whole to be at the expense of the said Andrew Simison.[14]

This case is fascinating for any number of reasons—the view of social relations among young adults in early-nineteenth-century New Madrid, the glimpse of gender-specific implicit moral conventions, the frankness of the witnesses in relating what they had heard, and so on—but for our purposes, the case stands as an excellent example of how most litigated disputes were resolved. In a case that took a great deal of time and effort to adjudicate, there was no need for written law. The entire case was resolved on the universally accepted premise (in the end, acknowledged even by one of the defendants) that it is wrong to spread false gossip. This idea did not exist in written form in Upper Louisiana. It was an unwritten custom at most, but that did not prevent it from being the governing rule in this and other libel cases.[15]

Many other noncommercial cases were resolved in similar fashion. When Louis Dubreuil and Charles Sanguinet petitioned to have Sanguinet's stepsister, Constance Conde, removed from the custody of her stepfather, Gaspard Roubieu, on the ground that he "struck her twice" and called her "only the most odious names," the litigation proceeded on the assumption, evidently shared by all concerned, that Roubieu had a duty to abstain from such conduct.[16] When Charles Vallé's oxen trampled the garden of his neighbor Peyroux, Peyroux's petition assumed the existence of a duty on the part of Vallé to enclose his oxen.[17] In both cases, the governing rule existed nowhere on paper. Yet its validity was never questioned; it was a custom understood by everyone involved to constitute the rule that would resolve the dispute.

Litigants sometimes appealed to these customs explicitly. When Cézar, a slave belonging to Charles Sanguinet, drowned in the Gingra River, Sanguinet sued Jacques Clamorgan for compensation, on the theory that Clamorgan was responsible because Cézar was working for Clamorgan at the time. Sanguinet alleged that Clamorgan "acted against the regulations and customs which prohibit exposing other people's slaves to danger." The allegation suggests that Sanguinet understood the two types of authority—"regulations and customs"—to be interchangeable in this context, as equally valid sources of the law governing the dispute. It is not even clear that there was any such "regulation" present in written form in Upper Louisiana at the time. If there was not, Sanguinet's blending of regulation and custom becomes even more striking, as he would have been citing the existence of custom as sufficient in itself to establish the existence of something understood to be "regulation."

In any event, Sanguinet's appeal to custom was matched by Clamorgan, who responded with a hypothetical predicated even more solidly on custom:

> I wish to suppose for a moment that this slave was rented out by his master . . . ; the well established custom of this place easily suggests that the risks of accidental death are assumed by the leased slave's owner, because, in the agreements made between individuals in this dependency, it is ordinarily stipulated that the leased slave will not be exposed to this or that danger; this proves that if such conditions are not inserted by the owner into the agreement, accidental death is his own risk.[18]

In Clamorgan's view, even more than in Sanguinet's, it is local practice that determines the governing rule, not vice versa. If slave owners have conventionally assumed the existence of a given rule, that rule is suitable for use in resolving disputes, whether or not it was ever reduced to writing or approved by any institution of government.

The same conflation of law and custom is evident in Silvestre Labadie's response to the petition of Elizabet Vachard seeking to hold him responsible for the loss of the boat full of lead, already mentioned in chapter 1. Labadie placed the blame on Vachard's son Louis, "who is the boat's driver, and who is consequently responsible for everything that may happen as a result of his negligence, up until he has delivered all the objects in his care; this is the law and custom of the area."[19] The use of "law and custom" as effective synonyms—like "rules and regulations" or "pattern and practice"—suggests that Labadie understood the two as equally valid sources of binding rules. Since there is no record of any written law in Upper Louisiana that related to the duties of boatmen, much less any written law that assigned responsibility for a boat's cargo to the driver until the cargo was delivered, it is reasonable to infer that Labadie was deriving the existence of this "law" solely from his knowledge of the customs of boatmen.

In 1779, when Auguste Chouteau attempted to prevent town residents from fishing in the pond adjacent to his water mill, custom played the same role. Chouteau's petition explained that he had recently purchased the mill and the pond, only to find himself "troubled today in his acquisition, due to some persons who go to fish in the mill's pond." Such unauthorized fishing, Chouteau argued, was "in mockery of the customs and laws, which consider the fish in a pond to be immobile and attached to the place, and properly belonging to the owner." Again, there was no such written law in Upper Louisiana; Chouteau was inferring the existence of "laws" from his knowledge of "customs." Lt. Gov. Fernando de Leyba's decision rested even more explicitly on custom. "[H]aving been informed by various other residents of the place, trustworthy people," he explained, "that fishing in the pond or stream in question has always been common to all the residents, . . . we nonsuit Sr. Chouteau of his demand."[20] Leyba's opinion makes no reference to any written law. The rule governing the case was derived entirely from repeated practice.[21]

Most litigated disputes in colonial St. Louis and the surrounding towns were of this character. Written law played no direct role, because the disputes were resolvable with reference only to the unwritten norms of the community—in mercantile disputes, the customs of merchants, and in other disputes, the norms of the wider white population.

HARD CASES

Such a system breaks down, of course, when there is no generally accepted norm at hand, or when a dispute could plausibly be governed by two opposing norms. In these more difficult cases, local officials tended to avoid having to reach any decision. Such cases were conventionally referred instead to arbitrators from the local community, chosen by the litigants.

Reliance on unwritten norms, on local custom, is even clearer here. It is conceivable (although not very likely) that government officials were surreptitiously using written law to decide cases, either by consulting it without citation or by being so steeped in it that they drew from memory, perhaps unconsciously. But this was not possible when cases were decided by traders and farmers. The local residents who served as arbitrators knew no written law from Spain or New Orleans. They may have been aware of the local ordinances promulgated by commandants and syndics, but these rarely applied to any litigated disputes. All an arbitrator had at his disposal in resolving a case was his sense of right and wrong. And that sense does not develop in a vacuum; it is derived from the unwritten norms of the community. This is particularly true when the sense of right and wrong pertains to commercial matters, where personal morality tends to play less of a role than a knowledge of how things are usually done.

In 1782, for example, merchants in New Orleans shipped a large quantity of taffia to Auguste Chouteau in St. Louis, with the shipping fee paid in advance to Eugène Pourée, the boat's pilot. On the way up the Mississippi, Pourée's boat was attacked at the Yazoo River "by a party of Englishmen"; he retreated to Natchez, where he had to raise the salaries of his employees to persuade them to continue; farther upriver, hearing of additional brigands farther north, he had to stop at the Arkansas post, where he had to rent a warehouse to store the boat's cargo and hire a new crew. When Pourée finally made it to St. Louis, he presented Chouteau with a bill for his additional expenses, which Chouteau refused to pay. Pourée petitioned Lt. Gov. Francisco Cruzat, asking:

> Doesn't [Chouteau] know that when a ship is obliged by force majeure to lay up en route, the shippers are bound to pay the captain the fees in their entirety, as if the ship had completed its voyage; and that if the captain makes a second assessment, the shippers are bound to pay it in proportion to what they have on board?

Chouteau responded with the observation that "it would be a great wrong to shippers to have to pay the fee twice for goods embarked in a ship whose fee had already been paid before it left port."

The case thus posed a classic question of commercial law: Who suffers the loss when the shipment of goods is unexpectedly costly, the master of the ship or the person sending the shipment? This is a question not readily answered with reference to the generally accepted norms of the community, and it was for this reason a question exceedingly difficult for a lieutenant governor to answer. Cruzat thus ordered the parties to choose one arbitrator each. The two men chosen, Joseph Marie Papin and Gabriel Cerré, were themselves merchants who were familiar with commercial practice. They concluded that Chouteau should pay only for the storage of the taffia at the Arkansas post "following mutual understandings," but not any of the additional expenses incurred by Pourée.[22] Given the backgrounds of Papin and Cerré, there can be little doubt that this decision embodies their understanding of commercial custom. They had no written law to consult, and even if they had, they would not have known where to start. Cruzat's decision to appoint arbitrators in the first place can thus be understood as an official decision to let unwritten norms serve as the rules of decision.

The same type of decision making can be seen in any of the cases submitted to arbitration during the period. When two English-speaking immigrants, James Ferrell and William Cowen, litigated over the effect of successive salt-mining agreements, for example, the dispute was submitted for arbitration to a panel of five English-speaking colleagues in Ste. Geneviève, whose opinions were clearly drawn from their understanding of contemporary contracting and record-keeping practices in the industry. In Ezekiel Able's opinion, "James Ferel has not got all his debt credits agreeable to all the resetes," and Ferrell thus stood indebted to William Cowen for the difference. Andrew Price agreed: "It is my opinion," he explained,

> that the first agreement between William Cowen & James Feril is void and of no effect and that the last is good and it appears frome the latter that sd Feril stand in debted to sd Cowen thirteen hundred & forty dollars & forty cents and that said Cowen keeps possion of the sd Furnace.

The remaining three arbitrators were likewise of the "oppinion that Ferell has not all his just Credits for Recepts."[23] These men were most likely fellow salt-miners; they were certainly not lawyers. Their view of how the dispute should be resolved could not have come from any source other than their knowledge of local custom.

The relationship between employers and employees, a source of many of Upper Louisiana's litigated disputes, was likewise often governed by unwritten norms discerned by arbitrators. In 1780, Silvestre Labadie and Auguste Chouteau sued a group of employees who failed to deliver provisions to a winter camp of Indian traders (who were presumably also employed by Labadie and Chouteau), and then failed to bring peltries from the camp back to town. The employees explained that because they had been robbed twice by Indians, they suffered from such severe hunger that they had been forced to leave their cargo unattended while they hunted for deer (at which time the provisions were apparently lost), and on the return trip were reduced to cooking and eating some of the peltries. Arbitrators chosen by the parties

> after due deliberation unanimously condemned Frederic Loise [one of the employees, apparently the supervisor of the others] to be responsible for the loss of the peltries and other effects he had under the direction of MM. Labady and Cheauteau for having failed to fulfill the duties of an employee, and particularly for having left with others the provisions he was given being easily able to carry them with him.

No written law in Upper Louisiana governed the relationship between employers and employees, much less spelled out the duties of an employee to his employer. Again, the arbitrators' decision appears to have rested on conventional unwritten understandings of who was responsible for what. And again, the local government official's choice to submit the dispute to arbitration in the first place is best understood as an official decision (taken at the local level) to let local norms rather than official written law govern disputes.[24]

Examples of this mode of dispute resolution could be multiplied further, but the result would be a tedious catalog of humdrum arbitrated cases, all to prove a point I hope has already been made. The multilayered structure of written law that theoretically governed the St. Louis area had next to no bearing on any actual litigated disputes. Most of these were resolved by local officials with reference to universally accepted norms—debts should be paid, contracts should be enforced, people should not spread false gossip. When the applicable rule was not obvious, officials generally referred disputes to arbitrators chosen by the parties, in what appears to have been a conscious decision to let community residents derive their law from conventional practices. This was especially true in commercial cases, where the relevant customs were those of the communities of traders, salt-miners, and so on. Because commercial cases constituted the overwhelming majority of litigated disputes, it is hard to know whether arbitration was particularly favored in such cases, or whether the instances of commercial arbitration that have survived simply reflect the preponderance of commercial matters in the universe of decided cases.

CHAPTER 4

Common Fields

In this chapter, I will move from a consideration of the legal system generally to a focus on one specific element of it, the way in which the residents of Upper Louisiana allocated property rights in their land. Chapter 8 will return to the subject, to discuss how property rights were reallocated after the Louisiana Purchase.

ORGANIZATION

The French residents of Upper Louisiana, like the earliest European colonizers of many parts of the present-day United States, held much of their productive land in common. They farmed in part in common fields, grazed their animals in common pastures, and gathered wood and other natural resources from common wasteland. French, Spanish, and English settlers replicated the property regimes they remembered from Europe, in which a significant portion of local productive land was understood as an asset belonging primarily to the community, and only secondarily to the individual. Despite the obvious cultural differences among colonists from different parts of Europe, their systems of property rights in productive land bore many similarities, corresponding to similarities among land ownership models across northern Europe.[1]

Both the French and Spanish influences in Missouri were part of this pattern. Common fields covered much of early modern France and Spain.[2] Spanish farmers and government officials brought the notion to the Spanish American colonies.[3] French farmers and officials did the same in the French colonies, where common field farming developed in Canada and was subsequently brought to the Illinois country.[4]

Many years after the 1764 founding of St. Louis, one of the founders recalled that "immediately after their arrival at this place, they commenced fencing for a common field."[5] Two years later, the residents laid out a second common field.[6] By 1767, when Spain first attempted to exercise sovereignty over the area, the common fields were already established; the Spanish order to plant fields of grain "for the common welfare, all the people sharing in them in common" only ratified local practice.[7] The French inhabitants of the area established common fields soon after the founding of most or all of the surrounding towns as well.[8]

There were two types of these fields. The first was a true commons, a large tract in which all inhabitants of the town had a right to graze animals and gather timber for firewood. The St. Louis area included a mixture of grassland and forest, each of which existed in sufficient quantity to permit each town in the area to have one such tract, referred to simply as "the commons."[9] While the evidence on this point is not completely clear, it appears that in principle these commons could be used by anyone, without racial or residential restrictions. In practice, of course, use of the commons would only have been available to people who lived close enough to utilize the resources located within them. The theoretical distinction between a resource open to an unlimited number of people and one open to a large but bounded number, a distinction with some importance today regarding globally accessible resources such as clean air, thus has little relevance to the commons of Upper Louisiana. Although the commons were most likely open to all, there were at most only a few thousand people who could have used any town's commons at any one time.

The second type of field was more complex. Farming was conducted in large common fields, divided into strips assigned to individual residents. St. Louis had five such common fields—the St. Louis Prairie, the Petite Prairie, the Grande Prairie, the Cul de Sac, and the Prairie des Noyers. The customary length of a strip was forty arpents, or nearly a mile and a half. The width of the strips varied according to the size and number of town lots held; a typical width was one arpent (192.5 feet), but widths of one and a half or two arpents were not unusual.[10] The most common width of strips in the Ste. Geneviève common field, for example, was one arpent; widths ranged from a low of one-third of an arpent to a high of nine arpents.[11] The shape of the strips presumably facilitated plowing by minimizing the number of turns needed, and may have also made it easier for farmers to share equipment.

Between spring planting and fall harvest, the only thing common about this second type of common field was the fence surrounding it, which all owners of strips were obliged to maintain. Each resident was entitled to whatever he could produce on his own strip of land. There is no surviving evidence of any restrictions on the types of crops each farmer was to plant. Once the harvest was in, however, the field became a true commons, in which the residents could graze their animals until the following spring. This two-season system was common throughout Europe, and was utilized in Spain's other North American colonies as well.[12] It is not clear whether in principle grazing was open to all residents of Upper Louisiana or only to those who possessed strips within the field. In practice, this distinction may have made little difference, as strips were available to anyone who wished to use them. Any farmer with animals needing to graze was already likely to own a strip.

Individual strips in the common fields were allocated by the government without charge, based on a minimal showing of need.[13] The location of each person's strip seems to have been determined on a first come, first served basis. In the one recorded instance where an entire common field was allocated simultaneously, after the Mississippi River flooded the original Ste. Geneviève common field, strip location was determined by lottery.[14] Like privately owned land, strips could be bought and sold.[15] When the owner of a strip died, the strip became part of the owner's estate, and passed along with the rest of the owner's real and personal property.[16] Property rights in the common fields were thus closer to a system of private parcels than to a true commons. Possession of a strip in a common field differed from fee simple ownership in only a few respects. Strip owners could not exclude others from their land for roughly half the year; they most likely could not use the land for any purpose other than farming (more precisely, no evidence suggests that anyone ever tried); and they were obliged to keep up their section of the fence. In theory, an enterprising farmer with enough resources could have consolidated numerous strips into a single large parcel. In practice, farming was never lucrative enough to warrant consolidation, most likely because of the small local population and the absence of any nearby export market. The area's entrepreneurs, in fact, abandoned farming altogether for more profitable ventures such as trading with the Indians and mining for lead.[17] (The Indian trade was governed by a private property regime, under which the government annually allocated exclusive licenses to trade with particular tribes.[18] The lead mines began as a commons, but toward the end of the eighteenth century became an uneasy mixture of commons and private land claims, resulting in years of sometimes violent disputes.[19])

As a large and very old body of economic theory has demonstrated, resources owned in common are susceptible to being used inefficiently, because the set of incentives facing each individual owner is not necessarily in line with the collective good. This is true in two complementary senses. First, each owner stands to gain personally by consuming more of the resource than he would if he were the sole owner. For each unit he consumes, he gains that entire unit, but the loss of the unit from what remains is spread over all of the co-owners. A sole proprietor consuming one unit has one less unit to consume in the future, and will accordingly balance his consumption between the present and the future in order to maximize his long-run best interests. But one of, say, ten co-owners consuming one unit has, like each of his colleagues, only 0.1 less units to consume in the future. Each of his colleagues faces an identical calculation. In balancing consumption between the present and the future, co-owners will overvalue present consumption, and undervalue saving for the future, relative to what the group as a whole would calculate its best interests to be. A resource owned collectively is thus susceptible to *overconsumption*, to being used up faster than would be optimal.[20]

Second, each owner has less of an incentive to maintain the resource than he would if he were the sole owner. A sole proprietor expending one unit of labor on repair will capture all the benefit of that labor, but one of ten co-owners expending an identical unit of labor will capture only one-tenth of its value, because the benefit of his work will be spread among all the co-owners. As each of his colleagues makes the same calculation, the resource will be maintained less carefully than if it had been owned by a single person. "[T]hat which is common to the greatest number," Aristotle explained long ago, "has the least care bestowed upon it. Every one thinks chiefly of his own, hardly at all of the common interest. . . . [E]verybody is more inclined to neglect the duty which he expects another to fulfil."[21] As Thomas Aquinas suggested, "every man is more careful to procure what is for himself alone than that which is common to many or all: since each one would shirk the labor and leave to another that which concerns the community."[22] Many economists have since repeated the point. Along with overconsumption, resources owned in common are susceptible to *undermaintenance*, to being repaired less carefully than would be optimal.

The division of the common fields into quasi-private strips enabled the residents to avoid the problem of overconsumption. Such was not the case with respect to winter grazing in the common fields, when the fields reverted to true commons, nor with those commons limited to grazing and wood-gathering. Overgrazing was never considered a problem in this period, however, simply because the number of animals in the area was never very large relative to the extent of available land. Overconsumption of wood was a more serious problem, as is discussed below. Undermaintenance, the other half of the collective action problem, was a constant threat to the survival of the common fields, which depended on secure fences to keep animals in during the grazing season and to keep them out during the planting season. Building and repairing fences required concerted action; a single hole in a fence could mean the loss of a year's crops or many animals, depending on the place and the time of year.

Outside observers of the commons, both American and Spanish, were quick to point out these collective action problems. There is no record of any of the French inhabitants expressing any view one way or the other, partly because of the low rate of literacy, but most likely also because this system of property rights was so much a part of everyday life that it hardly seemed worth discussing.

The American reaction was mixed. Washington Irving thought Ste. Geneviève's common field so successful that "strangers [were] apt to marry the Ste. Geneviève girls to get the right" to farm there.[23] Most visitors, however, must have seen the common fields as inefficient, because they tended to search elsewhere for explanations as to why people might choose to farm in this manner. Another traveler viewed farming in a common field as a necessary accommodation to natural conditions. "As the prairie has no timber upon it," he explained, incorrectly, "the trouble and expense of fencing would be very considerable: they have therefore but one fence around the whole." He thus concluded, also incorrectly, that the French had learned this technique from local Indian tribes, who also faced the same supposed shortage of timber.[24] Henry Marie Brackenridge, another visitor, attributed the common fields to the danger of Indian attack in the early years of French settlement, and the corresponding need for the inhabitants to work close together, a danger he suggested was no longer present.[25] Frederick Bates, one of the earliest American government officials in St. Louis after the Louisiana Purchase, chalked it up to a shortcoming embedded in French culture. "The French People," he sniffed, "for the most part live in villages and cultivate a Common Field. They cannot bear the idea of separation. To live in the country without a neighbour in less than half a mile is worse than death, and almost as bad as Purgatory."[26] The implicit comparison was to the pattern of Anglo-American settlement of the West, in which the home was part of the same large private parcel as the farmland, a pattern often resulting in long distances between homes and between workplaces.[27]

Spanish officials living among the residents had a closer view of the collective action problems inherent in managing the common fields, and perhaps for that reason were less interested in attempting to explain the common fields' existence than in correcting their defects. One official, Charles Delassus, twice reported to the governor in New Orleans, in 1793 and again in 1797, concerning "a great inconvenience prejudicial to the progress of agriculture"—the inability of any of the farmers to grow profitable crops during the winter, because of the custom of opening the common fields to livestock after the autumn harvest. His proposed solution, never adopted, was not privatization but better regulation: he suggested fencing the animals out for the entire year.

As Delassus saw it, the commons posed two more collective action problems as well. On the one hand, residents were underinvesting in maintenance: "I mean to speak of the fires of the fields, woods and prairies, . . . these fires are set and lighted without precaution and without any object of great utility, and often by the negligence of the numerous smokers of this country, white as well as Indians and slaves," each of whom faced a much smaller individual loss from a fire than if he had been smoking on his own land. On the other hand, residents were overconsuming the resources of the commons relative to what the rate of consumption would have been on privately held land, because of

> the vicious manner generally used as much by whites as by slaves who in order to cut fire wood with less difficulty use only the end of the top of large trees that they cut down for this purpose, in such a way that they leave and abandon more than three fourths of the length of each tree; also it is of the most evident notoriety that all of the woods of the environs of said villages are strewn with these great bodies of abandoned trees although still very healthy and good for burning.[28]

A decade later, residents of St. Charles experienced the same phenomenon. "[A] prodigious quantity of wood has been lost," a group reported, "because the residents, in cutting down trees for their heat, were content to take only the branches, and left the trunks to rot on the ground." The solution to these two difficulties was not privatization but better (and better-enforced) regulation; Delassus proposed simply banning fires in the woods and forbidding wasteful tree-cutting. In St. Charles as well, the solution proposed by the villagers and ratified by the government was not to divide up the commons, but rather to "prohibit all persons from felling any tree, or from taking any bark, on the commons of said place, for their heat, unless they take away the entire trunk of said trees."[29]

A more difficult collective action problem was posed by the annual need to repair the fences, as Lt. Gov. Zenon Trudeau pointed out:

> [S]ince the stockade which they have to make annually is extremely extended, and since the interest of all is not the same, in order that the stockade be kept up, the most exact vigilance is not sufficient to restrain the animals and in attending in time to its repair. Therefore, the crops are destroyed most years by said animals, and it will continue so in the future if that vicious custom is persisted in.

He predicted that eventually the problem of maintaining the fences would cause the inhabitants to "begin each one to enclose their farms."[30]

This prediction proved only partially correct. Sometime in the late 1790s, the fences surrounding two of St. Louis's common fields, the Grande Prairie and the Prairie des Noyers, lapsed into such a state of disrepair that they were taken down. Farming in these fields accordingly ceased.[31] (Farming resumed in the Prairie des Noyers about ten years later, after the fences had been rebuilt.[32]) Other commons and common fields remained in operation, however, until well after the Louisiana Purchase, despite what seemed to outside observers like obvious inefficiencies. These included the other three common fields of St. Louis, the St. Louis commons (the large tract used for grazing and collecting wood), and the commons and common fields of the smaller French communities surrounding St. Louis.[33]

GOVERNANCE

These commons (from here on, unless otherwise indicated I will be using the term in its general sense, to include what residents of the Upper Louisiana called the commons and the common fields) endured because the residents found ways to regulate themselves so as to solve, at least in part, the collective action problems inherent in managing a common resource.[34] Self-regulation was possible because of the way ownership of the commons was conceptualized.

The commons was understood to occupy a category of land ownership that barely existed in early nineteenth-century American legal thought, and barely exists in the United States today. American lawyers were and are accustomed to dividing land into two categories, private and public. Private land is owned by individuals, by groups of a given number, by fictional entities (such as corporations) that serve as proxies for groups of shifting size and membership, and so on. Public land is owned by the government, as a representative of all people with some defined connection to a particular geographical area. Thus one speaks of a vacant lot "owned by the city," a forest "owned by the state," and the like. When land is identified in this way, it is understood that in theory the land belongs to a shifting collection of people in a particular place, but that in practice the bundle of rights associated with ownership—the right to exclude, to sell, and so on—is held by a governmental organization.

The commons of the St. Louis area fell within neither category. The commons were not owned by any individual, any defined set of individuals, any organization, or any governmental body; they were owned *by the public directly*, without the intermediation of any government as the public's agent.[35] Residents of Upper Louisiana, like other inhabitants of Spanish North America, distinguished between government-owned public land and directly owned public land.[36] They referred to the former category as "public land," or "vacant land," or "the King's domain," in contrast to the latter category, which was called "the commons" (or the name of the individual common field). The contrast became manifest whenever a commons existed side by side with government-owned public land. Thus strip owners described the St. Charles common field as being bounded on one side by "Public land."[37] A landowner in Ste. Genevieve explained that his plot was located between "the S'Genevieve Big field [i.e., the common field]" to the east and "Vacant land" to the west.[38] The holder of a strip in the St. Louis Grande Prairie recalled that the common field was bordered on two sides "by Vacant land, or as it was then called the Kings Domain."[39]

The distinction between the two types of public land—land owned by the government and land owned by the people—became most apparent when government officials tried to grant private land concessions within an existing commons. Government-owned land was available for concession to settlers without charge; this was a routine aspect of local government. Every so often, however, when a government official would attempt to grant land within a commons, the public outcry was so great that the government was forced to recognize that it lacked any authority to dispose of land owned directly by the public.

In the late 1780s, for example, Lt. Gov. Francisco Cruzat purported to concede to five merchants, as individually owned plots, land located in St. Louis's Petite Prairie. More than fifty local farmers presented a request to Manuel Pérez, Cruzat's successor, to annul the concession. When Pérez did not respond, the farmers went over his head to the governor in New Orleans. Pierre DeVolsay, one of the more prominent citizens of St. Louis, first wrote to the governor to plead on behalf of the farmers (most of whom did not know how to write) "that it may please you to nullify all the concessions, which do considerable wrong to these poor wretches, and to give them back their commons."[40] Two weeks later, the farmers wrote their own letter to the governor. Over a few signatures and many more marks, the farmers explained how

> Mr. Pérez, lieutenant governor, wished to continue such concessions in this commons, saying that these lands were the King's domain, and the farmers had no title to them; yet for 24 years, they have benefitted from them (since the establishment of this village) . . . they never had any other place to pasture their beasts of all sorts; the commons was always surrounded with fences.

The farmers concluded by asking the governor to order the merchants who had received concessions "to hand these lands back over, for the public good, as they were not unaware that *these were public lands*, and their ownership would be detrimental to the public." The farmers thus understood the commons to be a form of public land not within the government's power to alienate, a category that would have been an oxymoron if there had been no distinction between public land and government land. Pedro Piernas, a former lieutenant governor, agreed with the farmers as to the distinction between land owned by the government and land owned by the people. He informed the governor that "during my long tenure and command in Illinois, for the reasons expressed by the inhabitants of Saint Louis, I did not issue any concessions in the territory of the Petite Prairie cited in regard to having always considered and held it to be a community possession." The governor declared Cruzat's concessions void, in an opinion that seemed to accept the views of Piernas and the farmers.[41]

A similar dispute erupted in early 1804, only a few days before American officials assumed control of St. Louis, when James Mackay, the commandant in St. Charles, began surveying land within the St. Charles commons for future concession, including a parcel he seems to have planned to grant to himself. The farmers of St. Charles immediately protested, and then protested again two days later that no action had been taken on their first petition.[42] Mackay admitted defeat. He agreed to "cede, abandon, and renounce forever, for myself and for my successors, any right, title, property, or pretention" to the land he had intended to claim as his own. He further declared "that I hand over said land to the common of St. Charles for the general use of anyone who will be a resident of said village of St. Charles, keeping for myself always the same communal rights as all other residents of said village to said land."[43] Again, public pressure had forced a government official to recognize the existence of a category of public land not within the government's power of alienation.

The government thus lacked the power to concede land within the grazing commons, and, once having conceded strips in the common fields, the government lacked the power to alter property rights there as well. But the government's power was even more limited than that. Whatever their nominal authority, Spanish officials tended to permit the French residents to regulate the commons themselves.

In St. Charles, for example, the farmers assembled in the presbytery after Mass to formulate rules governing the commons. They agreed to appoint a syndic each year, who "will make his inspection around the fences of the common field, and if he finds them open or broken, he will warn the farmer who owns the fence in question, to repair it immediately." If a farmer did not immediately repair the section of fence adjacent to his strip, the syndic was authorized to "seize the first objects he finds belonging to [the farmer], to be sold for cash, in order to pay for this repair; furthermore, this delinquent farmer will suffer 24 hours in prison for the first offense." The syndic was to make his inspection every Sunday, and on Thursdays during harvest time as well.

To facilitate the inspection, each strip owner was required "to create a navigable path, inside the common and along his fence, and put his name all along it on posts five feet in height, three feet from the fence." The syndic was authorized to have this done at the expense of any farmer who failed to comply. Finally, the farmers were required to "keep their fences closed starting April 15 at the latest," when the planting season began, "and will be allowed to open them on November 10 and no earlier," once the harvest was complete.[44] Residents of the other communities in the area enacted similar regulations.[45]

Even when government officials became involved in regulating the common fields, they understood their role as limited to helping the farmers regulate themselves. In 1793, for example, Lt. Gov. Zenon Trudeau traveled from St. Louis to Ste. Geneviève, where he "called an assembly of all of the inhabitants and citizens of the parish in order to deliberate as to the manner most convenient to the interests of everyone with regard to the fixing of the fences of the fields." By popular vote, the assembled farmers approved new regulations, which Trudeau "ratified, to remain immutable, in accordance with the wishes and the intentions of the majority of the inhabitants of the above said village."[46] In much the same manner, Charles Tayon, the commandant, assembled all the residents of St. Charles, "to decide if the bottom end of the commons would be enlarged or not." After deliberation, the residents agreed unanimously to enlarge the commons.[47]

It would be extremely helpful to have any evidence of how disputes within the commons were resolved, or evidence of exactly how syndics were selected and how they performed their work, but no such evidence appears to have survived.[48] Whether disputes were resolved with or without government officials, it is likely that they would have been resolved in oral proceedings that left no written record.

As best as one can tell, the conception of the commons as land owned neither privately nor by the government but directly by the unorganized public was thus understood to imply a corresponding division of political power. Government land was within the control of the government in both a sovereignty sense and a property sense, just like public land in the United States today; the government could both regulate it and convey it. Private land was within the control of the government in the sovereignty sense but not the property sense, just like private land in the United States today; the government could regulate it but not convey it. The commons was within government control in neither the sovereignty sense nor the property sense; in practice, the government could neither regulate it nor convey it. Because the land within the commons belonged to the people directly, without the government as intermediary, the people were understood to be able to govern that land directly as well. The commons was thus a zone of self-government, against the background of a political system that otherwise contained few formal representative institutions.

EXPLANATIONS

Why did the residents of Upper Louisiana choose to farm in common fields? They were following traditions well established in the places from which they had come, but that only pushes the question back a stage. Why were there common fields in Illinois and Canada, in France and Spain? It is unlikely that the common fields of Upper Louisiana were more productive than private farms would have been, because of the standard problems of overconsumption and undermaintenance. Even if there was a good reason for common fields in other places, why would local farmers persist in this method of land allocation? What benefit did they gain that offset the probable loss in productivity? Any attempt to answer this question requires a great deal of inference from the scanty surviving evidence.

One of the hypotheses offered by contemporary observers can surely be rejected: Private farms require more fences than a single fenced-in field, which might make a common field attractive where fencing material is scarce. In fact, wood was so plentiful in Upper Louisiana that tree trunks were left rotting on the ground after the branches had been cut. In addition, as I will show in chapter 8, American farmers preferred private farms, and apparently had no difficulty enclosing them. The expense of fencing is thus an unlikely explanation.

A bit more promising as a hypothesis for the existence of the common fields is another local circumstance mentioned by a contemporary, the need to farm close together so as to defeat or deter an Indian attack. In the early years of French settlement, the threat of an attack was always present. There was only one actual attack, in 1780, but the lingering possibility of one may have created a feeling of danger and a perceived need to avoid becoming separated by large distances.[49] If so, that danger subsided by the later part of the eighteenth century, and was gone by the time of the Louisiana Purchase. The increasing number of Americans in the area, who faced the identical risk of attack, showed no desire to farm in common fields. Their early fears of the Indians may, however, have caused the French to continue to prefer common fields, for two reasons. First, their experiences in 1780 may have caused them to overreact to what little danger remained, either by overestimating the chance of another attack in the future or by being so averse to that risk that they would sacrifice more agricultural productivity to minimize it than would the Americans. Second, once having organized themselves into common fields, the French may have found it costly to reallocate property rights in their land. A switch from one property regime to another is never without cost. If the productivity loss from overconsumption and undermaintenance was not high to begin with, it may have been less than the cost of switching to private farms, in which case the French would not have gained from privatizing their farmland. Unfortunately, the evidence necessary to assess these hypotheses is lacking. It is impossible to know the relative extent to which the French and the Americans feared Indian attack; the magnitude of the loss of productivity, if any, occasioned by farming in common fields; or what the costs of reallocating property rights would have been.

Several other possibilities are equally difficult to assess because of the lack of surviving evidence. The ability to graze animals in the common fields during the winter may have accounted for their existence. If there were returns to scale in grazing—if it was cheaper per animal to put them all in a large field rather than to put a few in each of several small fields—the gains from grazing may have exceeded any productivity loss from farming.[50] Common fields would have facilitated the sharing of farm equipment. If equipment were scarce, that may have provided a reason for farming close together.[51] The common fields may have provided a form of insurance, as Donald McCloskey has suggested with respect to common fields in Europe. If individuals in Upper Louisiana possessed strips in more than one field, the failure of one would not have been as catastrophic as the failure of a single private plot.[52] Again, an assessment of these possibilities is blocked; there is simply not enough evidence concerning the economics of grazing in Upper Louisiana, or the amount of equipment the local farmers had, or the pattern of strip ownership.

The same can be said about whatever social benefits might have been derived from working in the same place. Perhaps it was true, as Frederick Bates suggested, that the French did not like to work alone, and were willing to give up some productivity in exchange for a sense of fellowship. This is hard to determine, because most of the farmers were illiterate, and the records left by the literate do not discuss the issue. Without evidence independent of farming practices, any such explanation would be tautological: we would be inferring that the French liked farming in common fields from the fact that they actually did farm in common fields, and then concluding that they farmed in common fields because they liked to. Even if we had independent evidence of the farmers' preferences, moreover, attributing the common fields to those preferences would beg the question of why they had those preferences in the first place.

Finally, the farmers may have valued the political benefits conferred by the common fields. Under a formally unrepresentative Spanish government, where in principle most political power flowed down from the top, the commons was a mechanism for allocating power downward to the ordinary citizen. In governing the commons, the French farmers were in effect able to set up an unofficial alternative government, one which, unlike the official government, was popularly elected, was answerable to the people, and was most likely staffed by representatives drawn from the people themselves. It seems at least plausible that this outcome was viewed favorably by the farmers.

Again, there is no direct evidence that the farmers valued the commons for this reason. But the idea that people might own property in common in order to obtain political power is one that seems to accord with American experience. Groups of people have frequently set themselves apart from official institutions by agreeing to own property communally. Utopian communities throughout American history have held property in common, and some continue to do so today. Why? It is doubtful that members of communes expect land held in common to be more productive than private land. They have more likely experienced an alienation from official institutions strong enough to make them doubt their ability to have much of a voice in collective decision making. The decision to own property in common with others is a way of recapturing a sense of political participation. Among nineteenth-century utopian communities, the more successful were more likely to own land in common, and more likely to hold frequent meetings.[53] As one sympathetic observer of utopian communities in our own time observes,

> Intentional communities slake the thirst of their members for participation and for the management of their own destiny. The new communities devote many hours to deliberation and the resolution of great and small issues: how to select new members, whether to use chemical or organic fertilizers on their crops, how to allocate cars and other community resources, and how to rotate chores. In community both participation and responsibility are universal and visible.[54]

Or, as one member of a commune put it, "you are having a voice that counts in a minisociety. When there is no such possibility in society as a whole, you create your own society."[55] For many people, political participation seems to be an end in itself rather than a means to some other end. To obtain it, they are willing to sacrifice some productivity. Lawyers will be familiar with one version of this phenomenon, the persistent claim that procedural fairness is an end in itself, independent of substantive outcomes and despite its cost, because of the value perceived to lie in participation in the decision-making process.[56]

The analogy should not be pressed too far. Nineteenth- and twentieth-century American communes involved a degree of utopianism that was not present among the farmers of Upper Louisiana. The point is simply that people often perceive value, in a way that is difficult to put in monetary terms, in the ability to exercise a voice in collective self-government. Official institutions of government are often perceived to deny people a voice. Owning property in common sometimes provides the opportunity to carve out a zone of collective self-government.[57] It would be reasonable in such a situation for people to form a commons with respect to some resource even if a commons was not the most efficient way of exploiting that resource. If the farmers of Upper Louisiana thought this way, they would have been willing to exchange some productivity for the political power conferred by common ownership.

PART II

United States, 1803–1860

CHAPTER 5

Transition

With the Louisiana Purchase of 1803, sovereignty over Upper Louisiana passed to the United States. The larger and less populated northern portion of the Louisiana Purchase, including present-day Missouri, became the District of Louisiana, and was placed under the authority of the governor and judges of the Indiana Territory. A series of administrative reorganizations followed. In 1805, the area was separated from the Indiana Territory and became the Territory of Louisiana, governed by its own governor and judges. The Territory of Louisiana acquired its own legislature the following year. It was renamed the Territory of Missouri in 1812, when the name Louisiana was given to the state that still bears it. Missouri itself became a state in 1820.

The legal system of the United States, inherited from England, differed in many respects from that of Spain or France. More important to legal thought in the area, however, was the rapid influx of Americans into the area in the years after 1803. Many of these Americans were lawyers, who brought with them a way of thinking about law, and forms of resolving disputes, quite different from the accustomed thought and practice of the old inhabitants.

AMERICANS

At the time of the Louisiana Purchase, the area that became Missouri was, according to its first American government official, "less known than any other (inhabited by a civilized people) of the same extent on the globe." As a Spanish and French colony, it had been "almost inaccessible to us; nor were we influenced by motives of interest or curiosity to visit it."[1] If lawyers in the eastern United States knew anything about the area, their information would not have been professionally promising. Missouri contained only about ten thousand people, of whom only nine thousand were white, and most of the latter were French. For decades, they had managed without lawyers and largely without reference to written law. Yet within a year after the Louisiana Purchase there were already twelve lawyers in St. Louis, and many more flocked to the area after that.[2] Why?

The initial demand for lawyers came not from prospective clients but from the United States government, which intended to establish an American court system in St. Louis and needed judges with legal training immediately. Eastern lawyers quickly recognized that the "cession of Louissianna will . . . open a new field" of job opportunities in the West.[3] The jockeying began even before the cession occurred. John B. C. Lucas, a Pittsburgh lawyer (and newly elected member of Congress), began keeping close watch on the progress through Congress of the bill to ratify the Louisiana Purchase, and took care to solidify his ties with Secretary of the Treasury Albert Gallatin, an associate from western Pennsylvania.[4] Rufus Easton, a lawyer in upstate New York who believed his health required moving to a warmer place, began making discreet inquiries with highly placed friends about the possibility of an appointment in the soon-to-be-acquired territory.[5] Lawyers knew that theirs was an occupational group whose westward movement would in effect be subsidized by the federal government.

When Congress in late 1803 ratified the Louisiana Purchase, and then in early 1804 created positions for lawyers in New Orleans, the scramble for government money was on.[6] Easton promptly reminded Thomas Jefferson of his "strong attachment to the cause of Republicanism," and his "useful services rendered and personal sacrifices made" for the party's benefit, in the course of soliciting an appointment as United States attorney in New Orleans.[7] He rounded up letters of recommendation from anyone who he thought might have some influence. His friend Gideon Granger, the postmaster general, intervened on his behalf with Gallatin.[8] Thompson J. Skinner, a Republican member of Congress from Massachusetts, reassured Jefferson that Easton was not just "a very respectable Gentleman," but was also fortunately "A firm Undeviating Republican."[9] Correspondence poured into Washington, reminding Jefferson that Easton was "a Counsellor at law of respectable reputation" who had been "meritorious in the Republican cause."[10] Easton was not offered the post in New Orleans. He moved instead to the area around St. Louis, and waited for government positions to open up there.[11]

In early 1805, Congress detached St. Louis and the surrounding area from the Indiana Territory and provided it with officials of its own, including three territorial judges, three members of a Board of Land Commissioners, and one "agent" to represent the government in opposing fraudulent land claims.[12] Now the competition among lawyers for jobs in St. Louis began in earnest. Easton managed to secure one of the judgeships.[13] So did Lucas, who, as soon as his commission seemed safely in hand, informed his friend Gallatin for the first time that "owing to my deficiency in the practice and forms in the proceedings of court," it might be best if someone else were to be the chief judge.[14] (Lucas had been educated and had practiced law in France, and had briefly been a judge in Pennsylvania, but had apparently never practiced law in the United States.[15]) A month later, Lucas was back at the trough. He would not accept the judgeship he had pressed for, he told Gallatin, unless he could be simultaneously appointed land commissioner.[16] It was "the smallness of the salaries" of the judges, he explained to Secretary of State James Madison, and "the great expense which I should incurr in taking my family to Louisianna, and more than that the desire which I have to be honnored with the particular Confidence of government," that made him hold out for the second job.[17] Gallatin convinced Jefferson to accede to Lucas's request—Lucas now stood to earn a total of two thousand dollars as a land commissioner in addition to his annual eight-hundred-dollar salary as a judge—but in exchange Jefferson and Gallatin asked for one last political favor.[18] "[B]efore you leave your place of residence," Gallatin told Lucas, "you might render a last piece of service to a large body of your constituents, by drawing for them a petition both to Congress and to the State legislature applying for an amendment to the Constitution of the United States to limit the jurisdiction of the judiciary to objects of a federal or general nature." Such an amendment was necessary, in Gallatin's view, to undo the effects of a recent "opinion of the Supreme Court of the U. States."[19] With these arrangements made, Lucas was off to St. Louis.[20]

The same story was repeated many times over in the aftermath of the Louisiana Purchase. Clement Penrose, for instance, had very little legal experience—he had studied law in Philadelphia for eighteen months, but had never practiced. He had, however, several less tangible qualifications. He was a member of "two old and respectable Penns[ylvani]a families."[21] He spoke French. More relevant was that he was "a good republican" who had connections to Tench Coxe, a fellow Philadelphian and at the time a minor official in Jefferson's administration, and was the nephew of James

Wilkinson, the first territorial governor in St. Louis. Penrose became one of the land commissioners.[22]

Meanwhile, a young Baltimore lawyer named James Donaldson with "a disposition to reside in the Western Country" began making himself known to two fellow Baltimoreans, Robert Smith and Samuel Smith, respectively the secretary of the navy and U.S. senator from Maryland.[23] Donaldson congratulated Robert Smith on the recent reelection of Jefferson—"an event, which . . . fills with honest pride and satisfaction the breasts of those, who have only viewed, and admired him at an humble distance"; he applauded Smith's "appointment to your present high and honorable station, the duties of which I am satisfied will be discharged, with equal credit to yourself, and advantage to the country"; he reminded Smith of his "political opinions . . . which will transmit to future ages the glory of the present administration"; he mentioned that he had been practicing law for the past three years; and he finally asked if he might be appointed as a land commissioner.[24] Donaldson prompted Samuel Smith to bring to Jefferson's attention the fact that Donaldson had "written some useful pieces" for the Republican Party in Maryland.[25] Donaldson became a land commissioner and the recorder of land titles in St. Louis.[26]

In Kentucky, Judge John Coburn began to feel his "family and wants increase" beyond his salary, and accordingly asked Madison about the possibility of "some respectable appointment, either in Louisiana or elsewhere," which might provide more pay and the opportunity for some land speculation on the side. He was well suited for the job in the new territory, he advised Madison, "[h]aving a knowledge of the French language and being so long employed in the adjustment of the conflicting claims to Land in Kentucky."[27] It was not long before Madison was bombarded with letters in support of Coburn's request. From Caleb Wallace, another Kentucky judge, Madison learned that Coburn was "a Zealous unwavering and intelligent republican."[28] Coburn's "political character is and has been strictly republican," echoed Harry Innes, Kentucky's federal district judge.[29] Coburn's other associates emphasized his "firm inflexible republicanism," as well as his prior judicial service and his ability to read French.[30] Coburn was named one of the land commissioners in New Orleans, but as the position was intended to be temporary—it would expire when the commissioners had resolved all the land disputes—Coburn had to turn it down. He had sought a position in the West, Coburn explained, because of his desire "to obtain some more ample means of providing for a rising family than the economy of this State will permit." A post slated to expire was simply too great a financial risk.[31] Coburn was then appointed as a judge in New Orleans, but rejected that job too, due to "the delicate health of some of my family, and their extreme reluctance to risque the climate of that Country."[32] He asked instead for a position in St. Louis, "where the prospect of health is supposed to be better than in the more southern territory." Coburn eventually attained his goal of a St. Louis judgeship in 1807.[33]

The establishment of territorial government in St. Louis in the years after the Louisiana Purchase thus provided the initial impetus for lawyers to go there. Where the federal government created no jobs for lawyers, as in Arkansas, lawyers were scarce.[34] In St. Louis, the prospect of a government salary existed before the likelihood of finding private clients, and that salary, as in other parts of the West before and after, was enough to attract eager candidates.[35] Memories of ardent job seeking ran short, however. Easton, finding himself unpopular with many of his fellows, within a year was already complaining to Jefferson that "when I accepted this place of Judge I gave up a lucrative practice necessary" to the support of his family.[36] Two decades later, Lucas—still climbing the public ladder, this time unsuccessfully seeking to be governor of the Arkansas Territory—had convinced himself that "if instead of removing to Missouri 19 years ago I had remained in Pennsylvania it is probable that long before this time I should have acquired a standing which would justify my pretensions to a higher situation than this."[37] It was only Lucas's "self denyal by this retiring in the wilds of Missouri" that had held him back.[38] With such high-minded personal sacrifices, the first wave of lawyers arrived in Missouri.

INTERACTION

The first American officials to view the legal system of Upper Louisiana were appalled. "[T]he laws, rules of justice, and the forms of proceedings," Amos Stoddard reported from St. Louis two weeks after receiving possession of the area on behalf of the United States, "were almost totally arbitrary—for each successive Lieut. Governor has totally changed or abrogated those established by his predecessor."[39] Under "the despotism of the Dons," as Frederick Bates described the preceding four decades, the residents "knew that they had no rights and that they were absolutely dependent, in all things, on the will and pleasure of the Governor."[40] In New Orleans, William Claiborne described a legal "system in most points incongenial with the principles of our own Government," one in which "the executives of the collony have often exercised a dispensing power over th[e] Laws, and the people consequently have been habituated to the uncertain operation of rules occasionally modified by the wisdom or caprice of those in power."[41] In short, this was a government of men, not laws; the task at hand was to get rid of it as soon as possible. "[T]he wisest measure that can be adopted," asserted the Philadelphia lawyer Peter Du Ponceau, would be to "at once *plant* our excellent system of Laws into Louisiana."[42] As Bates explained to Meriwether Lewis, the future governor (and former explorer), "we are endeavouring to establish the empire of the laws; and to substitute those laws in the place of the arbitrary Rescripts of proconsular Agents."[43]

Anglo-American visitors to the southern part of the Louisiana Purchase territory gave similar accounts. "During the loose and irregular Government of Spain," one explained, "the laws were trodden under foot, crimes left unpunished or punished too severely, all was disorder and confusion."[44] Another traveler reported that the inhabitants "depend in all their civil and criminal affairs upon the whim or caprice or favour or folly of an upstart Spaniard who is set over them as their governor, and who, through pique or malice, or in a fit of drunkenness or insanity, has it in his power to sport with the[ir] lives and property."[45] As a result, concluded another, "[g]oing to law in Louisiana is going to the devil."[46]

This view must have been widely held among Americans, because years later, even after the legal system of Upper Louisiana had been dismantled, American visitors to the area were still reporting the same thing in the past tense. "All favours from the governor," one traveler recalled, "all grants of land, or even common privileges, could only be obtained by bribery."[47] Another described the pre–Louisiana Purchase system of criminal justice like this:

> When the commandant was raised in his temper, the object of his resentment was immediately brought before him, tried on the spot, and if found guilty, was sent straight to the *calaboza*. But to blunt the acuteness of his feelings, and render the reflections of his first hours as little bitter as possible, a suitable provision of whiskey was sent to the unhappy culprit, who would become very drunk; and after the long sleep that followed, was over, and he became clamorous for more whiskey, the commandant generally stipulated that the prisoner upon liberation should be gone, and then he was liberated.[48]

These accounts come from visitors who had not personally seen the legal system they were describing; their information thus most likely reflects the general view among Americans in St. Louis in the decade or two after the Louisiana Purchase.

The defects in Upper Louisiana's legal system, American officials believed, were in large part traceable to the character of the inhabitants. "[T]he people of Louisiana," reasoned Secretary of the Treasury Albert Gallatin, "seem to be but one degree above the French West Indians, than whom a more ignorant and depraved race of civilized men did not exist."[49] Gouverneur Morris agreed. "[T]hose who gabble the provincial Dialects of France and Spain," he observed when American law was being introduced to St. Louis, "will curse the Jury System which must to such men and in their present Situation be prolific of Injustice."[50] Americans tended not to hold the French inhabitants of Upper Louisiana in high esteem. William Carr, one of the first American lawyers in St. Louis, wrote back to his mother that "the French manner of living is not only extremely disagreeable to us, but is really very low." In particular, "[t]he french women are undoubtedly the greatest sluts in the world." Carr swore that he "would not marry a french girl if she [were] worth a million."[51] A legal system made up of such poor citizens, Americans concluded, could not help but be characterized by the arbitrary exercise of power. For the "ext[r]emely ignorant . . . crude and heterogeneous assemblage" that were his St. Louis neighbors, Amos Stoddard later recalled, "the theory and administration of their government were in most respects as perfect as their situation and circumstances would allow."[52]

But the shortcomings of the inhabitants, Americans also thought, were simultaneously attributable to having lived under such an oppressive legal system. "Do not imagine that I speak with prejudice of those People," Frederick Bates began.

> But I must say that Justice and liberty are words which they do not understand. You who have been bred up in Republican Habits will be surprized at this. Yet it is a mournful fact, that they do not comprehend the import of the words.
>
> The very name of *liberty* deranges their intellects, and it appears absolutely impossible for them to form accurate conceptions of the rights which Justice creates on the one hand, and obligations which it imposes on the other.
>
> The summary decree of a military officer however tyrannical or absurd is much better suited to their ideas of the fitness of things, than the dilatory trial by jury and "the glorious uncertainty of the Common Law."

> If their Commandant spurned them from his presence; deprived them of half their Estate or ordered them to the black Hole, they received the doom as the dispensation of Heaven, and met their fate with all that resignation with which they are accustomed to submit indifferently to sickness and health, to rain and sunshine.[53]

When a people's moral education had been so stunted, they could not comprehend the flaws of their own legal system. "[T]hey had not been accustomed," one lawyer argued, "to distinguish between the slow and cautious advances of *even-handed justice*, and the despatch of arbitrary power."[54] Nor could they appreciate the merits of the legal system about to be given to them. "Ignorant of all the principles of our Government," explained Moses Austin, "they View things with an evil eye."[55] For these simple, oppressed people, the establishment of an Anglo-American legal system was, at least to the officials running that system, much like a familiar event from long ago. "Since the American government commenced its operations," Bates reported, "a gleam of light, like the first blush of the morning has dawned on their bewildered imaginations. They were before in the impenetrable glooms of ignorance; but now, like the blindman cured by our Saviour, they 'See men as trees walking.'"[56]

Two old strands of American thought, one focusing on the French inhabitants and the other relating to their Spanish legal system, combined to produce this reaction. First, the brute presence of so many French people in the newly acquired territory was irreconcilable with the popular American conception of the West as virgin land.[57] The French were triply irritating: unlike the Indians, they could not be ignored on the ground of racial inferiority, many were plainly agriculturists who were using the land exactly as the Americans planned to use it, and many claimed ownership by virtue of formal written grants from a duly recognized government.[58] If American expansion into the area were to be justified, the French could not be productive farmers who worked as hard and appreciated the value of land as much as Americans. They had to be stupid, lazy, depraved, and incapable of forming or understanding sophisticated institutions of governance. This aspect of American thought drew upon the old stereotype of the indolent Creole, an image, as David Langum has persuasively argued, that was not held exclusively by Anglo-Americans, but was one in which Anglo-Americans had particularly strong incentives to believe.[59]

Second, the presence of Spanish government officials triggered, in the thought of early-nineteenth-century Americans, the so-called Black

Legend. Anglo-American writers had long conceived of Spanish government institutions, especially in Spain's colonies, as barbaric and tyrannical. To early-nineteenth-century Americans, as Richard Kagan has suggested, "America was the future—republican, enterprising, rational; while Spain—monarchical, indolent, fanatic—represented the past."[60] The appearance of unchecked power possessed by lieutenant governors in Upper Louisiana was understood by contemporary Americans as an instance of this phenomenon. The inhabitants of Upper Louisiana possessed none of the institutions of justice Anglo-Americans cherished as protections against tyranny—no trial by jury, no elected legislatures, no judiciary separate from the executive, and little written law to check the power of government officials. Americans had concluded a revolution only two decades before in which the advocacy of such institutional features had loomed very large. A legal system without them hardly deserved to be called law.[61] As in other parts of Spanish North America colonized by Anglo-Americans, the absence of these features was understood as the failure to establish a realm of "law" separate from a realm of pure power.[62]

American territorial judges occasionally spoke of "law" in ways indicating that they understood the pre-Purchase legal system not as consisting of unwritten rather than written law, but as embodying the absence of law altogether. Speaking sarcastically of Gov. James Wilkinson, Lucas predicted, "It is not to be expected that he will soon have time to convene the Legislature, lest his favorite spanish usages and regulations should be replaced and done away by certain and positive laws of an american stamp."[63] The opposition here of "spanish usages" and "certain and positive laws" suggests Lucas's view that these were two different categories. Usages, no matter how well established, were simply not the same thing as laws, because they lacked the certainty of a written text. Coburn similarly juxtaposed pre-Purchase "customs" with "our Laws" in explaining how the former could be given effect by incorporating them into the latter.[64] Like Lucas, he understood law and custom as two different things; "custom" could be enforced only by becoming "law," a process that required the formal sanction of authoritative government officials.

The Americans were nevertheless confident that the French residents of Upper Louisiana would welcome the new government and its legal institutions. "I have not been able to discover any aversion to the new order of things," Amos Stoddard reported shortly after arriving in St. Louis; "on the contrary a cordial acquiescence seems to prevail among all ranks of peoples."[65] William Henry Harrison visited St. Louis not long after, and discovered "that nine tenths of the people of this Country are warmly attached to the Government of the United States."[66] The transition promised to be a smooth one.

The French, however, soon grew as dissatisfied with the new legal system as the Americans were with the old one. Government authority was no longer local and easily accessible; it was now in Vincennes, in the Indiana Territory. As a hastily convened committee of local residents noted in protest to Congress, political power was now "not less than one hundred and sixty-five miles distant, and there is not a house to be met with on the road."[67] A recent immigrant from South Carolina explained that the prairie between St. Louis and Vincennes was "almost impassable in the Winter & in a manner uninhabited," a circumstance rendering "Communication almost impracticable" and causing the inhabitants to "Wish they could have a Governor and proper officers to reside amongst them."[68] The residents' voice in government was equally stifled by the fact that most of the officials set over them did not speak their language. The residents accordingly pleaded with Congress to have more officials "chosen from among those who speak both the English and the French languages," and to have "the proceedings of the courts of justice [kept] in both the English and French languages."[69] The latter two requests were never granted. As the population increased, however, Congress did remove the area from the authority of the Indiana Territory and establish local judges and executive officials.

The French residents then shifted the focus of their disapproval to the specific features of the American legal system that represented the greatest changes from previous practice. The French "are unhappy at this particular period," reported John Coburn in 1807. By local standards, he explained, "the administration of Justice is dilatory," in large part because of American legal procedure.[70] Not only was justice slower than before, but it was in the hands of people far less competent than Spanish colonial officials. Juries, the leading French inhabitants of St. Louis protested, were made up of "whatever individuals may happen to be present, without regard to character, standing or property." Jury trials thus endangered "the liberty, property or even life of the citizens by entrusting the most material interests of criminal justice, to Agents who having no stake in the community, have no interest to protect it."[71] Even when juries conducted themselves responsibly, moreover, an American judge could hardly supervise a jury composed of "old french settlers whose language he did not even understand."[72] This tension exploded into a crisis only a year after the onset of American government, when a largely French grand jury tried to investigate, on its own initiative, wrongdoing allegedly committed by Rufus Easton, one of the first American judges.[73]

American law differed from pre–Louisiana Purchase local law in a few substantive areas that caused the French residents equal concern. The foremost of these differences involved the recognition of land grants. Congress had promised to recognize grants made by local officials, but grants made after 1800—when Spain ceded Louisiana back to France in the secret Treaty of San Ildefonso, a treaty not known in Upper Louisiana—would be recognized only when the recipient had actually settled on the land.[74] As the residents angrily observed, the law in existence at the time such grants were made had placed no such condition, and there were many "who, ignorant as they must have been of a law not enacted at the time," had not settled on their land.[75] "The Cession of a country by one power to another," they argued, "cannot change the rights of Individuals to private property."[76] The new American government, unlike the Spanish, also required precise surveys in order to recognize land claims. But "[t]he extravagant fees for Surveying," Moses Austin pointed out, "rendered it impossible for numbers of the Poor to have their claims Survey'd." As a result, "one Third of all the claims in the Territory, are agreeable to the present Laws of Congress for ever lost.... Murmurs and Complaints are the Consequence. Under such circumstances," Austin wondered, "can the People of Louisiana be well dispos'd towards the United States[?]"[77]

"I will observe one thing to you Sir," a resident of Cape Girardeau informed Jefferson; "many people here do not like the Change & every Law that is pass'd that puts them on a Worse Situation than they would have been under the Spaniards is Criticiz'd & the Worst Construction put on."[78] In this climate, rumors of impending legal change flew. "[T]here exists amongst the Blacks a fermentation which may become dangerous," a committee of French slaveholders reported, "that they will be free Before Long." The committee pleaded with Amos Stoddard to reinstate the *Code Noir* and put the slaves "again under the Subordination which they were heretofore."[79] Legislation authorizing the removal of eastern Indians to the western bank of the Mississippi looked to the French like a plan "to exterminate from the face of the earth every inhabitant of Louisiana." Rumors of this relocation, they believed, were responsible for the fact that "depredations and assassinations by the Indians have already begun." French settlements, "dispersed at an immense distance from each other," would be "an easy and defenceless prey to the bloody rage of the merciless tomahawk. Is this protection? Is this justice?"[80]

American contempt for Upper Louisiana's old legal system was thus matched by French disappointment with the new one.

ACCOMMODATION

In the first few years after the Louisiana Purchase, the old settled into an uneasy coexistence with the new. The old French inhabitants and the new Americans both made necessary accommodations to the other. The result was a strange hybrid, with some characteristics of both the old legal system of Upper Louisiana and the Anglo-American system that for a time could not completely replace it.[81]

The French, despite their reservations about Anglo-American law, knew very well that they could not afford to turn their backs to it. From the beginning, French residents agreed to serve as jurors and as judges of the lower courts, positions for which formal legal training was not a prerequisite.[82] The elite French mercantile families, who litigated in the new American courts as frequently as they had litigated before Spanish officials, promptly began hiring American lawyers to represent them.[83] Members of the non-elite French community soon did the same.[84] (In Arkansas, by contrast, where American immigration took place more slowly and the French remained a significant fraction of the local population for a longer time, they took much longer to participate in American legal institutions.[85]) The French in Missouri were very gradually losing their Frenchness and merging into the larger American population.[86] Participation in the American legal system, and the slow erasure of memories of an alternative, was part of that process.

American lawyers, meanwhile, quickly occupied the most important administrative and judicial positions in the new Territory of Louisiana. But they took their new posts under the authority of a statute requiring them to keep existing law in force until modified by new legislation.[87] Because that legislation was slow in coming, American lawyers sometimes found themselves, to their chagrin, serving as judges within the old legal system of Upper Louisiana. They faced the same routine disputes, mostly commercial matters, that constituted the majority of litigation under the Spanish government. They also faced a steadily growing number of disputed land claims. Congress recognized all land claims arising from "any bona fide grant, made agreeably to the laws, usages and customs of the Spanish government."[88] As discussed earlier, Spanish land grants were in theory regulated by written law from New Orleans, but these procedures were generally ignored in favor of adherence to an earlier unwritten local tradition. The new American judges thus faced some difficult questions concerning land. What was Spanish "law" governing land allocation—the written law or the local unwritten practice? Should local practice be recognized as among the "usages and customs" mentioned in the statute? If so, what exactly was that practice? In answering these questions, as well as in resolving the ordinary commercial and other disputes that formed the daily work of the local courts, American judges found themselves administering in public the same legal system they derided in private.

They did not like it one bit. "It is an endless task," Amos Stoddard complained right at the start, "to find out the laws and steady maxims of the late Spanish Government."[89] Part of the problem, admitted J. B. C. Lucas, was that "not one of the judges of the superior court understand spanish."[90] Since, as Stoddard lamented, "all the papers in this quarter relative to land matters, and to debts and contracts, are either in French or Spanish," the American judges were at an immediate disadvantage in construing what documents existed.[91]

Language, however, was not the most serious problem. Much worse, in the view of American judges, was the absence of any written law governing the types of disputes they most frequently encountered. "[I]n this place," Lucas discovered, there was not "one single spanish Law Book, yet we are left in the humiliating position of being judges of spanish Law."[92] William Carr, appointed to represent the interests of the United States in opposing invalid land claims, reported his despair at ever finding any Spanish law, or indeed any Spanish records at all, on the subject. A "regular record of the proceedings of no branch or department of the former government of Louisiana, was ever kept," he complained to Albert Gallatin, "or if kept whilst in the possession of France or Spain, . . . few traces of them are to be found at this day."[93] The difficulty of deciding cases in the absence of written law moved Lucas to plead with President Jefferson for relief. "[T]he territory of Louisiana," Lucas explained, "stands in a peculiar predicament, that from the doubts existing as to what is spanish Law, spanish usage & spanish abuse, there is no country that stands in greater need of Legislative provision."[94]

Without any written texts to guide them, the American judges of the Louisiana Territory determined preexisting law as best they could, often by taking testimony from pre-1804 residents as to how things were done in Upper Louisiana. But, as John Coburn pointed out, "[t]he dangers attendant on this practice are obvious. The recollection of uninformed men, and the interested views of others, both as to the existence or extent of a decree of a Commandant, or a particular custom, is in general too imperfect, to afford a proper guide to a decision." For want of a better guide, however, the practice became common. The old informal norms of Upper Louisiana, which for decades had served as rules for resolving litigated disputes, especially in commercial cases, continued to play that role even after decision makers who shared those norms were no longer in office. Soon after he took his seat on the territorial court, Coburn explained:

> To meet the wishes of the French inhabitants, we were induced to incorporate in our Laws, several leading commercial customs; existing in the Country for a series of years. Those customs are peculiar to the Country, and are perhaps necessary for the convenience of the trading part of society. For example, we permit a debtor in certain contracts, to have the alternative, to pay his creditors in peltry, lead or cash. We permit the Merchant who advances the merchandize for a trading voyage with the Indians; to retain a species of lien, on the peltry and furs produced by the voyage, in preference to subsequent or other debts contracted by the voyager. It was our wish to assimilate by insensible means, the habits and customs of the American and French inhabitants.[95]

As Lucas put it, he and the other Americans administering the local legal system became "Judges of Laws of which we know nothing."[96]

This uncomfortable role for American judges withered away within a decade, at first gradually as more and more legislation occupied the gaps formerly filled by custom, and then with one final stroke in 1816 when the territorial legislature declared "[t]he common law of England" to be in force.[97] Thenceforward any spaces in the written law would in principle be filled by Anglo-American legal precedent rather than local custom. For the first few years after the Louisiana Purchase, however, local civil disputes were often resolved through a hybrid form of justice, in which American judges resorted to local substantive rules developed under Spanish colonial authority and established by the testimony of French Creoles, in proceedings whose form was copied from England. In California and New Mexico, Americans would overwhelm the earlier population more quickly, and the switch in legal systems was accordingly faster, without the several-year period of transition that characterized Missouri.

In land cases, this mixed legal system lasted much longer. Disputes arising from Spanish land grants in Upper Louisiana were litigated for the rest of the century. In nearly every case, the validity of a grant under Spanish law was at issue. Local judges and lawyers were thus obliged to learn so much of Spanish law as was necessary to evaluate the claims under dispute. Missouri was similar in this respect to other parts of the United States that had been acquired from Spain or Mexico.[98] In 1844, Hamilton Gamble explained that a judge in St. Louis needed "an acquaintance with branches of law which are of but little use in other portions of the State. Many of our land titles run back to the times of the Spanish Government & involve questions which are to be decided by the Spanish Law." Forty years after the Louisiana Purchase, it was still the case that "litigation in the Circuit Court embraces a vast number of suits for property in which such questions arise."[99] Samuel Treat, a state judge around the middle of the century, recalled that much of his work involved "the whole body of law pertaining to Land titles in this District resting on Spanish, French & U.S. grants—an unsettled & fiercely litigated state of controversy."[100]

Because disputes over Spanish land grants often involved tracts worth substantial sums of money, many such cases were appealed to the United States Supreme Court. Spanish land grant cases formed a significant part of the nineteenth-century Court's docket. These cases have largely been forgotten, because they generated little precedent that still has force today. From the St. Louis area alone, however, the Court decided at least twenty-five cases involving Spanish land grants in the nineteenth century, the last of which was not decided until 1888, eighty-five years after the Louisiana Purchase.[101] Like local courts, the Supreme Court thus frequently found itself applying Spanish law, within disputes conducted according to Anglo-American procedures.

With this one exception, however, older legal traditions died out within a decade after the Louisiana Purchase. By the time Missouri became a state, it had a legal system little different from that of any other western state. Other aspects of the local French culture lived on slightly longer. In the early twentieth century, in the small lead-mining towns south of St. Louis (by then devoted to mining barite rather than lead), there were still people who spoke only French. As late as the 1930s, "conteurs" were telling old French folktales, using words whose meaning was no longer remembered. This culture has now disappeared, killed off by mass media, compulsory public education, and the lack of local employment caused by the development of mining machinery.[102]

CHAPTER 6

Lawyers

"Lawyers spring up like mushrooms," complained a resident of tiny Fayette, Missouri, in 1841. "There are in this town perhaps ten lawyers."[1] The observation could have come from most of the towns in the state. Lawyers were even more noticeable in St. Louis, the state's largest city, where by 1845 there were 131 listed in the city's business directory, serving a population of approximately thirty-five thousand. Forty-one years earlier, when the United States had taken possession of St. Louis as part of the Louisiana Purchase, there had been none.

Why did so many lawyers come to Missouri in the early nineteenth century? What did they do when they got there? This chapter will address these questions.

ARRIVING

If the federal government directly subsidized the emigration of one small group of lawyers, as discussed in the previous chapter, it indirectly subsidized the emigration of the rest. The prospect of a territorial court and a board of land commissioners—joined simultaneously by locally created lower courts of common pleas, quarter sessions, and probate—in a country that lacked lawyers, was like a vacuum that sucked lawyers west.[2] By financing a legal infrastructure, the federal government indirectly encouraged many eastern lawyers to move to Missouri. As in the other western territories, lawyers were among the first occupational groups to arrive in large numbers.[3]

Some of the lawyers started arriving even before the newly appointed judges. Gov. James Wilkinson anxiously awaited the arrival of J. B. C. Lucas, the last of the three territorial judges to come to St. Louis, who he hoped would "attempt a System of Jurisprudence, calculated to discourage litigation and discountenance pettifoggers who begin to swarm here like locusts."[4] By mid-1805 there were already "a few high accomplished lawyers" in St. Louis, one resident reported.[5] As the courts and the board of land commissioners swung into operation, the number of lawyers steadily grew. Ste. Geneviève, slightly to the south, was by 1810 already "crowded equally as much if not more with Legal characters, than our courts are in Kentucky."[6] "[L]awyers are flocking here from all parts. The profession here will soon be overstocked," Lucas advised his son in 1817. Lucas accordingly preferred that his son "learn brewing beer or stilling," trades in which "great business might be done here."[7] The urban expansion of the 1820s attracted professionals of all types to St. Louis, including lawyers.[8] A similar boom in the 1840s caused a similar influx of lawyers.[9] As newer, smaller towns were formed in other parts of the state, lawyers headed there too.

Incoming lawyers were responding to a perceived demand for their services. "I fear no evil," the newly arrived Edward Hempstead reassured his father back in Connecticut in 1805, "as long as my present share of the business continues."[10] Charles Drake, who emigrated to St. Louis in 1834, recalled the city as "the best field in the United States for a young lawyer, so far as quick success in getting practice was concerned."[11] Eastern lawyers repeatedly heard from friends already in Missouri that the demand for lawyers far exceeded the supply. "Law business is very good here—much more so than at the East," one St. Louis lawyer informed a colleague from Massachusetts. "Fees are much higher—pay is better in regard to certainty." In short, "you can here obtain a livelihood easier than in N. England."[12] I "urge you to come immediately," James Cowan advised a colleague who had remained in Virginia. "My impression is you could very soon do well at the *Bar* there is every advantage here to bring a man of your turn and genius into notice."[13] A law student in Massachusetts heard from a friend in St. Louis that lawyers "can get a good living here at present. . . . Money is easier certainly to be obtained here than at the North with you, we are paid far better—we always take say, three or more times the sum, for the same amount of labour."[14] Young lawyers in particular understood the opportunities available in a place where older competitors were scarcer than they were back east. In a small Missouri town without an established bar, a single well-delivered argument could put a young lawyer "at the head of the bar as a Jury and criminal lawyer."[15]

Most of this demand for lawyers came from the Americans, who quickly outnumbered the older French residents. By 1830, Americans made up 90 percent of Missouri's white population. These emigrants, mostly from Kentucky, Tennessee, and Virginia—the older states at the same latitude—brought with them the habits of Anglo-Americans, including the habit of hiring lawyers to resolve disputes.[16] But, as discussed in the previous chapter, much of the demand came as well from the French, who realized very quickly that in the Americans' legal system the lack of a lawyer could be a serious disadvantage.[17]

The demand for lawyers was sensitive to wider economic conditions. In recessions, demand could suddenly drop, creating temporary local gluts of lawyers. "We have been in a perfect state of stagnation here this winter, no business in the mercantile line," reported one St. Louis lawyer in 1838, a year of nationwide recession. "Law business is improving," but only because "starvation begins to 'thin off' the stragglers and canaille of the host."[18] When merchants had trouble earning money, another reported, "[t]he court is in session but there is little business."[19] In such circumstances, competition among lawyers for clients intensified. "A man who wants law business attended to will go from one to another getting one to bid against each other until he reduces him to the very least fee a man will take," complained a rural lawyer in 1841. "I am somewhat disappointed in this country, and the prospects of a lawyer." When lawyers' incomes dropped in rural Missouri, so did their social status, and that may have hurt even more. "Our profession is regarded much in the same light that cobbling is," the same lawyer continued. "My heart is sick with what I have seen, it is leveling with a vengence."[20]

But such complaints were the exception, not the rule. And even when the demand for lawyers seemed to slacken, there were other reasons for lawyers to emigrate to Missouri. As elsewhere in the West, lawyers were heavily overrepresented in politics.[21] In the newer towns that lacked an established political structure, political opportunities for beginners were greater than they were back east. The disappointed rural lawyer quoted in the previous paragraph resolved nevertheless to stay put, because "[i]t is a fine political field and in that line perhaps something may be done in time."[22] Even in St. Louis, there were "large meetings of some sort every few days, and always an opportunity for Speechifying," where young lawyers might use talents developed in the courtroom to launch a political career.[23] Politics and law practice could be symbiotic: in practice one met many people and interacted regularly with public officials, which provided a sound basis for entry into politics; while in politics one acquired power and a familiarity with government institutions, qualities attractive to prospective clients. And in an era when both were often part-time occupations, one could pursue them simultaneously. As J. B. C. Lucas explained to his son, "you will see your brother Charles doing himself considerable honour both in his law practice and in the Legislature and bettering himself fast in a pecuniary way."[24]

The other great spur to emigration by lawyers, as by others, was the chance to profit from land speculation. As in other parts of the West, a growing population meant rising land prices, and some dramatic profits for landholders.[25] "All the gentlemen of the legal profession, who have means, engage in speculation in the west," remarked a New York lawyer visiting St. Louis. Lawyers with "small capital, by taking advantage of the time, make fortunes here in a few years."[26] A St. Louis lawyer reminded an eastern friend in 1837 that "there are other chances of making money" besides the practice of law. "[T]he chances for speculation are numerous," he advised, "though the best times have passed for this."[27] When Hamilton Gamble advised a Virginia client who inherited property in St. Louis to "come and live upon the land, grow rich on its products and add to the agreeable & improving society of St. Louis," he had to have been mindful that every new emigrant drove up the value of land, including land Gamble owned himself.[28] Lawyers were uniquely well placed to engage in land speculation, because so much of the process of securing title to land—purchasing it, registering it, disputing with others over title—passed through their hands, which meant that they were likely to learn of profitable opportunities. When Robert Heath and John Heath "concluded to become land jobbers," their first course of action was to write to a St. Louis lawyer, asking if he might wish "to enter into a liberal arrangement with us," under which the lawyer would presumably share the Heaths' gains in exchange for his services.[29] With land ownership inevitably came agriculture, and many Missouri lawyers were accordingly farmers as well, like many lawyers farther east.[30] William Lucas, for example, was not too concerned when legal work turned scarce in the fall of 1829; "[t]he tide of emigration is upon us with considerable rapidity," he explained, "and promises to afford some market for the . . . cribs of corn that we shall house this fall."[31]

As a result, the number of lawyers in Missouri increased rapidly over the first half of the nineteenth century. The earliest St. Louis business directory, published in 1821, listed 31 lawyers in a city of approximately 4,700.[32] This concentration of lawyers—6.6 per 1,000 population—is astonishingly high for the period. Massachusetts, by contrast, was the home of only 0.9 lawyers per 1,000 population at the time, or less than one-seventh that of St. Louis.[33] A ratio of 6.6 lawyers per 1,000 would be very high even in the late twentieth century. As of 1991, there were only

2.3 lawyers per 1,000 people in the United States as a whole, and even in New York, the state with the highest concentration of lawyers, there were only 5.1 lawyers per 1,000.[34] Even by modern standards, St. Louis grew thick with lawyers in the first two decades after the Louisiana Purchase.

The number of lawyers in St. Louis rose in subsequent years, but the concentration of lawyers steadily *declined*, as shown in table 2 and the corresponding chart.[35] The aberrant steep drops in the concentration of lawyers in 1836 and 1851 (and the decline in absolute numbers in 1836) may be due to inadequacies in the business directories for those years. With due allowance for those two years, the concentration of lawyers in St. Louis decreased steadily between 1821 and 1860, from 6.6 per 1,000 to 2.3 per 1,000, as nonlawyer emigration gradually caught up with that of lawyers. This declining trend in the concentration of lawyers after a sharp initial increase is consistent with the pattern found in other western communities, where the percentage of lawyers relative to the overall population was at first disproportionately large and then decreased over the following years.[36] In contrast, the concentration of lawyers in Massachusetts between 1820 and 1840 held approximately steady.[37] Data have been collected for only a few locations, but they are consistent with the general hypothesis that while the concentration of lawyers in eastern cities over the course of the nineteenth century was stable or gradually rose, the concentration of lawyers in western cities over the same period exhibited the St. Louis pattern of a sharp upward spike at the initial Anglo-American settlement followed by a long period of slow decline. The lawyers came early, in short, and the nonlawyers followed.

This conclusion supports recent efforts to debunk a popular misconception of western development, according to which lawyers arrived relatively late in the process and introduced eastern legal forms, for better or worse, to a population that had been living without them.[38] If St. Louis and the other western communities where lawyers have been studied are typical, the truth is nearly the reverse. John Reid has shown that a disposition to follow the law headed west with the first white settlers, even in areas where no sovereign existed to enforce the law.[39] It appears that the lawyers were not far behind.

WORKING

When lawyers arrived in Missouri, how did they integrate themselves into the professional community already in place? What kind of work did they do? What sort of social status did that work provide?

Table 2 and Corresponding Graph

NUMBER OF LAWYERS PER THOUSAND RESIDENTS, ST. LOUIS, 1804–1860

Year	Population	Lawyers	Lawyers per Thousand
1804	1,183	0	0.0
1821	4,723	31	6.6
1836	9,414	20	2.1
1840	16,469	64	3.9
1845	35,930	131	3.6
1851	84,800	160	1.9
1855	97,672	242	2.5
1860	160,733	367	2.3

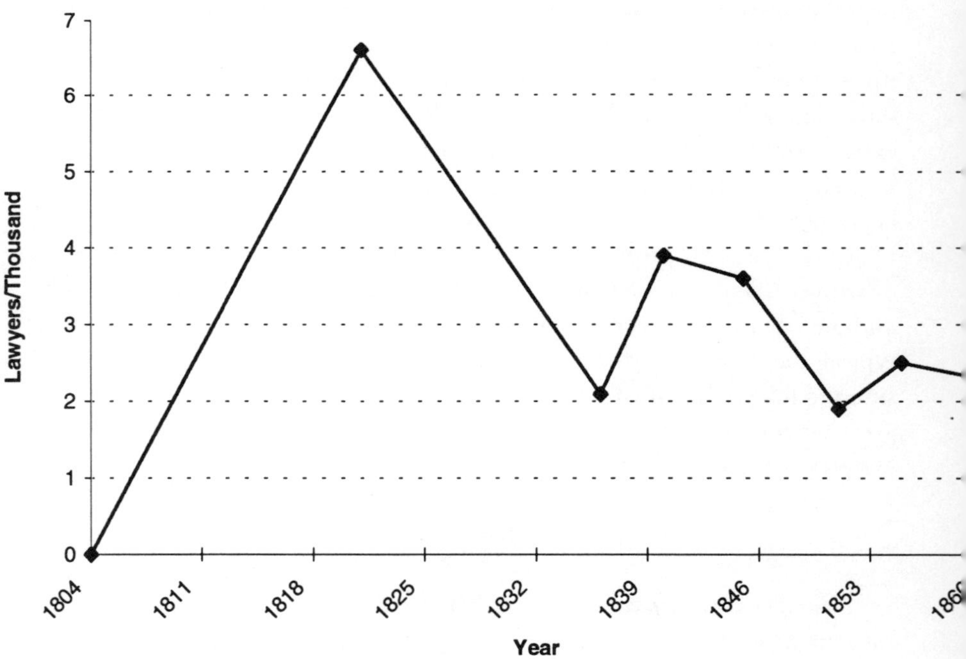

Getting Started

Lawyers arriving in Missouri routinely bore letters of introduction testifying to their experience and good intentions. Solomon Ward, for example, carried from Baltimore to St. Louis a letter from Henry Marie Brackenridge, addressed to J. B. C. Lucas, explaining that Ward "has been for a number of years in the practice of the law in this city."[40] When Jason Chamberlain determined to leave Vermont for Missouri, he secured a similar letter stating that "he has been in the practice of the law for some time & goes to our Territory with a view to settle himself & follow his profession."[41] It was so generally assumed that any reputable lawyer would have such letters that their absence could be interpreted as a warning sign. "Bring Documents, letters from the right sort of men of both parties," one St. Louis lawyer advised a friend coming from Virginia. "[E]verything here with a stranger depends upon his recommendations, and references."[42] When Charles Drake decided to cease travels and settle down to practice law in St. Louis, he kicked himself for not having thought farther ahead. "Not having anticipated locating in St. Louis," he later regretted, "I had not supplied myself with letters of introduction, as I could have done, to any desirable extent, if I had expected that to be my home."[43]

Even aspiring lawyers could take advantage of this informal professional network. Henry Cassidy moved from Arkansas to St. Louis armed with two letters from lawyers under whom he had studied; that was enough to encourage Rufus Easton to take Cassidy in as a student, and to certify two months later that Cassidy had learned enough to be eligible for admission to the bar.[44] When John Rankin moved from Pittsburgh to St. Louis, he bore a letter from Pittsburgh lawyer David Ritchie to Hamilton Gamble, in which Ritchie explained that he had advised Rankin to seek to study law under Gamble's supervision.[45] In towns where almost everyone was from somewhere else, lawyers were likely to have many colleagues in other states, so many prospective emigrants who anticipated practicing law in Missouri could easily obtain a letter of introduction. Of course, personal connections could be even better. Edward Bates, the future attorney general (under Abraham Lincoln), moved to St. Louis at the age of twenty-one and had no trouble reading law and joining the bar, a path smoothed by the fact that his older brother Frederick was the secretary of the Missouri Territory.[46] Most lawyers and would-be lawyers, however, had no such advantage. Obtaining the proper letters of introduction was the first step to success.

In order to practice in Missouri, as in any other part of the country, lawyers with experience elsewhere first had to gain admission to the local bar. Bar admissions were administered locally, not at the state level; a lawyer wishing to practice in multiple courts thus had to gain admission to the bar of each one.[47] In this respect, Missouri was like most states at the time.[48] Admission was not difficult for emigrants. "An Atto. licensed to practice elsewhere," Frederick Bates explained, "is admitted to our Bar on a slight examination & perhaps without one."[49] Examinations were conducted by the judges of each local court, without any prescribed length or content, and so there were wide variations in practice from judge to judge, and from applicant to applicant. One 1817 examination lasted, as the judge explained, only so long "as to satisfy my self that he is qualified to practice law."[50] Thomas Hart Benton, already a Tennessee lawyer when he moved to St. Louis at the age of thirty-three, promptly joined the bar and began practicing.[51] Hamilton Gamble arrived in St. Louis in 1818 with recently acquired licenses to practice in Virginia and Tennessee; he likewise was able to start working almost immediately.[52] David Holmes Conrad came from Virginia at the very end of 1819; he was practicing within a couple of months, and by the end of 1820 he was clerk of the court of chancery.[53]

Those without prior legal experience faced a tougher road, but again it was the same road faced by prospective lawyers anywhere else in the country at the time. The first step was to "read law" in an attorney's office—in effect, to apprentice oneself to a practicing lawyer. A student would have the opportunity to use the lawyer's library and watch the lawyer in action, and would be called upon to perform tasks that required little skill, like copying and delivering documents. Lawyers, like other employers in the early nineteenth century, experienced no clear division between workplace and home.[54] A student was likely to sleep in his employer's house and eat at his employer's table. These circumstances contributed to aspects of the lawyer-student relationship that could make it difficult for students to find a place to begin their studies. From the lawyer's perspective, taking in a student often required much more than finding an extra chair. Lawyers were not likely to be able to accept more than one or two students at any one time. And the ordinary obligation to provide room and board imposed substantial costs on the lawyer, who for this reason often had to charge the student a fee in exchange for the opportunity to study. In 1835, Stephen Hempstead was grateful to find a lawyer who says "that if I can procure board I shall be welcome to read under him gratis." The offer was a great improvement over his only other option, studying under

Hamilton Gamble, "for Mr. Gamble would certainly charge something considerable."[55] Nearly all the aspiring lawyers in Missouri began this way. A handful of the more cosmopolitan attended one of the law schools that were beginning to pop up back east. (None existed in Missouri.) J. B. C. Lucas, for instance, sent his son William to Connecticut to study at the Litchfield Law School, the most well known law school in the country, under Tapping Reeve, the former Connecticut chief justice.[56] But William Lucas was unusual; most law students had to find an experienced lawyer under whom to study.

After a period of study lasting typically two or three years, a prospective lawyer was ready to be examined by the judges for admission to the bar. Again, the difficulty of the examination could vary widely. "[T]he examinations are very slight here," one St. Louis lawyer explained in 1837 to a friend studying law in Massachusetts.[57] A few years later, however, in the lead-mining area to the south of St. Louis, a newly admitted lawyer reported that "the whole day was consumed in my passing an examination before Judge Stone and Mr. Cole. Mr. Cole examined me for about four hours and the Judge kept me with him all the afternoon."[58] After passing the exam, the applicant was admitted to the bar, and could begin practicing law.

Practice

Most litigation in antebellum Missouri, just like most litigation in the area before the Louisiana Purchase, consisted of suits to recover voluntarily contracted debts.[59] Of the 163 matters in which Hamilton Gamble was employed in 1818 and 1819, for example, 122 were suits to recover money that the defendant had promised but failed to pay the plaintiff.[60] Lawyers played a crucial role in the process of debt collection, a role created and rendered important by the manner in which commercial development took place.

Any newly settled part of the state was for many years thereafter an importer of goods manufactured in the eastern United States. It did not take long after the Louisiana Purchase for St. Louis to become the site of a large volume of transactions in goods shipped from the east.[61] In the 1830s and 1840s, as St. Louis grew and other parts of the state were settled, St. Louis became the hub for trade between the east and the small towns to the north and west. Ocean-going vessels carried goods from Atlantic ports to New Orleans, where the goods were loaded on smaller river steamboats bound for St. Louis, where they were again reloaded on still

Edmonton H.
Buckingham H.
Manchester H.
Hudson H.
Saskashawan R.
Blood Indians
Black Foot Indians
Serpent Indians
Fall Indians
South Branch
Red Deer R.
Chesterfield H.
Carlton H.
Probable North Boundary of the Missouri Territory
Canada H.
Assiniboin L.
Assiniboin R.
Cattanahowes
Long Hair Indians
Flat Head Indians
Grosventers
Mandans
Maria's R.
Falls
Missouri R.
Little Missouri R.
Cannon Ball R.
Snake Indians
White R.
Queen Charlotte's S.
Vancouver's I.
Nootka
C. Flattery
Destruction I.
P. Grenville
Gray's Har.
Whidby Har.
Mt. Rainier
Columbia R.
Mt. St. Helens
C. Gregory
C. Foulweather
C. Orford
Multnomah R.
P A C I F I C
N E W A L B I O N
B. of Trinidad
C. Mendocino
R. La Platte or Shal R.
Probable Southern Boundary
R. S. Rafael
R. Zaguananas
R. Dolores
Port Francis Drake
P. de los Reyes
S. Francisco
P. Pinos
R. Jasquevillo
N E W M E X I C O
Red R.
Cadodaquious
St. Fee
Cenis
R. Colorado
R. Gila
Copper Mines
P. Arguello
St. Catalina
S. Diego
O C E A N
GULF of CALIFORNIA
N E W N A V A R R E
Passo
R. Puerco
Rio del Norte
Chihuahua

Map 2. Missouri Territory, 1814, attributed to Matthew Carey. St. Louis is the only significant city in this immense area. Its location at the center of a network of rivers would make it the focus of east-west trade for decades, which created debt-collection work for a large population of lawyers. (Courtesy of the Missouri Historical Society, St. Louis.)

smaller ships heading farther up the Mississippi, Missouri, and Illinois Rivers. These goods were sold and resold on credit, from eastern merchants to merchants in St. Louis, from merchants in St. Louis to merchants in the small towns, and then from merchants in the small towns to consumers. Payment flowed the other direction; as the farming season drew to an end, consumers could pay their debts to local merchants, who could then pay their debts to St. Louis merchants, who could then pay their debts to their eastern suppliers. Any break in the chain was likely to set off a series of subsequent defaults; a local merchant unable to collect from consumers would be unable to pay a merchant in St. Louis, and so on.[62]

This network of debt was created within a legal framework in which litigation was the primary mechanism for collecting unpaid debts. In the second half of the century, it would become common for merchants and banks to take security interests in the property of their debtors, which would enable them, in the event of default, to seize the property and sell it to satisfy the debts. In the first half of the century, however, such arrangements were unusual. The Missouri Supreme Court ruled in 1823 that mortgages of property other than land could not be foreclosed upon, on the ground that no statute authorized such mortgages, "and it is not pretended that any such proceedings are known to the common law."[63] By 1835, the state legislature authorized mortgages of personal property and established a recording system for them and a procedure for foreclosing upon them.[64] In subsequent years, if the reported cases are representative, such mortgages were most often used for purchasing slaves.[65] But where other kinds of personal property were the subjects of transactions, secured credit appears to have remained unusual through midcentury. In most situations, in practice, there was no way for a Missouri creditor to collect other than by bringing suit. "It has come to an impossibility," one resident of Jefferson City complained, "to collect any money here without sueing."[66] As a result, recalled Thomas Anderson, "[t]he collection of debts furnished a very lucrative practice," even in places as sparsely settled as northeastern Missouri.[67]

Such was the bread-and-butter work of most Missouri lawyers. Lawyers in and around St. Louis spent much of their time collecting debts from local residents for trade creditors back east. Hamilton Gamble, for instance, received in June 1836 from Baltimore merchant John Keirle a draft drawn on a St. Louis merchant. Keirle urged Gamble "to pursue this claim as you would were it your own."[68] St. Louis lawyers received similar letters from eastern attorneys representing creditors, such as the New York law firm of Miller & Burke, who hoped Archibald Gamble might help their client recover a debt from a local brewer.[69] As two St. Louis lawyers explained in what appears to have been a circular sent to New York businesses, they had "for upwards of three years devoted our almost entire time in the collection of debts throughout this state and in the City of St. Louis."[70] In the smaller towns, lawyers' work consisted largely of collecting debts from local residents on behalf of trade creditors in St. Louis. B. F. Hagerman, a lawyer in Alexandria, Missouri, had a stable roster of St. Louis clients in the 1850s, who regularly forwarded notes signed by residents of Alexandria and other nearby small towns. Hagerman also represented eastern merchants seeking to collect from rural Missouri debtors. These matters were so routine that Hagerman could receive his work in preprinted form letters, with the debtor's name and the amount of the debt written in the blanks.[71]

Commercial development in other parts of the nineteenth-century West proceeded along similar lines. The debt-collection work of Missouri lawyers was accordingly typical of the work of western lawyers generally, so far as the issue has been studied.[72] The largest part of the western demand for lawyers was thus attributable to a combination of (1) the way westerners bought things from easterners, and (2) the absence from the legal system at the time of any superior method of debt collection.

Missouri lawyers did other things as well, of course. As elsewhere in the West, the process of claiming land provided a steady stream of work, as did the conflicts that frequently arose from inconsistent claims. Eight of Hamilton Gamble's 163 cases in 1818 and 1819 involved disputes over the right to possess parcels of land. This sort of work was particularly plentiful, as discussed in the last chapter, in the parts of Missouri settled before the Louisiana Purchase, where the validity and location of the Spanish colonial government's land grants were often contested.[73]

As anywhere else in the United States, heirs quarreled over the division of estates, accused criminals could sometimes afford representation, victims of violence sought damages, public officials occasionally needed advice as to their powers, and suits were brought by workmen to be compensated for work done and by the hirers of workmen to be compensated for work performed negligently. In taking on this sort of work, lawyers in Missouri did not differ from American lawyers generally. Hamilton Gamble's files contain one intriguing departure from the norm: of 163 suits in 1818–19, fourteen were filed by slaves seeking freedom. In thirteen of these Gamble represented the slave; in one he represented the slave's owner.[74] This was almost certainly an unusually large proportion of a lawyer's caseload to be devoted to the subject.

Most lawyers worked alone. The occasional partnerships that existed were all two-man enterprises until 1860, when the business directory listed five three-man firms. Partnerships were often formed when a student reading law under an experienced lawyer became a lawyer himself and simply remained in the office. When Charles Lucas, for instance, finished studying under Rufus Easton's supervision, Easton took him in as a partner for four years. Easton provided the office and the library, and probably most of the clients as well at the beginning. In return, he received three-fourths of the firm's proceeds in the first two years, and two-thirds in the last two years.[75] The relationship between a senior and junior lawyer could be even more one-sided. Edward Hempstead paid David Barton five hundred dollars a year, plus board, to attend to Hempstead's business in the outlying counties around St. Louis, but specified that "all the profits of the business done by you during the time you receive the Salary from me shall be *exclusively mine* (the Salary being in my opinion fully sufficient for you to appropriate all your time to my affairs)."[76] It could also be fully equal. John Scott furnished Beverley Allen with an office, the use of Scott's library, room and board, washing, and "a horse till next June to attend the court on," and Allen was still entitled to half the proceeds from all business conducted by either.[77] Lawyers of approximately equal experience on occasion formed partnerships as well. When Allen was older, for example, he proposed to Hamilton Gamble "a partnership formed with the view of engrossing, if possible, the collection business in Illinois & Missouri."[78]

Sole practitioners were not completely on their own, however. The population outside of St. Louis was so widely dispersed that lawyers with business in more than one court had to travel long distances by horseback, and sometimes found themselves with litigation scheduled in more than one place at the same time or within a period too short to allow for travel. "I am perplexed about the courts," William Lucas confessed to his father in 1832. "[T]he circuit court at Montgomery, where I have some twelve or fifteen cases to try occurs the same day with the District Court at Jefferson City and the court of Warren where I also have several engagements follows the Thursday after the Montgomery court."[79] Lawyers, although formally unaffiliated, thus sometimes had to ask one another to stand in. "I find it will be utterly impossible for me to attend the St. Charles court at this term," Henry S. Geyer informed Hamilton Gamble in 1829. "I beg of you therefore to attend to the little business I have in which you are not concerned."[80] The distances between towns also meant that litigation could occur without any meeting, or even without any prior acquaintance, between lawyer and client. When Robert Hood, in Boonville, Missouri, was sued by George

Sibley, whose witness was to be examined more than a hundred miles to the east, in St. Louis, Hood had to find St. Louis representation by mail. Hamilton Gamble was his first choice, but, in case Sibley had already hired Gamble, Hood asked Gamble to "please place this letter in the hands of my friend Mr. Bates or some other worthy member of the Bar."[81]

If lawyers sometimes had to cooperate, they were nevertheless aware of the competition for work in which they were engaged. Some lawyers advertised. Hamilton Gamble, for instance, placed a notice in the St. Louis newspaper early in his career.[82] The firm of Williams & Curtis, which specialized in land claims deriving from the French and Spanish governments, published a handbill announcing that it possessed its own "translated abstracts of the *French and Spanish Archives* in the office of the County Recorder . . . all arranged in such order as enables us to refer to and ascertain the exact tenor of all the conveyances made by any one person, in less time than is necessary at the Recorder's office."[83] Competition seems to have driven many lawyers either out of business or farther west. Of the sixty-four lawyers listed in the 1840–41 St. Louis business directory, thirty were no longer around to be listed in the 1845 directory. In their place were ninety-seven new lawyers who had not been listed four years earlier. In towns where people were constantly moving in and out, the population of lawyers was just as fluid.

Status

Lawyers thought of themselves as highly paid men. Thomas Anderson, who practiced in rural Palmyra, in the sparsely populated northeast corner of Missouri, from the 1830s through the 1860s, earned between $3,000 and $5,000 annually for most of his career. Anderson considered his practice "large and lucrative," and by local standards it was.[84] (Back east at around the same time, associate justices of the Supreme Court were making $4,500 per year, and the most prominent lawyers, such as Daniel Webster and William Pinkney, were earning up to $20,000 annually. In 1840, $3,000 carried the purchasing power of approximately $43,000 in 1993.[85]) Abiel Leonard, one of the leading lawyers in central Missouri at the middle of the century, earned $1,686 from the practice of law in 1849.[86] In St. Louis in the 1830s, Charles Drake was satisfied that "success was with me" when he "began to make pretty regularly from $75 to $100 per month."[87] One could possibly make more in aggressive land speculation, or simply by the good fortune of having been early to acquire land in urbanizing St. Louis, but as a steady income one could not do much better in antebellum Missouri. Lawyers were particularly prevalent among the upper-income earners in the newer, smaller towns, where there was less of a commercial elite than in St. Louis. In Boonville in 1837, for example, the largest property holder was the estate of lawyer Charles Lucas.[88] Lawyers most likely spanned the spectrum of wealth, but enough of them were rich enough for an anonymous 1821 poet in Franklin, Missouri, to refer to lawyers as "Those bloated [a]ristocrats of wealth / Who pride themselves on money."[89]

The nature of lawyers' work meant that no individual fee was likely to be especially large; a lawyer had to represent many clients simultaneously on numerous small matters in order to accumulate a substantial income. Even while earning between $3,000 and $5,000 annually, Thomas Anderson "would very frequently, nay, every week almost, go to LaGrange in Lewis County, 18 miles distant and attend a case before a Justice of the Peace for five dollars." As Anderson explained, "[t]he litigation was generally of a small nature," but fortunately "there was a great deal" of it.[90] Charles Drake's $100 per month was composed in large part of "a good run of cases before magistrates," any one of which netted a relatively small fee.[91] Abiel Leonard received an occasional fee of over $200, but like Anderson he was eager to take on matters in which he could charge as little as $5. Leonard's mean fee in 1849 was $32; the median was only $20.

From Leonard's records one can get a sense of how he earned a living. The following table lists each payment Leonard received, in each month of 1849, in exchange for legal services.[92]

January: $10, $40, $10, $15
February: $20, $50, $29.80
March: $5, $87.53, $10, $5, $10
April: $25, $15, $40, $102.30, $35, $15, $20, $10, $57.50, 11.75
May: $47.40, $15, $220.50, $75, $20
June: $15, $62.08, $50, $10
July: $75, $22.90
August: $75, $5, $5, $26.10, $40
September: $20, $7.20, $30, $25
October: $20
November: $10, $25, $31.50, $10
December: $15, $25, $10, $49.76, $20

These figures suggest, first, that the income of a lawyer could fluctuate widely from month to month. Leonard took in $377.90 in May, helped by the single largest fee he received all year, but he earned only $20 in October and only $75 in January. The numbers further suggest that lawyers simultaneously used at least two different methods of pricing. Most of Leonard's smaller fees are round numbers—$5, $10, $20, and so on—which suggests that Leonard was either (a) charging a single lump sum for an entire case, or (b) billing $5 per hour, rounding off to the nearest hour, and not spending many hours on any individual case. The occasional explanations for fees entered by Leonard in his account book are consistent with either method. In March, for instance, the first fee of $5 was in exchange "for verbal advice"; the last fee of $10 was "from M. Leintz for defending his slave." These fees might represent Leonard's rough estimates of the value of his services, or they might mean that the oral advice took only an hour and the slave trial only two. Leonard's larger fees tend not to be round numbers—$87.53, $102.30, $62.08. One of these ($62.08) Leonard referred to as "my collection fees." When Leonard was employed to collect debts, he appears to have charged a percentage of the sum collected, as any other pricing method would have been unlikely to result in such uneven numbers. These cases, moreover, seem to have been Leonard's most lucrative, which sheds further light on why lawyers were so eager to enter the collection business.

Whatever the pricing method, lawyers typically sought payment only after their work was done, which on occasion turned lawyers into creditors of their former clients. "I beg to remark that your charge of $100," explained W. G. Wells to his lawyer, "for the part you took in the Garrison trial, on which occasion a verdict was *obtained*," could not be paid, because "not one cent [was] ever collected the Garrisons being candidates for the *Bankrupt Law*." As a result, Wells concluded, "I think your charge not only too high, but entirely out of my power to *attempt* to pay."[93] In such circumstances, a lawyer had no more power to compel payment than any other creditor. The risk of nonpayment had to be taken into account from the beginning, in deciding whether or not to accept new business and how to price one's services.

Along with wealth came social standing. Near the end of his life, St. Louis lawyer Charles Gibson recalled anticipating in the 1840s how proud his mother would be when he became a lawyer, "which in those days meant a great deal more than it does now."[94] In rural parts of the state, lawyers riding circuit "could stop anywhere in the country and not pay anything," Thomas Anderson remembered, because "the settlers were very anxious to have us stay all night in order that they might find out what was going on in the world—but very few of them taking newspapers."[95]

In St. Louis, lawyers were as socially prominent as any other occupational group. This social status contributed to lawyers' political influence, both formally, as lawyers moved in and out of political office, and informally, as lawyers worked behind the scenes to encourage or discourage the appointment of particular people as government officials, especially judges.[96]

St. Louis was a small town relative to some eastern cities, of course, and it was far from anywhere else with a substantial population, so much of the status of local lawyers was attributable to the absence of serious competition. But not all St. Louis lawyers were merely big fish in a small pond; some would have been big fish even in bigger ponds. When J. B. C. Lucas sent his son Charles on a tour around the country "to endeavour, whilst he is young, to enlarge his mind and improve his manners on the national standard," he fortified Charles with letters of introduction from St. Louisans familiar with the leading residents of the cities Charles planned to visit. Charles showed up in Tennessee with an introduction to the governor; he arrived in Philadelphia with an introduction to Alexander Dallas, a leader of the Philadelphia bar.[97] For a few years in the early 1820s, one of the lawyers practicing in St. Louis was Joseph J. Monroe, the president's brother.[98] The short-lived position of state chancellor, in existence only from 1820 to 1822, was occupied by William Harper, who would later return to South Carolina and attain national fame as a judge and states' rights advocate. Nathaniel Beverley Tucker, who arrived in St. Louis in 1815 and served as a judge for several years, was part of a family well known in Virginia legal and political circles; his brother was the prominent lawyer Henry St. George Tucker, and his half-brother was John Randolph.[99] Some of the St. Louis lawyers were well connected on a national scale. Others made some effort in that direction. At least twenty-nine antebellum St. Louis lawyers argued cases in the U.S. Supreme Court, for example.[100] They were:

Edward Bates: *Mackay v. Dillon*, 45 U.S. 421 (1846)

Montgomery Blair: *West v. Cochran*, 58 U.S. 403 (1854); *Willot v. Sandford*, 60 U.S. 79 (1856); *Dred Scott v. Sandford*, 60 U.S. 393 (1856); *Sigerson v. Mathews*, 61 U.S. 496 (1857); *Berthold v. McDonald*, 63 U.S. 334 (1859); *Jones v. Soulard*, 65 U.S. 41 (1860); *Massey v. Papin*, 65 U.S. 362 (1860); *Berthold v. Goldsmith*, 65 U.S. 536 (1860)

Louis V. Bogy: *Mills v. Brown*, 41 U.S. 525 (1842)

Mann Butler: *Choteau v. Marguerite*, 37 U.S. 507 (1838); *Marsh v. Brooks*, 55 U.S. 513 (1852)

James H. Carlisle: *Berthold v. Goldsmith*, 65 U.S. 536 (1860)

John F. Darby: *Burgess v. Gray*, 57 U.S. 48 (1853)

Hamilton Gamble: *Chouteau v. Eckhart*, 43 U.S. 344 (1844); *Mackay v. Dillon*, 45 U.S. 421 (1846); *Missouri v. Iowa*, 48 U.S. 660 (1849); *Bissell v. Penrose*, 49 U.S. 317 (1849); *Mills v. Stoddard*, 49 U.S. 345 (1850); *Mills v. St. Clair County*, 49 U.S. 569 (1850); *Landes v. Brant*, 51 U.S. 348 (1850); *Easton v. Salisbury*, 62 U.S. 426 (1858); *Fenn v. Holme*, 62 U.S. 481 (1858); *Berthold v. McDonald*, 63 U.S. 334 (1859)

Alexander Garesché: *Jones v. Soulard*, 65 U.S. 41 (1860)

Hugh A. Garland: *Burgess v. Gray*, 57 U.S. 48 (1853); *Denise v. Ruggles*, 57 U.S. 242 (1853)

Henry S. Geyer: *Farrar v. United States*, 30 U.S. 373 (1831); *Strother v. Lucas*, 37 U.S. 410 (1838); *Marsh v. Brooks*, 49 U.S. 223 (1850); *Marsh v. Brooks*, 55 U.S. 513 (1852); *Delauriere v. Emison*, 56 U.S. 525 (1853); *McCabe v. Worthington*, 57 U.S. 86 (1853); *Guitard v. Stoddard*, 57 U.S. 494 (1853); *Kissell v. St. Louis Public Schools*, 59 U.S. 19 (1855); *Ham v. Missouri*, 59 U.S. 126 (1855); *Griffith v. Bogert*, 59 U.S. 158 (1855); *Long v. O'Fallon*, 60 U.S. 116 (1856); *Meegan v. Boyle*, 60 U.S. 130 (1856); *Garrison v. Memphis Ins. Co.*, 60 U.S. 312 (1856); *Dred Scott v. Sandford*, 60 U.S. 393 (1856); *Goodman v. Simonds*, 61 U.S. 343 (1857)

Charles Gibson: *Easton v. Salisbury*, 62 U.S. 426 (1858); *Fenn v. Holme*, 62 U.S. 481 (1858)

[Samuel or John] Glover: *Lessieur v. Price*, 53 U.S. 59 (1851); *Long v. O'Fallon*, 60 U.S. 116 (1856); *Willot v. Sandford*, 60 U.S. 79 (1856); *Massey v. Papin*, 65 U.S. 362 (1860)

G. W. Good: *Bissell v. Penrose*, 49 U.S. 317 (1850)

T. P. Green: *Missouri v. Iowa*, 48 U.S. 660 (1849)

Charles S. Hempstead: *Smith v. Honey*, 28 U.S. 469 (1830)

Britton A. Hill: *Boone v. Missouri Iron Co.*, 58 U.S. 340 (1854); *West v. Cochran*, 58 U.S. 403 (1854)

[Nathaniel or Samuel A.] Holmes: *Gamache v. Piquignot*, 57 U.S. 451 (1853)

Thomas C. Johnson: *Denise v. Ruggles*, 57 U.S. 242 (1853); *Guitard v. Stoddard*, 57 U.S. 494 (1853); *Kissell v. St. Louis Public Schools*, 59 U.S. 19 (1855); *Stanford v. Taylor*, 59 U.S. 409 (1855); *Dred Scott v. Sandford*, 60 U.S. 393 (1856)

Luke E. Lawless: *Smith v. Honey*, 28 U.S. 469 (1830); *Lagrange v. Chouteau*, 29 U.S. 287 (1830); *Strother v. Lucas*, 37 U.S. 410 (1838);

Chouteau v. Eckhart, 43 U.S. 344 (1844); *Mackay v. Dillon*, 45 U.S. 421 (1846)

[unknown first name] Lawrence: *Menard's Heirs v. Massey*, 49 U.S. 293 (1850)

Abiel Leonard: *Fenn v. Holme*, 62 U.S. 481 (1858)

Miron Leslie: *Lessieur v. Price*, 53 U.S. 59 (1851)

Robert E. Phillips: *Belcher v. Linn*, 65 U.S. 508, 533 (1860)

Louis Picot: *Gamache v. Piquignot*, 57 U.S. 451 (1853)

Trusten Polk: *Montgomery v. Anderson*, 62 U.S. 386 (1858)

John H. Rankin: *Montgomery v. Anderson*, 62 U.S. 386 (1858)

Frederick P. Stanton: *Hale v. Gaines*, 63 U.S. 144 (1859); *Belcher v. Linn*, 65 U.S. 508, 533 (1860)

Joseph P. Wells: *McCabe v. Worthington*, 57 U.S. 86 (1853)

[Henry W. or Willis] Williams: *Guitard v. Stoddard*, 57 U.S. 494 (1853); *Stanford v. Taylor*, 59 U.S. 409 (1855); *Meegan v. Boyle*, 60 U.S. 130 (1856)

That St. Louis lawyers ordinarily handled these arguments themselves, rather than deferring to Supreme Court specialists or eastern lawyers generally, suggests that St. Louis lawyers had a certain degree of confidence in the sophistication of their own practice relative to practice in the east. (That said, none of the St. Louis lawyers had a national reputation as a lawyer rather than for holding political office, while a handful of eastern lawyers did have such a reputation; and in some cases St. Louis lawyers *did* hire well-known eastern colleagues.[101]) Because of the difficulties of travel from St. Louis to Washington and back, moreover, these arguments must have been occasions for spending some time in the east, and probably occasions for socializing with eastern lawyers as well. When one adds the substantial collection work Missouri lawyers performed for eastern clients, the not uncommon travel back east, and other opportunities for informal contact—such as Hamilton Gamble's subscription to the *New York Observer*—it becomes clear that many Missouri lawyers had a field of vision broader than Missouri.[102]

The income and standing enjoyed by Missouri lawyers gave rise to the same kind of antilawyer sentiment that could be found anywhere else in the country.[103] The state legislature was sharply divided along social lines, one legislator recalled, between "the Farmers & Mecaniciks" on one side and "the big bugs Lawyers & C." on the other. It was the "big bugs," to the resentment of the others, who dominated debate.[104] As one local writer explained,

What glorious privilege we have
To chuse the men to rule us;
What dolts and blockheads we should be
To let the lawyers fool us.

The author made clear that "I am a farmer firm and free / Who ne'er read Coke and Chitty," and contrasted the productivity of farmers with lawyers, who "Do little for the public good / As drones in making honey."[105] Lawyers, another contemporary charged, were people who "will seize you by the collar with one hand, and thrust the other into your pocket; and while they strip your back of the one, they will empty the other of its contents."[106] This sort of criticism drew on a long Anglo-American tradition of disliking lawyers because of their money, their power, and their apparent failure to contribute to the national wealth. Lawyers were wealthy, powerful, and disliked almost from the moment of their arrival in Missouri.

CHAPTER 7

Written Law

Antebellum Missouri lawyers and government officials understood themselves to be establishing and operating a legal system where none had existed before. People, to be sure, had been present in Missouri for as long as anyone could remember; the French had been there for half a century, and the Indians far longer than that. But the lawyers understood "law" as a set of rules found in written government documents—statutes, court decisions, and the like. By this definition, the pre–Louisiana Purchase residents of Missouri had been without law. That would soon change.

AUTHORITY

The first order of business after the Louisiana Purchase was to enact written law, to fill the perceived legal vacuum. Late in 1804, before any American legal institutions were actually in operation in St. Louis, the governor and judges of the Indiana Territory enacted the District of Louisiana's first fifteen statutes all at once. These were copied from previous statutes in other American jurisdictions. At least ten were taken from the laws of the Northwest Territory, the jurisdiction with which the Indiana officials would have been most familiar. The district's first statute, for instance, provided a list of crimes and punishments nearly identical to the one contained in a 1788 Northwest Territory statute; the district's statute omitted the crimes of disobedience, drunkenness, and Sabbath-breaking, but it otherwise tracked the Northwest Territory statute word for word.[1] The district's third statute regulated the institution of slavery; for obvious reasons the Northwest Territory could not serve as a model, so various Virginia statutes were copied instead.[2] Many other statutes followed quickly, from the Indiana territorial government at first, then in 1805 from the governor and judges of the reorganized Territory of Louisiana, then from the new legislature of the Territory of Louisiana as of 1806, then from the assembly of the reorganized Territory of Missouri in 1812, and finally from the legislature of the new state of Missouri beginning in 1820.

At the same time, the officials with legislative power quickly moved to create a court system similar to that existing elsewhere in the country. The system was made up of two tiers—an upper level staffed by judges with legal training for the more important cases, and a lower level staffed by lay judges for the less important ones.[3] As more lawyers arrived in Missouri, the inferior judges would soon also be men with legal training. At the very top, the Supreme Court began publishing its opinions when Missouri became a state. From then on, Missouri was indistinguishable from any other state in terms of the structure of its legal system and the reliance of its lawyers on written authority.

From the beginning, Missouri lawyers adhered to the same formality of procedure as that which characterized eastern legal practice.[4] Forms of common law pleading were used as rigorously as they were anywhere. Hamilton Gamble, for instance, carefully noted the writ appropriate to commence each dispute in which he was involved; his collection cases were dominated by assumpsit and debt, while his land cases tended toward ejectment and the occasional trespass quare clausum fregit. Peyton Hayden, a lawyer who practiced in four rural central Missouri counties in the 1830s, painstakingly recorded the procedural history of each of his cases, including each plea and replication.[5] As in other western communities, one finds none of the procedural informality once thought to permeate court proceedings on the so-called frontier.[6]

Nor, where lawyers were involved, were legal proceedings informal in substance. Like lawyers in the east, Missouri lawyers relied heavily on written authority, rather than on arguments from public policy or intuitive morality. Court records, and the notebooks of individual lawyers, are full of references to legal treatises, English cases, and American cases, mostly from Missouri, of course, but often from New York and elsewhere.[7] Lawyers' preference for written authority was so strong that in 1833 one rural Missouri lawyer believed "that a handsome speculation may be made by publishing a Digest of the laws," for sale to lawyers. Such a digest was so badly needed, he predicted, that "the enterprise will come out a clean profit of 5 or 6000 dollars."[8] Again, this reliance on written authority accords with our knowledge of lawyers in other parts of the

West, which cumulatively discredits the older view to the contrary. As Elizabeth Gaspar Brown concluded with reference to early Michigan lawyers, "the practising lawyer in Wayne County did not find his sources of law in theoretical abstractions of justice or local conceptions of right and wrong. Rather, he possessed and used the same sources of law as his contemporaries in Philadelphia or New York."[9] The same could be said of Missouri lawyers.

Reliance on written authority made a library an essential part of a lawyer's office. The quality of lawyers' libraries varied widely. The lower end may have been near zero; the upper range most likely included the 111 volumes possessed by Rufus Easton when he died in 1834, and the 220 volumes owned by Abiel Leonard in 1838. Most of Easton's books were English. Leonard owned a wide range of authorities, including mostly English treatises and case reports, but also treatises by American jurists such as James Kent, Joseph Story, and Nathan Dane; statutes and case reports from Missouri; case reports from the U.S. Supreme Court; and statutes and case reports from other states.[10] Local statutes and cases were published locally, but the other authorities were not. Sometimes they could be purchased in St. Louis, but the selection fluctuated in quality; when Leonard sent an agent to St. Louis to purchase books in 1846, for instance, the agent reported that the seller "had previously sold all the books on your memorandum except two." Lawyers' trips to eastern cities thus sometimes included visits to eastern publishers to purchase law books.[11] Such efforts meant that although law books could be hard to obtain, and although some lawyers had many more books than others did, there were enough in Missouri, as in other parts of the West, to support a practice based largely on written authority.[12]

CULTURE

Why were American lawyers and government officials so eager to establish a text-based legal system? Several factors—some local, some national—played a part in forming this consensus.

First, there were local causes. Many of the Americans clearly felt uncomfortable operating within the remnants of the Spanish colonial legal system, and wanted to replace it as quickly as possible with the system they already knew. Whether one calls this chauvinism or a preference for the familiar depends entirely on where one's sympathies lie. Either way, given the federal statutes that maintained the old regime until modified by new legislation, the Americans knew that the only way to get the law they remembered from home was through the enactment of new statutes. Much of the Americans' distaste for the old unwritten norms of Upper Louisiana no doubt stems from the simple fact that in the earliest years they were effectively managing a foreign government. Much of their preference for written law can be attributed to a purely local circumstance, that written law allowed them a way out of this predicament.

As the government was changing, so too was the composition of the population. The French residents of Upper Louisiana varied widely in wealth and education, but in many respects they participated in a single culture. They practiced the same religion, they observed the same holidays, and they came from the same places. By the first decade of the nineteenth century, however, the area's population was growing larger and more diverse every day. Every American immigrant was one more person who was unfamiliar with local ways and unlikely to become socialized into Creole life. It is a familiar phenomenon that the smaller and more homogeneous a group is, the more likely its members will be to govern themselves with unwritten norms.[13] Small communities of people with similar backgrounds can resolve disputes according to local norms or "industry practices" familiar to all concerned.[14] Large diverse communities have more need to resort to written law, simply because of the many inconsistent sets of norms possessed by members of heterogeneous cultures. With the pattern of immigration that characterized early-nineteenth-century Missouri, it would have been increasingly difficult for the French residents to maintain their legal system even if they had possessed the governmental power to do so. That this power was possessed by the immigrants instead made adherence to the old system even more unlikely.

Local land issues provided another reason for many of the lawyers to exhibit a strong desire for written law. Soon after the Louisiana Purchase, the American community split into two factions, each with a different interest in land policy. On one side were those who had come to the area earlier and who, like the French mercantile elite, had received substantial land concessions from the Spanish government. On the other were the more recent arrivals, whose fortunes depended in large part on their ability to block congressional confirmation of the first group's Spanish land claims. The second group included most of the American lawyers and government officials in St. Louis. When Gov. James Wilkinson sided with the first group, the American lawyers sought any means possible to limit his power. Because Wilkinson had effectively stepped into the shoes of a Spanish commandant, there was little written law defining the scope of his authority or providing a basis for any other person or institution to assert rights in opposition to him. One method of limiting Wilkinson's power was the enactment of that sort of legislation. For American lawyers in St. Louis, the establishment of written law was a tool in a local power struggle. Some of their reluctance to accord legitimacy to a legal system without written law has to be understood in this light.[15]

Meanwhile, the distribution of much of the area's wealth turned on whether Congress would confirm the thousands of land concessions made by local Spanish lieutenant governors but never approved by Spanish governors in New Orleans. If American land commissioners were to recognize unwritten pre-Purchase land allocation practices, members of the French elite and early American arrivals would hold on to their land, a rapidly appreciating asset in the first decade of the nineteenth century. But if the pre-1803 inhabitants were to be held to the letter of the official written Spanish law, very few would have valid claims, and the same land would be opened up to the incoming Americans. This context no doubt influenced the jurisprudential views of some American land claimants. Whether the same motive can be attributed to government officials, however, is a more difficult question. On the one hand, officials claimed land themselves and shared their personal and professional lives with other American land claimants. They had an undeniable personal stake in the land controversy that could easily have contributed to their general preference for written law. On the other hand, like all theories resting on unstated personal motivation, this one is impossible to document. There appear to be no surviving written records explicitly linking a preference for written law with the opportunity to obtain more land. The most that can be said is that if American lawyers and government officials had searched for a coherent jurisprudence supporting their land claims, the privileging of written over unwritten law would have been their best bet.

Equally difficult to prove or disprove, for the same reason, is the likelihood that American lawyers rightly perceived that their employment opportunities depended in large part on the adoption of the legal system in which their training qualified them to play a leading role. A norm-based legal system has less need for a class of professional advocates. The demand for lawyers, had the legal system of Upper Louisiana been retained, would not have been zero. Lawyers' skills in public speaking, for instance, would still have commanded fees. But to survive in that kind of system would have required a significant degree of reeducation among the lawyers arriving from the eastern United States. Lawyers would have had to learn how to operate within a very different legal system from the one to which they were accustomed. The prospect of that effort, when a much easier and more lucrative alternative was available, no doubt propelled lawyers to advocate the alternative—the simple adoption of the familiar Anglo-American system of written law. Again, there is no record of anyone saying as much, but this is another sentiment unlikely to find much explicit written expression.

A variety of local circumstances thus played a part in causing American lawyers and government officials to exhibit a strong preference for the replacement of the unwritten norms of Upper Louisiana with a legal system based on written law. It is worth noticing, if only because of their prominence in some earlier accounts of frontier legal history, two sets of local factors that appear to have been much less important in shaping the area's legal system. Geography and population size have often been asserted to be significant determinants of the formality or informality of a legal system.[16] Such a claim would be difficult to reconcile with the experience of Missouri. No local geographical features changed with the Louisiana Purchase. The population grew substantially in the early nineteenth century, but, with the exception of the very end of the period covered by this book, there were at all times parts of the state that were on the so-called frontier. Throughout the area, the switch from a norm-based to a text-based legal system occurred far too quickly to be explained by the area's removal from frontier status. At the same time, lawyers and officials in remote and sparsely populated parts of the state, areas unmistakably on the frontier by any definition, were nevertheless scrupulous about adhering to written law. The location of the frontier thus apparently exerted little influence on the legal system of Missouri.

Similarly unimportant in shaping the legal system was another local factor, the size and complexity of the local economy. It is sometimes asserted that participants in larger and more complex economies increasingly value written law for its certainty, its predictability, and its uniformity.[17] In assessing California's transition from a Mexican to an Anglo-American legal system, for instance, David Langum has concluded that the desire of American merchants for "certainty and predictability in the law" was an important driving force.[18] The economy of Missouri did grow larger and more complex in the early nineteenth century. The leading French merchants in the area *before* the Louisiana Purchase, however, were large operators with far-flung enterprises. They did not complain about the legal system in which they litigated, and their complaints after the Louisiana Purchase suggest that they would not have minded retaining it. It is not at all clear that the American legal system provided them with any greater certainty, predictability, or uniformity than the system with which they were already familiar. After the Louisiana Purchase, the most ardent advocates for a text-based legal system were not American merchants seeking certainty, predictability, or uniformity; they were lawyers and judges, whose interest in the subject had much more to do with their own well-being than that of the merchants. They urged the change as early as 1803 and 1804, long before it was possible for the region to undergo any significant economic change from pre-Purchase conditions. And the legal change occurred within the compass of a few years, much too fast for it to have been in response to economic change. Local economic change was thus not a primary force driving local legal change.

The new territory was part of the United States, obviously in a political sense, but more important, in a cultural sense as well. National circumstances, as well as local, thus also contributed to legal development in the area in the early nineteenth century.

Cultural influences were the most important of the national factors in shaping the legal system of Missouri. American lawyers in the early nineteenth century participated in a professional culture that valued textual authority as a limit on the discretion of governmental decision makers. States were beginning to publish their statutes and court opinions in easily accessible form. American lawyers were beginning to write treatises collecting and sorting judicial decisions into logical categories. The power to declare the law was shifting from juries composed of ordinary citizens to legally trained judges, men familiar with the standard texts of the profession.[19] Arbitration, once an informal norm-based alternative to the official legal system (and one that closely resembled the method by which disputes had been resolved in Upper Louisiana), was becoming more and more like litigation in official courts.[20] Custom, often given normative force in the years leading up to the American Revolution, was losing its place as an accepted source of law.[21] Lawyers trained in this text-based professional culture brought it with them to Missouri, where they replicated it. The law-related desires of an American lawyer in Missouri were far more attributable to his status as an American lawyer than to his presence in Missouri. In the early nineteenth century, regardless of local political controversies and economic interests, an American lawyer was far more likely than a French farmer or fur trapper to understand law as composed of texts issued by authorized agents of the sovereign.

National economic influences were far less important. To be sure, the first decade of the nineteenth century saw what the closest student of the subject has called "a minor revolution in the general avenues of trade," as

St. Louis quickly became part of a commercial network including Philadelphia, Baltimore, and Pittsburgh.[22] Unwritten norms work well enough in a local community, one might suppose, but they will be poor guides for resolving disputes between trading partners from different communities, particularly communities far from one another. Again, however, the pressure to transform the legal system did not come from merchants trading with easterners; it came from lawyers. This was not, moreover, the first national or international trading network to include St. Louis. Before the Louisiana Purchase, French merchants also traded with people far away, in New Orleans, Canada, and Europe. Yet they do not appear to have desired a more text-based legal system to accommodate the wishes of their trading partners. That is most likely because norms are not necessarily local, and are not necessarily bounded by geographic space. A national or international community of merchants is likely to have its own set of norms, despite the distances between members of the community, independent of the local norms in any of the places the merchants reside. International commerce had, of course, been regulated for centuries in just this fashion, through the law merchant, a supranational set of business norms existing outside the sovereign power of any of the nation-states in which the merchants lived. There is no evidence that Missouri businesspeople desired written law in order to establish rules identical to those present elsewhere in the United States and thus facilitate trade. Like Missouri lawyers, Missouri traders more likely shared a professional culture with their counterparts back east, a culture far more important than the law in structuring trade relationships. National economic influences were thus less significant than national cultural influences in shaping the general preference for written law in Missouri in the decades after the Louisiana Purchase.

That preference was clearly related to the Americans' general contempt for the legal system of pre-Purchase Upper Louisiana, but the causal relationship between the two opinions is much less clear. The relationship may well have run in both directions. To justify their demands for written law, American lawyers must have found it useful to discount the ways in which the norms governing Upper Louisiana did function as law. Disparagement of the pre-Purchase legal system was thus in part a rhetorical strategy, a method of highlighting the case for written law by exaggerating the darkness of the background against which it was placed. To call the Spanish colonial legal system "arbitrary" and "tyrannical" was to add urgency to the call for change. At the same time, however, the Americans' contempt for what they encountered in Upper Louisiana no doubt stemmed in part from simple prejudice. The preference for written law was a handy way of justifying their rejection of a system they would have rejected anyway, for reasons of unfamiliarity and national pride, regardless of whether it was largely composed of unwritten norms. A coherent jurisprudential position always sounds better than the expression of a naked personal preference, but, probably more important, it *feels* better to someone making the pre-rational choice between the two. A preference for written law and a contempt for the eighteenth-century legal system thus reinforced one another, creating the picture of Spanish colonial St. Louis that dominated American legal thought in the years after the Louisiana Purchase.

STYLE

With lawyers representing the parties to disputes, and with legally trained judges deciding disputes, the style of judicial decision making in Missouri scarcely resembled that which characterized the pre–Louisiana Purchase legal system. The differences were all attributable to the perceived importance of written law. They can be seen in any randomly chosen subset of the surviving litigation records. The examples in the next two paragraphs all come from volume 4 of the *Missouri Reports* (the series of volumes that includes the reported opinions of the Missouri Supreme Court), covering Supreme Court decisions from 1835 to 1837, but they could just as easily have come from any other contemporary local source.

The reliance on written law produced a procedural formality that had been unknown in the area before the Louisiana Purchase. William Gordon's conviction of challenging an opponent to a duel, for instance, was reversed because the state's attorney had forgotten to prove a fact that everyone knew was true—that the challenge was issued in the state of Missouri. That omission, the Missouri Supreme Court explained, was "a fatal error."[23] Another conviction was reversed because the indictment described a note as purporting to be "payable to the holder," when in fact the note purported to be "payable to the bearer." Although the legal effect of the words "holder" and "bearer" was the same, the indictment was "clearly a wrong description of the note," and a new trial was thus held to be necessary.[24] When the loser of a case concerning who would inherit a slave attempted to appeal the decision to the Supreme Court, the court refused to hear the case, on the ground that the appellant ought to have called the document in which he sought review a "motion for a new trial" rather than a "motion to dismiss the bill for defect of evidence."[25] In a suit to recover on some bonds, where one defense was that the plaintiff had already recovered from the defendant in a different court on the same bonds, the Supreme Court held that the defense had properly been stricken, and judgment properly awarded to the plaintiff, because when the plaintiff had denied the existence of any record of the former judgment, the defendant had failed to *reassert* the judgment's existence.[26] None of these outcomes would have been imaginable in the area before the Louisiana Purchase. All rested on the existence of written authority specifying procedures for resolving disputes.

Rather than drawing upon local practices to guide decisions, local judges relied upon written authority, much of which had been produced quite far away. In the course of deciding that the state legislature lacked the authority to grant divorces, the Missouri Supreme Court cited the American commentators Joseph Story, James Kent, and David Hoffman; the English writers William Blackstone, Edward Coke, and Matthew Hale; French legal authorities including Robert Pothier and the Napoleonic Code; cases from the supreme courts of the United States, Missouri, Massachusetts, Connecticut, and New Hampshire; and a wide range of other sources, including the *Federalist*, Jefferson's *Notes on the State of Virginia*, and Plutarch's *Lives*.[27] To decide whether a ditchdigger could recover at least partial payment before he had completed his work, the Missouri Supreme Court relied largely on precedent from England.[28] In such cases, the judges were self-consciously presenting themselves as part of a single Anglo-American (and sometimes Euro-American) legal culture, whose norms barely varied between eighteenth-century London and nineteenth-century St. Louis. English common law authority, ironically enough, was itself widely understood to have originated in custom.[29] In using English decisions as sources of law, Missouri judges were in effect substituting the customs of a people long ago and far away for those of their neighbors.

By borrowing statutes from older American jurisdictions, and by relying upon precedent from England and the other states, lawmakers quickly caused Missouri law to become part of a largely uniform body of law throughout the country. While this process was most obvious in the formation of common law, because citation practices made the borrowing explicit, Missouri's constitution and statutes were equally important in bringing state law into line with the law in other states. Constitutional provisions were borrowed primarily from Kentucky.[30] A series of statutes governing wills provided the same doctrines of probate, intestate succession, and dower as could be found elsewhere.[31] Even the 1816 statute declaring the English common law to be in force, along with English noncriminal statutes "of a general nature" enacted before 1607, was substantively identical to similar provisions found in other states, which in turn differed only slightly from the similar statutes present in every state other than Louisiana.[32] Most of the state's residents, and nearly all of its lawyers, had come from other states. They created a body of law with no discernible local characteristics. Like their French predecessors in the area, they established law that conformed closely to the law in the places from which they had come.

In the years that followed, Missouri law underwent the same major changes that visited antebellum American law generally. Many American states at midcentury abandoned the system of common law pleading that had structured Anglo-American lawsuits for centuries, and replaced it with a simplified method for bringing disputes into court, a method that has remained in place ever since. New York was the first state to make this change, in the famous Field Code of 1848, but Missouri was second; Missouri abandoned common law pleading the following year.[33] Most states converted from an appointed to an elected judiciary in the 1840s and 1850s. Missouri did as well, in an amendment to the state constitution in 1850.[34] Most states passed statutes at midcentury allowing married women to own separate property, free from the debts incurred by their husbands. So did Missouri, in 1849.[35]

Missouri's most well known contribution to antebellum American law, the *Dred Scott* case, was another instance in which the state followed the mainstream of American legal development. In the 1820s and 1830s, Missouri courts shared the general view among American courts that slaves brought to reside in a free state became free, but that slave owners traveling through a free state retained property rights in their slaves. In St. Louis alone, over two hundred slaves brought suit to claim their freedom between 1806 and 1865. Most of these claims were based on a previous period of residence in a free state, typically Illinois, the most convenient place from which to enter Missouri for emigrants from the east. Seventy-eight of these freedom suits were successful, nearly all before the mid-1840s.[36] In the 1830s, this consensus among American courts began to break down. Northern courts began to hold that slaves became free as soon as they entered a free state. Courts in slave states began to hold the opposite, that even a period of residence in a free state did not terminate slave status.[37] Missouri followed the latter trend. In the *Dred Scott* case itself, the Missouri Supreme Court overruled its prior decisions, and concluded that a slave brought to reside in a free state, and then brought back to Missouri, would remain a slave. "Times now are not as they were when the former decisions on this subject were made," the court explained. "Since then not only individuals but States have been possessed with a dark and fell spirit in relation to slavery, whose gratification is sought in the pursuit of measures, whose inevitable consequence must be the overthrow and destruction of our government."[38] The court was participating in widening the gulf between north and south, and was doing so in part because it perceived danger from the growing antislavery movement in the north. The case would later be refiled in federal court, where it would of course soon attain even greater notoriety.[39] In the Missouri courts, it stands as another example of the state's participation in general antebellum American legal change.

"There are no state legal histories," Gordon Bakken has pointed out, and although his study of early California law was intended in part to fill that void, the experiences of California and Missouri both suggest why. An American state in the nineteenth century was simply not a meaningful unit in the development of the law. Lawyers participated in a single, nationwide culture. (In fact, they participated, to only a slightly lesser extent, in a single worldwide British imperial and ex-imperial culture, embracing places as far as Australia and New Zealand.) Individual states bore very few state-specific legal characteristics. That was particularly true in the West, where in the earliest decades of the development of each state, the period potentially most significant for the creation of a unique local legal culture, all of the lawyers necessarily had to have come from somewhere else. Bakken concludes that "[i]n law in books, California's experience was very much a part of the American legal experience," and one could say the same about Missouri.[40]

DISAPPOINTMENT

The ideal was a system of law as formal written sovereign command, but the goal receded as quickly as the lawyers could progress toward it. At each step, the lawyers discovered that informal unwritten convention could often be powerful enough to supersede written law. They were repeatedly forced to realize that their legal system was shot through with unwritten convention, and that the standard picture of rule-based government was in practice rarely attainable. Sometimes they complained about it, sometimes they joked about it, but they could never resolve the tension between the ideal and the actual, between two inconsistent but simultaneous visions of the law.

Sometimes, when the unwritten norms were those of the lawyers themselves, the results could be benign. The system of common law pleading, for instance, was not required by any statute or any executive decision. It was brought to Missouri as part of the stock of knowledge possessed by lawyers and judges, who continued to use it as they had used it in their earlier careers, but if there was any feeling of compulsion it was generated within the profession itself, not by the government. When American courts first opened their doors after the Louisiana Purchase, common law pleading was used from the start.[41] The territorial assembly's wholesale adoption of the common law in 1816 could be interpreted to require the employment of the common law forms of action, but by that time those forms had been in use for over a decade. The professional culture of Anglo-American lawyers was a set of unwritten conventions that were not *imposed* by law, but rather *constituted* part of the law despite the absence of any written sovereign authority for them. This was hardly troubling to the lawyers, of course, although it provided ammunition for the standard antilawyer belief that common law procedure was designed by the lawyers for their own benefit.[42]

Often, however, the law on paper was effectively trumped by unwritten norms that lacked the consensus of the legal community. Such occasions were more troubling to the lawyers. Sometimes the relevant norms were those possessed by jurors, who had the disconcerting habit of resolving cases according to criteria other than those favored by lawyers. "The juries look as if they had been vomited forth from some whisky kennel on the levee," one St. Louis lawyer complained in 1838. "You might as well argue with so many wild beasts, especially on a criminal case. They make up their minds, and to change them is impossible except you should offer to treat them with an extra glass of whiskey or gin cocktail."[43] Charles Drake attributed his success before juries to the fact that "I had a loud voice, and talked with a great deal of physical force."[44] Timothy Flint sat through some trials in the late 1810s or early 1820s, and concluded that "classical taste and discipline . . . were too often thrown away upon the jury in a region, where noise and flourish are generally mistaken for sense and reason."[45] Behind such complaints doubtless lurked a great deal of class-based snobbery, but it was snobbery grounded largely on jurors' willingness to substitute an intuitive sense of justice for formal rules of law. Lawyers' attitudes toward this phenomenon were mixed. On the one hand, they deplored what they perceived as jurors' inability to follow the law; on the other, successful lawyers could build a livelihood upon this same divergence between law and action, by developing a rhetorical style designed to exploit it.[46] The result was a cynicism toward the institution of jury trial hardly different from that which permeates the profession today.

If lawyers had mixed feelings when jurors reached decisions contrary to the formal law, they were irate when they perceived that judges themselves had the power to do the same, whether through incompetence or malice. "I have lost three" cases, Edward Bates groused, "by what I consider gross blunders, if not perverse errors of the Circuit Court (Judge Krum)." Bates would have won, he believed, if only he could have argued before a judge who understood the law correctly. "I do not mean to say that Judge K is ignorant of law books," he explained. "But he does not seem to know principles for the use of them. His mind is so loaded down & confused with a multitude of odds & ends of cases, that it has not the faculty to grasp a principle."[47] In a small town outside of St. Louis, William Lucas saw the local circuit judge in a more sinister light. "[T]he appointment of N. B. Tucker as Judge," he informed his father, is "one of the greatest misfortunes that can happen to us now." Lucas believed that Tucker harbored a personal dislike for him, and that Tucker's feelings had influenced the outcomes of Lucas's cases when Tucker had been a judge in St. Louis. "I shall act cautiously until I discover clearly the course that Tucker will pursue here," he resolved, "until I see whether the same system of favouritism is to [be] adopted here, that was pursued on the St. Louis Bench."[48] Any system of law, no matter how formal, had to be implemented by men; the force of the written law thus depended in large part on the identities and the motives of the men with the authority to pronounce it. The judges' power effectively to nullify the written law, whether intentionally or inadvertently, constantly hovered beneath the surface of the legal system, ready to erupt unpredictably. The unwritten beliefs of the people who managed the legal system could never be completely suppressed.[49]

While most lawyers appear to have battled this tension between written law and actual practice, some concluded that the tension was inevitable. Rather than reading a law book, Charles Gibson recalled, he would "work out in my own mind, the rule of action that would apply to a particular case." Only then would he "examine the authorities" for the rule he had intuited, a search that was invariably successful, because "the vast accumulation of authorities furnish decisions on every side of every case." Gibson had no respect for "[m]ere book lawyers," who "never become great; they never get above the artificial."[50] The same point was made more cynically by another St. Louis lawyer in a letter to a friend studying law. "How do you like Law after progressing thus far in the science?" he asked. "You will find the practise very different from the theory . . . the Judges here go pretty much according to common sense they decide as whim and caprice dictates."[51] These lawyers were moving toward a proto–Legal Realism nearly a century before such views attained highbrow jurisprudential respectability.

In antebellum Missouri, however, the dream of law as a system of written rules persisted despite its evident unattainability in practice. Despite the occasional dissenting view, lawyers generally continued to treat divergences between the real and the ideal as aberrations rather than the norm, as attributable to the inadequacies of individual jurors or judges rather than to the impossibility of the task the overall system was asked to perform. The system was one that served them well, of course; it would not have been in their interest to question its presuppositions too closely. The profession's text-based conception of law played a part in maintaining the profession's authority, in that other conceivable grounds for a legal system—popular intuitive justice, for instance—would have been less likely to require specialists to manipulate. (Of course, for the profession to maintain its authority the *clients* had to share the professional conception of law, because nothing forced them to use lawyers when they litigated.)[52] If anything, the extent to which lawyers' collective self-interest was intertwined with an understanding of law as a system of written rules would intensify later in the century, as Missouri lawyers, like members of similar occupational groups, became more self-consciously professional, and developed an even greater self-conception as possessors of specialized knowledge inaccessible to others.[53] The tension identified by the more reflective lawyers in antebellum Missouri thus would not go away during their own lifetimes, nor has it in ours.

While the legal system often failed to approach the ideal held by the lawyers who operated it, it nevertheless came much closer than the system it replaced. Even in practice, Missouri's legal system relied much less on local unwritten norms, and much more on the written word, than had the legal system of Upper Louisiana. A century after the area was first inhabited by people of European ancestry, Missouri had become the eighth most populous of the thirty-three American states, with a population of nearly 1.2 million, most of whom were from elsewhere in the United States. Like any other thickly settled Anglo-American jurisdiction, it governed itself primarily through written law.

CHAPTER 8

Private Land

After the Louisiana Purchase, the residents of St. Louis and the surrounding towns slowly acquired formal institutions of representative government. As that happened, their conceptualization of the public nature of the commons began to change. Meanwhile, the area's population skyrocketed, with the influx of thousands of American immigrants with experience in farming only in privately owned plots. The French and American inhabitants both began to rethink how best to use their common land.

The United States assumed sovereignty over the area with a promise to recognize all land grants "made agreeably to the laws, usages and customs of the Spanish government."[1] This promise generated considerable uncertainty as applied to the commons, which had never been the subjects of any formal Spanish grants. When the "Inhabitants of St. Louis" filed a claim for their grazing commons in 1806, and when the inhabitants of St. Charles and Carondelet did the same for theirs, it took the Board of Land Commissioners six years to reject the claims.[2]

Meanwhile, owners of strips in the common fields faced a different sort of uncertainty. They had received concessions from local Spanish officials, but few (if any) residents had gone to the expense of obtaining formal confirmation from the Spanish government in New Orleans. A group of leading residents of St. Louis petitioned Congress nevertheless to recognize land claims in the common fields. "[I]t is . . . well know[n]," they observed,

> that the Inhabitants of these villages possess other Lands Commonly Called *terres de champs* or out lots for Cultivation and that the Condi-

> tions annexed to such grants, were, that each of the grantees or their assi[gn]s should Contribute in their respective proportion the fencing of said lands & should Cultivate the same; . . . .
>
> It will appear obvious to the honorable Congress that thoze various Conditions were not grounded on the Caprice of the Comandants & lieutenants gouverneurs, but on a uniform system . . . well adapted to the state of the Colony.[3]

Congress clarified the status of titles to strips in the common fields with an 1806 statute recognizing the land claims of those who could prove they had been actually cultivating the land as of 1800, despite the absence of formal approval from the Spanish government.[4] Farmers of strips eventually became fee simple owners of long, thin pieces of land.[5]

In 1812, Congress resolved the controversy over title to the commons, in a statute with inconsistent wording that perfectly captured the ambiguous status of "public" land in a new political order. The statute provided:

> That the rights, titles and claims, to town or village lots, out lots, common field lots and commons, in, adjoining and *belonging to the several towns or villages* of Portage des Sioux, St. Charles, St. Louis, St. Ferdinand, Village a Robert, Carondelet, St. Genevieve, New Madrid, New Bourbon, Little Prairie and Arkansas, in the territory of Missouri, which lots have been inhabited, cultivated, or possessed, prior to the twentieth day of December, one thousand eight hundred and three, shall be and the same are hereby *confirmed to the inhabitants of the respective towns or villages aforesaid, according to their several right or rights in common thereto*.[6]

In a single sentence, Congress thus described the commons as belonging (1) to the towns, and (2) to the inhabitants of the towns. In conventional Anglo-American political understanding by that time, there was no difference between the two. The distinction had little practical effect in other parts of Spanish North America, in which Spanish or Mexican municipal governments had been in existence and had controlled local commons, and common land could accordingly be confirmed to towns rather than to the public directly.[7] For the French residents of the territory now called Missouri, however, in which there had been no municipal governments, these were still two separate ways of thinking about land ownership.

In the first two decades after the Louisiana Purchase, claims to the land in the commons were *not* filed by towns; they were filed by the *inhabitants* of towns. Petitions to Congress regarding the commons were not sent by units of local government; they were sent by self-styled representatives of an unorganized local public. In 1817 and 1818, for instance, when private land claimants threatened to settle in the Carondelet commons, the petitions pleading with Congress to take action were still being drafted in the names of the inhabitants of Carondelet directly, who still spoke of the land as having "descended to them from their forefathers who settled said village & used said commons."[8]

But this conception of the commons as land owned directly by the people would soon change. By 1808, the legislature of the Territory of Louisiana had already authorized towns to incorporate themselves and to elect trustees, who would have the power to regulate the commons.[9] As towns incorporated, the commons thus lost its status as a zone of direct popular sovereignty. For a while, the commons retained its sense of direct popular ownership. In cases of trespass or waste in the commons, for example, suits were authorized only in the names of individual residents with rights in the commons, not in the names of towns.[10] By 1824, however, the legislature of the new state of Missouri authorized towns to sue in their own names for trespass and waste in the commons.[11] The commons was gradually losing its sense of direct public ownership as well.

One can get a sense of the ambiguous status of the commons during this transitional period from the claim filed in 1825 to the St. Louis commons. In 1806, remember, an identical claim had been filed by the "Inhabitants of St. Louis." In 1825, however, the commons was now claimed by "[t]he Mayor, Aldermen and Citizens of the City of St. Louis."[12] The commons no longer belonged purely to the inhabitants, but it was not yet owned purely by the city either. The government of the city and the city's inhabitants instead collectively claimed the land, in a verbal formula that, although by no means an unusual way of describing a city, nevertheless revealed the shift in understanding of who exactly the owner of the commons would be.[13] Equally revealing of the transition in the conception of the commons was how Theodore Hunt, the recorder of land titles, transcribed the testimony of Henry Duchouquette, the city's primary witness. The key portion of Duchouquette's testimony is rendered like this: "He allways knew there was a Common belonging to the ~~Town~~ Inhabitants of the Town of St. Louis."[14] Perhaps Hunt's initial transcription of the stricken word "Town" was only a typographical error. But it seems just as likely that when Duchouquette, an old French resident, recalled property rights in the inhabitants, Hunt, an American newcomer, at first understood Duchouquette to refer to property rights in the town, and only afterward recognized that Duchouquette was talking about something slightly different.

The transformation in the popular understanding of the commons was complete soon after. In 1832, the Missouri legislature authorized the town of St. Charles "to sell in fee simple forever, all, or any part, of the town lots, out-lots, common-field lots, or commons, belonging to said town." In 1835, the legislature gave the same privilege to the villages of Owens' Station and St. Ferdinand.[15] In conventional thought, the commons was no longer owned directly by the public. It had been recategorized as public land in the present-day sense of the term, as land owned by the government, which the government had the authority to convey in fee simple.

Occasional vestiges of the earlier understanding of the commons, tiny hints of discontent at what had become of the commons, appeared from time to time in the years following. Residents of St. Ferdinand must have questioned the right of the town government to sell land owned directly by the people, because two years after authorizing the sale, the state legislature found it necessary to appoint a commission to determine whether the commons could in fact be sold by the town government, or whether it would have to be divided up among all the individuals with rights in it. The commission was to inquire into

> whether the commons were conveyed to the inhabitants of the village as an aggregate mass, or to the specific owners of lots; whether they were conveyed to the inhabitants in being at the period of the grant, and to their successors in all time to come, or whether to the lot-holders and their assigns.[16]

If the commission ever reached any result, it has apparently been lost. Given the general climate of opinion permitting local governments to sell off the commons, however, it would be surprising if the commission decided otherwise.

In St. Louis, where the political power of the old French elite lasted longer, the older conception of the commons appears to have endured slightly longer.[17] In 1835, the legislature required a poll "to determine whether the proprietors of the commons of St. Louis consent to the sale of the same." The "proprietors," the only people eligible to vote, were free whites who had owned property in St. Louis as of 13 June 1812, the date Congress confirmed the inhabitants' claims to the commons.[18] There was not much doubt as to what the outcome of the vote would be. The week before the election, the *Missouri Republican*, the leading newspaper in St. Louis, devoted its entire discussion of the issue to the question of what would be done with the proceeds of the sale; that the commons would be sold was too obvious to mention.[19] Soon after the election, the City of St. Louis ordained "[t]hat the Commons of St. Louis be sold to the highest bidder."[20] The city established a Committee on the Common, which began selling and leasing lots in the commons, prosecuting trespassers in the commons, and generally behaving as an ordinary owner of land.[21]

The last ember of the older conception of the commons was snuffed out by the Missouri Supreme Court a few years later. *City of St. Louis v. Morton* was an action of covenant, brought by the city against the lessee of a lot in the commons who failed to pay his rent. In defense, Morton alleged that the city lacked the authority to dispose of the commons "without having first obtained the consent of a majority of the owners of lots and parts of lots within the limits of the town of St. Louis as it was limited on the 13th of June 1812," that is, that the *inhabitants* of St. Louis, not the city government, were the owners of the commons. The court did not reach the merits of this defense. "These pleas amount then to a denial of the title of the plaintiff," the court held, and Morton, as a lessee, was estopped from denying his lessor's title.[22]

Apart from these occasional controversies, the change in popular thought about who owned the commons seems to have gone unnoticed. In 1800, all would have agreed that the commons was owned by the people, not the government. By 1850, these two categories had become one. All would have agreed that the people owned the commons, and all would have agreed that the government had the power to sell it. Residents spoke without hesitation of the commons as "property owned . . . by the City."[23] Litigation over the commons pitted city governments against other city governments.[24] A way of thinking about land had vanished.

Meanwhile, conventional ideas about the best *use* of the commons were changing as well. As late as 1817 and 1818, residents were still arguing that the "Commons always was & still is the only Support of ourselves & our families being our only Dependance for Building our houses, Fencing our Cornfields, our Firewood & Pasture for our Stock."[25] Without the commons, the farmers of Carondelet predicted, "them & their Families must Perish having no other resource left, as their lots & fields would be totally useless without the Commons."[26] But land was beginning to be valued for new purposes. As an 1818 correspondent to the *Missouri Gazette* observed,

> Of the policy and utility of appropriating a tract of land in the vicinity of towns and villages, as a cheap and convenient resource to their inhabitants, for the pasturage of cattle, fuel and timber necessary of

Map 3. St. Louis Common, drawn 1838 by Charles De Ward, lithograph 1842 by Edward Hutawa. By 1838 the common was understood to be owned by the government of the city of St. Louis, and was being divided into blocks for sale.

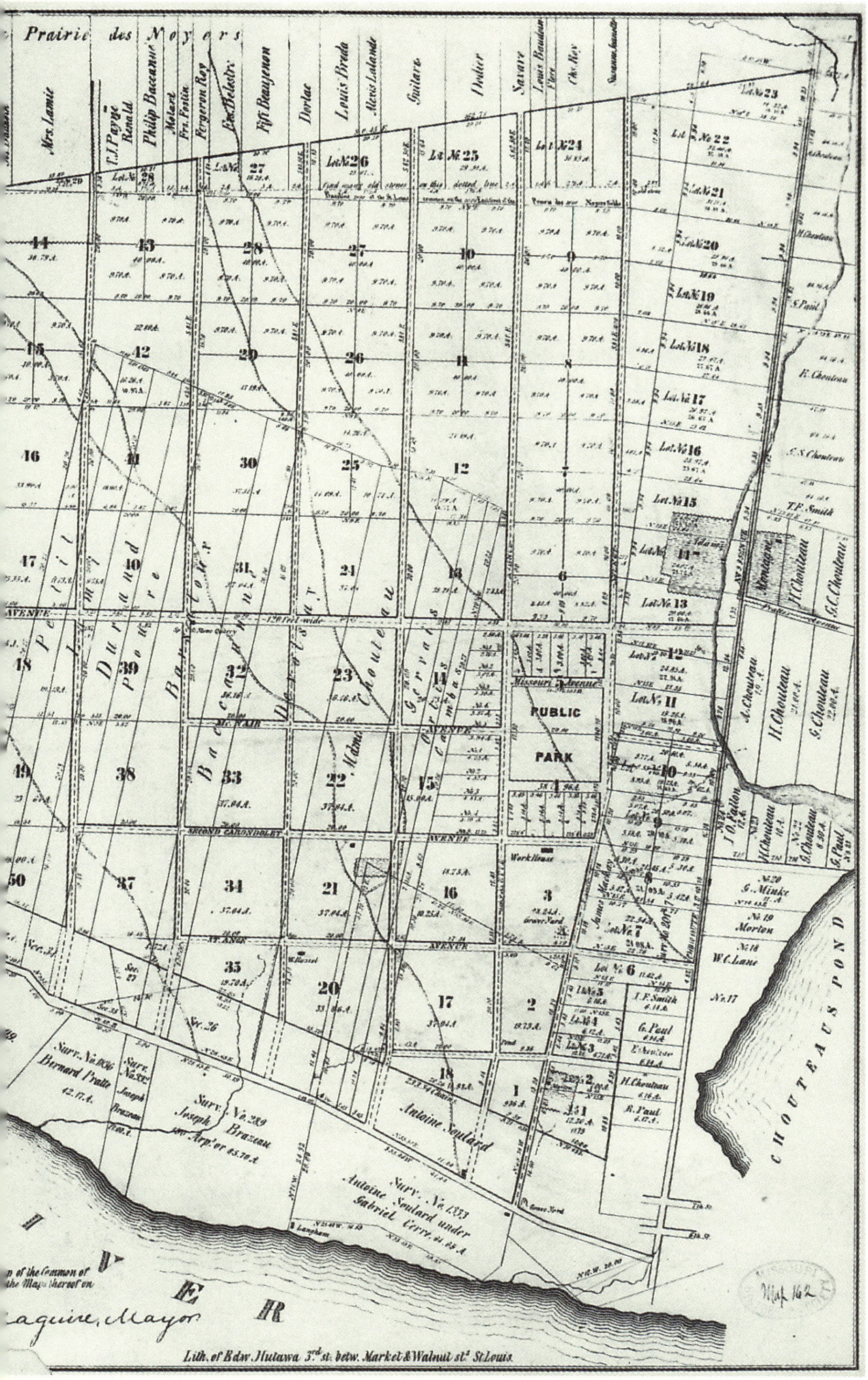

The long thin strips of land at the top of the map are vestiges of the old common fields. (Courtesy of the Missouri Historical Society, St. Louis.)

> fencing, building, etc., it may be premised different opinions are entertained. The ancient inhabitants are, from custom, much attached to that privilege. Others . . . view commons as an injury to the growth and prosperity of towns: as creating a waste around them: as preventing the settlement and cultivation of lands valuable for agricultural purposes.

Both opinions were correct, in the correspondent's view, and both could be accommodated simultaneously. "There can be no doubt," he wrote,

> but a certain extent of common land proportioned to their size and situation is desirable to all villages and towns:—and it is equally clear that the prosperity of a town may require occasional appropriations of such land to extend its limits, or for the attainment of useful objects—as the erections and support of schools, public edifices, etc., etc.[27]

Within a short time, newer ideas about the value of a commons had supplanted older ones. When the residents of St. Charles petitioned Congress in 1819 to preserve their commons, they did not mention the importance of pasturing, wood gathering, or any of the traditional uses of the commons. They asked Congress instead to confirm their claim to the commons so that they could "lease, sell, divide or dispose of the same for the benefit of the inhabitants of said Town." The inhabitants of St. Charles were already planning "a fund of at least twenty thousand dollars . . . to be raised out of the sale" of lots in the commons, "for the support of an academy or seminary of learning," as well as sites "for public buildings" and "for the college or university."[28] In St. Louis, public sentiment was just the same. "It is desirable," the *Missouri Republican* editorialized soon after the vote to sell off lots in the commons, "that they be brought into market as speedily as possible." Such haste had a little to do with the demand for land convenient for new housing, but more to do with the revenue to be gained from selling the commons, which would facilitate substantial municipal expenditure. "Few cities, indeed," exulted the *Republican*, "are better provided with the means of raising funds for improvement and ornament, as necessity or a liberal taste may require."[29]

Thus by the 1830s, it was generally believed that the commons could be put to better use than pasture. By selling off the commons and using the proceeds for other local government expenses—schools, buildings, and the like—the residents of the St. Louis area were not privatizing the commons so much as they were exchanging one kind of commons for another. The inhabitants traded an agricultural commons for an educational commons, a transportation commons (to the extent the city budget was devoted to roads and bridges), a public safety commons (for St. Louis's new police force, established in 1843), and so on. In this sense the sale of the St. Louis commons resembles similar acts of so-called privatization in our own time, in which governments sell off assets such as telephone companies, not to decrease the total amount of public assets relative to private, but rather to obtain the cash necessary to acquire *other* public assets instead. As expectations of services from local government grew, so did the demand to convert the old commons into all sorts of new commons. St. Louisans once had public farmland and private night watches; now they had private farmland and public employees.

Like the change in conventional thought as to who owned the commons, the change in conventional ideas about the best use of the commons occurred almost without being noticed. Unlike in England, where enclosure had significant distributional consequences—in E. P. Thompson's well-known phrase, enclosure "was a plain enough case of class robbery"[30]—enclosure in Missouri seems not to have harmed any group very much. The quantity of land remaining available for exploitation was still so large that, unlike in England, there was no class of landless poor to suffer (except of course for slaves and Indians, who never had rights in the commons in the first place, and who in any event had problems much more serious than this). At a time when private farming had largely replaced common field farming in St. Louis, local whites of even "the poorest class," observed one traveler, "generally possess a cart, a horse or two, a small stock of cattle, and cultivate small plots of ground."[31] Because no group lost much when the commons was sold, the shift in public attitudes toward the best use of the commons occasioned little controversy.

These changes in popular thought about the commons were composed of two distinct trends. On the one hand, the views of the original French inhabitants were changing; individual farmers, such as the farmers of St. Charles, were conceptualizing the commons differently and valuing it for different uses. On the other hand, the area was experiencing demographic change, as Anglo-Americans with Anglo-American ideas about property soon outnumbered the French. Because both trends moved in the same direction, it is hard to assess the relative importance of each.

What was the relationship between (1) the change in the conception of the commons, from land owned directly by the people to land owned by the government, and (2) the change in conventional notions of the best use of the commons? The two transformations bear no necessary logical relationship. It would have been possible, had the first change occurred but not the second, for the commons to have turned into a city-owned pasture. It would have been conceivable, had the second change occurred but not the first, for the proprietors of the commons to have either (a) simply divided the land up among themselves, for each individual to sell or farm as he saw fit, or (b) united in a sale and then used the proceeds to establish nongovernmental roads, nongovernmental schools, and a nongovernmental security force. (All three of these institutions are hardly unknown today, particularly the second, and in fact the first and third seem to be growing more popular.)

A causal relationship between the two changes could plausibly have run in either direction. It might be that as the commons' value as nonpasture began to exceed its value as pasture, the residents needed a way to sell it off; that an asset owned by a unit of government is administratively much easier to sell than an asset owned by an unorganized group of thousands of people; that the new types of metaphorical commons to be established with the proceeds of the sale are also more easily managed by a unit of government than by an unorganized mass of people; and that this desire to reduce the transaction costs of selling off the commons and managing the proceeds is what drove the conceptual transformation of the commons from land owned by the unorganized public to land owned by the government.

One might also say the exact opposite. It seems just as plausible that in a Spanish colonial political structure with no formal institutions of self-government, the commons served as an institution affording residents an opportunity to exercise power in matters closest to their economic livelihood; that when the United States assumed sovereignty, official institutions of self-government began to come into existence; that the commons then became redundant in a political sense, because the management structure of the commons was now hardly different from the management structure applicable to government-owned land; that the commons thus lost much of its value in this sense; and that with this loss of value, other uses of the commons began to appear to the residents as relatively more attractive. In this version of events, there is simply no place in republican legal thought for a category of land owned directly by the people rather than by the government. The government *is* the people, in the sense that the government is assumed to be the agent of the people in managing the people's property, and in the sense that the process is a transparent one, in which there is no divergence between what the government wants to do with the land and what the citizens want to do with it.

Either way, when the commons was broken up, it was not simply privatized. The commons was first *public*ized; it was converted in popular understanding into an asset owned by the government, so that it could be traded for other kinds of public assets. In the end, the move was not from public to private, but from nongovernmental public power to governmental public power. The public did not possess any more or any less property; the public just possessed property in a different way.

The Americans who streamed into Missouri in the first half of the nineteenth century preferred private plots to common fields. Farmland in common fields was already prepared for farming, while undeveloped land required an initial investment of labor to turn it into a private farm. Every prospective American farmer faced a choice: he could invest money, by buying into an established common field, or he could invest labor, by buying undeveloped land. It appears that every American immigrant chose the latter. There is no direct evidence as to why that was so, but the preference of American farmers in this respect has not changed in the past two centuries, so it seems fair to assume that the reasons people farm on private land today are much the same as those present at the time. Farmers starting anew with undeveloped land avoided the problems of overconsumption and undermaintenance associated with collectively owned fields. Private property had so many cultural resonances as well—the same ones people feel today—that one suspects that private plots would have been preferred even if costless solutions to those problems could have been devised. Americans soon so outnumbered the French that they would have been able to convert the pre-Purchase system of property rights into one closely resembling that with which they were already familiar, regardless of the preferences of the French.

As far as one can tell, however, the reallocation of property rights in Missouri was not imposed upon the French by the Americans. After a decade or so of resistance, the French seemed just as eager as the Americans to break up the commons. Part of this change in attitude was no doubt due to American cultural influence. As the older French colonists died, and as their land descended to younger people who had lived significant fractions of their adult lives in an American jurisdiction surrounded by Americans, many of the old ways died too. Among these was almost certainly a preference for farming in common fields. Part of the change can also be chalked up to rising land prices. The inefficiencies of overconsumption and undermaintenance grow progressively more expensive along with the value of the asset being consumed. As prices of an asset rise, people accordingly tend to pay greater attention to assigning clear property rights in that asset. When the value of Missouri land rose, so too did the number and the importance of property lines.

The common fields were also a political institution, and their demise most likely had political roots as well. American farmers would have seen no need to join a common field in order to exert political authority over their farmland. Institutions of local government would have seemed equally effective at the very least, and did not require working side by side with non-English-speaking people. After some experience with the new institutions, French farmers no doubt saw the political aspects of the commons in a new light. Municipal governments differed little in their representativeness from the governance structures peculiar to the common fields. As institutions of local government came into existence, the commons became useless as a political device. Ownership quietly shifted from the people to the government. To the extent French farmers perceived any benefit from the ability to manage the commons themselves, that benefit disappeared.

Conclusion

Frederick Bates was partly right. The United States did establish an "empire of the laws" in Missouri. Lawyers and government officials, many of whom were lawyers as well, took Anglo-American legal institutions and practices from the eastern United States and transplanted them to the newly acquired territory. They replicated the forms of dispute resolution and property ownership with which they were familiar. The imposition of one's own legal structures on another people in a new place is not the only aspect of empire, but it is an important one.

Bates, of course, meant much more than that. To describe American territorial legal policy as an "empire of the laws" was implicitly to describe pre-Purchase Upper Louisiana as a place without laws, where individual official power was unchecked, where Spanish officials could exercise tyrannical discretion. In this sense, Bates was wrong. The legal empire in which he participated was the second, not the first, in the area. In the decades before Bates and his colleagues arrived in St. Louis, Spanish officials and French residents had constructed a legal empire as well—a very different sort of empire, but an empire nonetheless. No less than the Americans, they transplanted the legal practices and institutions familiar to them from the places they had left.

In the conversion of Upper Louisiana to Missouri, the area's legal system changed considerably. The contrast was particularly striking in two respects. One concerned sovereignty, or the issue of how the residents identified the legitimate source of law. The other concerned property, or the issue of how the residents allocated rights to use their land.

First, where the pre–Louisiana Purchase legal system relied largely on unwritten local norms to resolve disputes, the post-Purchase system relied primarily on written authority—statutes and common law cases—

produced by authorized officials of government, often distant in time and space. This contrast was conspicuous at the level of actual practice, but it was even more so at the level of theory. The residents of Upper Louisiana understood quite well that their law bubbled up from the unarticulated norms of everyday life, and they intended that it should. The residents of Missouri (or at least the lawyers and government officials, whose views on the matter are the only ones to have survived) believed that their law flowed downward, in the form of rules and precedents embodied in texts issued by the sovereign. They ascribed normative force to this belief: a legal system not organized that way, like the one they replaced, was synonymous with tyranny, because it did not adequately cabin the discretion of government officials. When their own legal system failed to live up to this ideal, they tended to fault the individuals working within the system rather than the principle upon which the system was organized.

Second, where productive land before the Louisiana Purchase was often held in common, productive land afterward was allocated in private plots, and the common fields were eventually broken up into more private plots. Despite an initial attachment to the common fields, even the French farmers eventually pressed for land privatization. By 1860, the pattern of land distribution in the parts of Missouri settled by the French was indistinguishable from that anywhere else in the West.

In both respects, I have argued, the changes in Missouri's legal system in the years surrounding the Louisiana Purchase cannot be adequately explained without close attention to the legal cultures in which the residents were immersed. Purely material explanations, focusing on matters such as population, geography, and economic exchange, are insufficient to account for either shift. This is not to say that material explanations are irrelevant—particularly where the common fields are concerned, the productivity of land was obviously an important consideration—but such accounts leave large gaps, which can be filled only by an awareness of the thought and the habits of the people involved.

The approach taken by this book has been an unusual one, in that it has traced changes in legal thought and institutions as one set of people largely succeeded another in a single location. Most studies of transitions in legal culture have been organized in the opposite way: they have followed a single set of people as it moved from one location to another. Where these studies have kept the people nearly the same but varied the surroundings, I have kept the surroundings nearly the same but varied the people. Despite these differences in approach, however, the results of previous studies have been identical to the results of this one. Where one set of people has moved to a radically different place, its legal culture has tended not to change very much. This has been found true of English immigrants to North America, for instance, and of Americans headed west on the Overland Trail, into an area beyond the effective control of any sovereign.[1] In such cases, as in Missouri, cultural factors have proven more important than material environment in determining legal thought and practice.

Notes

INTRODUCTION

1. Frederick Bates to Meriwether Lewis, 28 Apr. 1807, Marshall, *Life and Papers of Frederick Bates*, 1:107.

2. The exception is Ekberg, *Colonial Ste. Genevieve*.

3. Nicollet, "Sketch of the Early History," 158.

4. Scharf, *History of Saint Louis*, 1:300; Vogel, *Social Life in St. Louis*, 24. The early local historians, in their haste to get past those dark Spanish years, sometimes lost track of exactly what was wrong. Scharf's "offensively paternal system" was, on the previous page, "patriarchical but not paternal."

5. Primm, *Lion of the Valley*, 35.

6. An earlier collection of essays included some on colonial Louisiana. Haas, *Louisiana's Legal Heritage*. Much relevant material can also be found in Dargo, *Jefferson's Louisiana*.

7. Kerr, *Petty Felony*; Cutter, *Legal Culture*. Relevant essays can also be found in Ebright, *Spanish and Mexican Land Grants*.

8. Bakken, *Practicing Law*; Fritz, *Federal Justice*; Haywood, *Cowtown Lawyers*; Wunder, *Inferior Courts*.

9. The more general history of land use in the United States, particularly in the West, has received substantial recent attention. See, e.g., Lewis, *Neither Wolf Nor Dog*; Boag, *Environment and Experience*; R. White, *Land Use*; Worster, *Nature's Economy*.

10. Usner, *Indians, Settlers, and Slaves*, 108–9 n.3.

CHAPTER 1: UPPER LOUISIANA

1. C. H. Chapman and E. F. Chapman, *Indians and Archaeology*, 128, 16.

2. Stout, Wheeler-Voegelin, and Blasingham, *Sac, Fox and Iowa Indians*, 175–76.

3. Rollings, *The Osage*, 47–48; C. H. Chapman, *Origin of the Osage*, 55–56; Din and Nasatir, *Imperial Osages*.

4. Balesi, *Time of the French*, 196–97.

5. There has been a longstanding controversy as to the date of Ste. Geneviève's founding. Carl Ekberg makes a persuasive case for 1750 in Ekberg, *Colonial Ste. Genevieve*.

6. 1752 Census for "Vilage Ste Junnievieve," Census Collection, box 1, Missouri Historical Society (hereafter cited as MHS).

7. McDermott, "Myths and Realities," 8–9.

8. Holt, "Shaping of St. Louis," 499.

9. Amos Stoddard to W. H. Harrison, 3 June 1804, Stoddard Papers, box 1, MHS.

10. Pittman, *European Settlements*, 49–50.

11. Hutchins, *Historical Narrative*, 25.

12. Whitaker, *Mississippi Question*; Lyon, *Louisiana*; Levasseur, "Major Periods," 585.

13. De Finiels, *Upper Louisiana*, 51–54.

14. Din and Harkins, *New Orleans Cabildo*.

15. The trip between Spain and Havana took approximately two months each way in the early seventeenth century. Burkholder and Johnson, *Colonial Latin America*, 71. I have found no estimates of the time necessary to travel between Spain and New Orleans in the eighteenth century, but I doubt it could have been significantly less.

16. Nasatir, *Borderland in Retreat*, 52–53.

17. Leyba to Galvez, 16 Nov. 1778, Kinnaird, *Spain in the Mississippi Valley*, 1:310.

18. Perez to Miró, 27 Oct. 1790, Kinnaird, *Spain in the Mississippi Valley*, 2:387; see Musick, *St. Louis*.

19. Manuel Gayoso de Lemos, "Political Condition of the Province of Louisiana," 5 July 1792, Robertson, *Louisiana under the Rule*, 1:283–84.

20. Ulloa to Grimaldi, 4 Aug. 1768, Kinnaird, *Spain in the Mississippi Valley*, 1:59–60.

21. Gitlin, "Boundaries of Empire," 85.

22. Belting, *Kaskaskia*, 21; W. Briggs, "Le Pays des Illinois," 30, 40.

23. Ste. Geneviève Colonial Archives, doc. 5, MHS.

24. Ste. Geneviève Colonial Archives, doc. 28, MHS; St. Charles common field regulations, 6 Jan. 1802, Emmons Collection, box 1, MHS.

25. *American State Papers, Miscellaneous*, 1:377; Din and Harkins, *New Orleans Cabildo*, 119.

26. Ekberg, *French Roots*, 123–37.

27. Belting, *Kaskaskia*, 21; Ste. Geneviève Colonial Archives, doc. 30, MHS; Expansion of St. Charles common, 18 Jan. 1801, Emmons Collection, box 1, MHS.

28. Population statistics in this paragraph are for St. Louis in 1800. In earlier years and in smaller towns, the percentage of white men was slightly higher, and the percentage of slaves, free blacks, and white women slightly lower. Holt, "Shaping of St. Louis," 502–3.

29. St. Louis Colonial Archives, box 9, folder 4, doc. 956, MHS; Gilbert, "Esther and Her Sisters," 14. On the free blacks of colonial New Orleans, a larger and more frequently studied group that was doubtless similar in many respects to the free blacks of Upper Louisiana, see Ingersoll, "Free Blacks"; Hanger, "Personas de Varias Clases y Colores"; Gould, "In Full Enjoyment."

30. Boyle, "Did She Generally Decide?"

31. See, e.g., Victoire Chouteau Gratiot to St. Gemes, 10 Aug. 1794, Semsrott Collection, box 1, MHS.

32. Leyba to Galvez, 16 Nov. 1778, Kinnaird, *Spain in the Mississippi Valley*, 1:312-13.

33. Thorne, *Many Hands*; Cleary, "Contested Terrain."

34. Kinnaird, *Spain in the Mississippi Valley*, 1:125–26, 167–79.

35. "Acknowledgment of M. Maxent of two negresses which belonged to MM. A[ugus]te and P[ier]re Chouteau which they exchanged for Lizette, savagess, and her son named Paul, 1777," Chouteau Papers, box 1, MHS; Magnaghi, "The Role of Indian Slavery."

36. New Madrid Colonial Archives, box 9, doc. 882, MHS.

37. Beckwith, *Creoles of St. Louis*.

38. Estate Inventory at 6, Laclède Papers, box 1, MHS; William C. Carr to Mrs. Charles Carr, 21 June 1804, Carr Papers, box 1, MHS.

39. See, e.g., Promissory note of Jacob Filie, 26 Apr. 1782, Promissory note of M. Labuxiere, 4 Oct. 1785, both in Chouteau Papers, box 1, MHS; Foley and Rice, *First Chouteaus*, 39.

40. See, e.g., "Statement of various promissory notes delivered to Monsieur Sarpy, by William Grant, to be recovered if possible at St. Louis in Illinois 22 March 1785," Berthold Collection, box 1, MHS.

41. McDermott, *Private Libraries*.

42. Gitlin, "Boundaries of Empire," 72.

43. Dickinson, "New France," 44–45; Din and Harkins, *New Orleans Cabildo*, 122; Briggs, "Le Pays des Illinois," 46.

44. Ste. Geneviève Colonial Archives, Litigation 132, MHS. Parts of the commandant's order are illegible, so it is difficult to tell exactly what relief he gave. Rather than giving Dame Gadobert actual possession of the property, he may have only placed her ahead of Catalan's other creditors. The earliest surviving litigation records from Ste. Geneviève are from the late 1760s. Only fragments have survived; there are no complete cases until the 1770s. The earliest surviving record of litigation in St. Louis is from 1779.

45. Ste. Geneviève Colonial Archives, Litigation 45, 73, 121, and 122, MHS; see also a largely incomprehensible petition from a lead miner named Larose, in the Vallé Papers, box 1, MHS.

46. Ste. Geneviève Colonial Archives, Litigation 52, MHS.

47. On the uprising, see J. P. Moore, *Revolt in Louisiana*; Texada, *Alejandro O'Reilly*; Korn, *Early Jews*, 29–34. English translations of O'Reilly's order have been published in *American State Papers, Miscellaneous*, 1:369; and "Ordinances of Don Alexander O'Reilly," 27. The Spanish original is published in Ramirez, *Alejandro O'Reilly*, 203. The original printed French version is in Archivo General de Indias, Cuba, leg. 2357, doc. 374 (hereafter cited as AGI).

48. Cutter, *Legal Culture*, 105–46.

49. Din and Harkins, *New Orleans Cabildo*, 117–18.

50. This order, in Spanish manuscript, is at AGI, Cuba, leg. 2357, doc. 396. I have found no published or printed versions, nor any translations into any other language.

51. Houck, *Spanish Regime in Missouri*, 1:127, 258; 2:262.

52. See, e.g., Clamorgan against Bouvet (11 July 1803), Litigation Collection, MHS; Ste. Geneviève Colonial Archives, Litigation 32, MHS; New Madrid Colonial Archives, box 14, doc. 1392, MHS. This jurisdictional limit appears not to have been taken very seriously in Arkansas either. Arnold, *Unequal Laws*, 53–56. A similar hundred-peso jurisdictional limit in Mexican California was likewise ignored most of the time. Langum, *Law and Community*, 39–40.

53. Penick, *New Madrid Earthquakes*.

54. Cottu against Langlois (July 1800), Amoureux-Bolduc Collection, box 1, MHS.

55. Sanguinet against Roy's estate (1797), Poepping Collection, MHS.

56. Baade, "Law of Slavery"; Foner, "Free People of Color," 410.

57. Valuation of Victoria, June 1796, St. Louis History Collection, box 1, MHS.

58. "Arbitrage entre Clamorgan y Sanguinet," 10 June 1800, Litigation Collection, MHS.

59. Vachard against Labadie (June 1785), Litigation Collection, MHS.

60. Langum, "Introduction of Conciliation," 329–30.

61. Gayoso to Delassus, 16 May 1799, Nasatir, *Before Lewis and Clark*, 2:598. Gayoso's reference to "arbitral judges" meant arbitrators appointed by a judge; "friendly arbitrators" were appointed by the parties. The latter were much more common in Upper Louisiana, although the former were not unknown. I am indebted to David Langum for pointing this out.

62. Stoddard to W. C. C. Claiborne, 26 Mar. 1804, Stoddard Papers, box 1, MHS.

63. On the role of the *auditor de guerra*, see Cutter, *Legal Culture*, 55–57.

64. Some of the documents related to this case are in the Chouteau Papers, box 1, MHS. These include DeVolsay's 1777 petition, his 1779 petition, statements from Gilles Duchemin, Paul Guitard, François Trolier, Louis Marchetaud, Nicolas Royer, Pierre Moutardy, and an unidentified person; a 1779 order from

Leyba requesting more such statements; additional statements from Jean-Marie Cardinal, Diego Blanco, and someone named Perrault; a notation from Leyba finding the testimony of these witnesses true; and a letter from Leyba to a judge in Cahokia asking him to give a copy of DeVolsay's petition to de Villiers. More of the documents are in AGI, Cuba, leg. 193b. These include de Villiers's response, doc. 657; Leyba's order sending the case to the governor, doc. 664; de Villiers's petition to prevent DeVolsay from selling any of the community property in New Orleans, doc. 666; Leyba's order granting that petition, doc. 668; and a letter from the priest in St. Louis taking de Villiers's side, doc. 994. DeVolsay complains about the priest's meddling in leg. 192, doc. 1104.

65. The many documents that make up the record of this case are in the Chouteau Papers, box 1, MHS. Cruzat's letter to Miró is at AGI, Cuba, leg. 12, doc. 188. Miró discusses the sentencing of the runaway Indians at AGI, Cuba, leg. 117a, doc. 96.

66. Langum, *Law and Community*, 97-104; Ebright, *Land Grants and Lawsuits*, 62–64.

67. Langum, *Law and Community*, 131–44.

68. See, e.g., Lukes, *Individualism*; Bender, *Community and Social Change*.

69. Konig, *Law and Society*, xiii–xiv, 117–35.

70. Langum, *Law and Community*, 113–16.

71. Piernas to O'Reilly, 31 Oct. 1769, Houck, *Spanish Regime in Missouri,* 1:70–71.

72. Leyba to Galvez, 9 Dec. 1778, Kinnaird, *Spain in the Mississippi Valley*, 1:316.

73. Trudeau to Carondelet, 26 Sept. 1795, Nasatir, *Before Lewis and Clark*, 1:350.

74. Cruzat to officials of Kaskaskia and Cahokia, 4 Aug. 1782, Kinnaird, *Spain in the Mississippi Valley*, 2:48.

75. Leyba to Galvez, 13 July 1779, Kinnaird, *Spain in the Mississippi Valley*, 1:349.

76. Pérez to Vallé, 1 Mar. 1792, Vallé Papers, box 1, MHS.

77. Portell to Vallé, 14 Nov. 1794, Vallé Papers, box 1, MHS.

78. Ste. Geneviève Colonial Archives, Litigation 114, MHS.

79. See, e.g., Turner to Vallé, 10 Mar. 1795, Vallé Papers, box 2, MHS; Permission of Delassus to William Glass and John Fery to enter New Bourbon to search for "Jacqueson, accused of stealing horses," 14 Aug. 1799, Litigation Collection, MHS; Trudeau to Vallé, 5 Sept. 1792, Vallé Papers, box 1, MHS; Delassus to Tayon, 17 Aug. 1799, Poepping Collection, MHS; Delassus to Vallé, 29 May 1801, Vallé Papers, box 3, MHS; Williams to Delassus, 27 Sept. 1803, Vallé Papers, box 3, MHS.

80. Cf. Kerr, *Petty Felony*, 103.

81. Prosecution of Buteau and Baribeau, Nov.–Dec. 1779, Litigation Collection, MHS. For a similar example, involving two men who diverted a barge

to Ste. Geneviève against the wishes of the passengers and crew, see Prosecution of Motard and Basquez, June 1779, Governors Collection, MHS.

82. Ekberg, *Colonial Ste. Genevieve*, 371.

83. New Madrid Colonial Archives, box 13, doc. 1342, MHS.

84. Petition of William Clark and Elisabeth Tigner against Samuel Greffeth, 10 Mar. 1803, Emmons Collection, box 1, MHS.

85. Petition of Cerré, 2 Sept. 1784, Litigation Collection, MHS.

CHAPTER 2: SOURCES OF WRITTEN LAW

1. "Ordinances of Don Alexander O'Reilly," 27.

2. Grimaldi to Unzaga, 24 Mar. 1770, Kinnaird, *Spain in the Mississippi Valley*, 1:163; see also *Strother v. Lucas*, 37 U.S. 410 (1838).

3. Grimaldi to Unzaga, 24 Mar. 1770, Kinnaird, *Spain in the Mississippi Valley*, 1:163–64. The husband's right to kill an adulterous spouse, although explicitly permitted under classical Greek and Roman law, had long since been abandoned by European states. Boswell, *Same-Sex Unions*, 108 n.2.

4. Baade, "Marriage Contracts," 37. Before 1769, the Spanish government had explicitly chosen not to subject Louisiana to Spanish colonial law. "Royal Decree Commissioning Don Antonio de Ulloa Governor of Louisiana," 21 May 1765, Kinnaird, *Spain in the Mississippi Valley*, 1:1.

5. Haring, *Spanish Empire*, 105.

6. Walton, *Civil Law*, 525.

7. Van Kleffens, *Hispanic Law*, 263; Ebright, "New Mexican Land Grants," 19.

8. Burkholder, "Honest Judges," 248.

9. Kagan, *Lawsuits and Litigants*, 25–38; Ebright, "Introduction," 3.

10. Meyer, *Water in the Hispanic Southwest*, 106–8.

11. Cutter, *Legal Culture*, 36–37; McKnight, "Law Books," 75–77.

12. Cutter, *Legal Culture*, 34, 38–40.

13. Ebright, "Frontier Land Litigation," 201–3.

14. Langum, *Law and Community*, 125–27; Cutter, *Legal Culture*, 38–39, 69, 78; Ebright, *Land Grants and Lawsuits*, 23–24, 83; Meyer, *Water in the Hispanic Southwest*, 160–61.

15. Weber, *Spanish Frontier in North America*, 325.

16. Houck, *Spanish Regime in Missouri*, 2:261, 273, 1:126, 258.

17. Houck, *Spanish Regime in Missouri*, 2:331; Inventory of Ste. Geneviève documents transferred to American officials, Vallé Papers, box 3, MHS; Inventory of St. Louis documents not transferred, Delassus Papers, box 3, MHS; Amos Stoddard to Jean Baptiste Vallé, 30 Sept. 1804, Governors Collection, box 1, MHS.

18. Houck, *Spanish Regime in Missouri*, 1:259, 2:275, 1:128.

19. McDermott, *Private Libraries*, 24, 33, 36, 132, 111.

20. AGI, Cuba, leg. 190, doc. 475, at 4.

21. *Riddick v. Walsh*, 15 Mo. 519, 536 (1852).

22. Ekberg, *Colonial Ste. Genevieve*, 186–88.

23. Baade, "Marriage Contracts," 66–72.

24. W. Briggs, "The Forgotten Colony," 154.

25. Din and Harkins, *New Orleans Cabildo*, 117–18.

26. Morales to Delassus, 24 May 1802, Delassus Papers, box 7, MHS.

27. Tanner, *Decrees*, 1:357. I am grateful to Richard Helmholz for pointing this out.

28. Miró to Cruzat, 25 Jan. 1787, AGI, Cuba, leg. 4B, doc. 28.

29. Kinnaird, *Spain in the Mississippi Valley*, 2:1, 3, 1:45, 46, 197. On the difficulty of enforcing such regulations, see Kinnaird, *Spain in the Mississippi Valley*, 1:76–77.

30. D. A. Bell, *Lawyers and Citizens*, 22–23; Berlanstein, "Lawyers," 165.

31. Wallach, *Bibliographic History*, 18–21; Dickinson, "New France," 32.

32. Baade, "Marriage Contracts," 66–72.

33. AGI, Cuba, leg. 217b, doc. 100.

34. Baade, "Law of Slavery."

35. AGI, Cuba, leg. 190, doc. 475.

36. Representative wills can be found in the St. Louis Colonial Archives, boxes 19–20, docs. 2164–2293, MHS. Pre-1770 wills include Will 14 and Will 18, Ste. Geneviève Colonial Archives, MHS; St. Louis Colonial Archives, box 19, folder 4, docs. 2163–65, MHS.

37. For sample contracts, see the St. Louis Colonial Archives, boxes 1–12, docs. 1–1389 (contracts conveying property), boxes 12–15, docs. 1501–1756 (promissory notes), and boxes 28–29, docs. 2671–2825 (appointments of agents), MHS.

38. Merryman, *Civil Law Tradition*, 105–6.

39. Langum, *Law and Community*, 163–64.

40. For French examples, see Promissory Note, 22 Nov. 1780, from Pierre Lasigeure dit Brouillet to Auguste Chouteau, Chouteau Papers, box 1, MHS; Contract, 3 Sept. 1789, signed by P. Tabeaux, Chouteau Papers, box 1, MHS.

41. St. Charles Colonial Archives, box 1, doc. 49, MHS.

42. A "secret contract" is in P. Tabeaux to Joseph Marie Papin, 3 Sept. 1789, Chouteau Papers, box 1, MHS; a "private agreement" is in the Clamorgan-Hortiz litigation, Sept. 1793, Poepping Collection, MHS.

43. St. Louis Colonial Archives, box 1, folder 5, doc. 23, MHS.

44. Ste. Geneviève Colonial Archives, Agreements-Contracts 20, MHS; see also St. Louis Colonial Archives, box 1, folder 2, doc. 2; box 1, folder 3, doc. 13; box 1, folder 4, doc. 16, MHS.

45. For a sample of the continuity in the language of contracts before and after 1770, see the following very similar contracts for the sale of goods on credit, all from the St. Louis Colonial Archives, box 13, folder 9, doc. 1502 (1766); box 14, folder 1, doc. 1523 (1769); box 14, folder 2, doc. 1561 (1771); box 14, folder 6,

doc. 1627 (1778); box 14, folder 6, doc. 1631 (1781); box 15, folder 1, doc. 1669 (1788); box 15, folder 3, doc. 1696 (1792); box 15, folder 4, doc. 1734 (1799), MHS.

46. Houck, *Spanish Regime in Missouri*, 1:1, 10; Crouch, Garr, and Mundigo, *Spanish City Planning*, 116–55.

47. Din, "Immigration Policy of Governor Esteban Miró"; Din, "Spain's Immigration Policy in Louisiana"; Arena, "Land Settlement Policies"; Kinnaird, "American Penetration into Spanish Louisiana"; Burns, "Spanish Land Laws of Louisiana"; *American State Papers, Miscellaneous*, 1:376; AGI, Cuba, leg. 2365, 378; *American State Papers, Public Lands*, 3:432–35; Galvez to Galvez, 27 Jan. 1778, Houck, *Spanish Regime in Missouri*, 1:152–53; Clamorgan to Carondelet, 4 Oct. 1793, Kinnaird, *Spain in the Mississippi Valley*, 3:208; Report of Zenon Trudeau, 15 Jan. 1798, Houck, *Spanish Regime in Missouri*, 2:247; Delassus to Peyroux, 21 Sept. 1799, New Madrid Colonial Archives, box 15, doc. 1419, MHS.

48. The same was true in Arkansas, another place where complying with Spanish land law was too costly to be worthwhile. Arnold, *Unequal Laws*, 105–9.

49. See, for example, the three 1752 Ste. Geneviève land grants in the Guibord Collection, box 1, MHS, or the 1766 St. Louis concession in the Pettus Collection, box 1, MHS.

50. *American State Papers, Public Lands*, 5:709.

51. François Roy, 7 June 1797, Parker-Russell Collection, box 1, MHS; John Long, 27 Aug. 1797, Long Papers, box 1, MHS; Antoine Gautier, 20 Jan. 1801, Emmons Collection, box 1, MHS; Jacques Clamorgan, 1 Mar. 1797, St. Charles Collection, box 1, MHS.

52. Daniel Boone, 9 Nov. 1799, Boone Collection, box 1, MHS; Faragher, *Daniel Boone*, 274–319.

53. St. Louis Colonial Archives, box 9, folder 5, doc. 973, MHS; Gayoso to Trudeau, 26 Apr. 1798, Missouri Register of Land Titles Collection, box 1, MHS; cf. Konig, *Law and Society*, 35–46.

54. Violette, "Spanish Land Claims in Missouri"; Richardson, "Private Land Claims in Missouri."

55. Langum, "Legal System of Spanish California," 5.

56. Houck, *Spanish Regime in Missouri*, 1:13–15; Kinnaird, *Spain in the Mississippi Valley*, 3:205; Nasatir, "Anglo-Spanish Rivalry"; Order of Charles Dehault Delassus, 19 Feb. 1803, Emmons Collection, box 1, MHS.

57. Kinnaird, *Spain in the Mississippi Valley*, 1:89–90, 150; *American State Papers, Miscellaneous*, 1:380–81.

58. Kinnaird, *Spain in the Mississippi Valley*, 2:58–59.

59. Kinnaird, *Spain in the Mississippi Valley*, 1:93, see also 1:237.

60. Kinnaird, *Spain in the Mississippi Valley*, 3:139; see also *American State Papers, Miscellaneous*, 1:377–79.

61. Houck, *Spanish Regime in Missouri*, 1:126, 128.

62. "Proces entre les Srs. Labadie Et Chouteau Contre Duchesne, Larche, et Lecompte," June–July 1779, Litigation Collection, MHS; Vallé and Datchurut

against Dame Lardoise, (Dec. 1783–Mar. 1784), Governors Collection, box 1, MHS; Ste. Geneviève Colonial Archives, Litigation 6 (Dec. 1771), MHS.

63. Kinnaird, *Spain in the Mississippi Valley*, 3:67.

64. Order of Trudeau, 8 Aug. 1799, Poepping Collection, MHS.

65. Houck, *Spanish Regime in Missouri*, 1:243.

66. Ste. Geneviève Colonial Archives, doc. 7, MHS.

67. Houck, *Spanish Regime in Missouri*, 1:246.

68. Houck, *Spanish Regime in Missouri*, 1:240–50.

69. New Madrid Colonial Archives, box 11, doc. 1092, MHS.

70. Ste. Geneviève Colonial Archives, docs. 5 and 30, MHS.

71. Expansion of St. Charles common, 18 Jan. 1801, Emmons Collection, box 1, MHS.

CHAPTER 3: UNWRITTEN NORMS

1. Bouligny to Miró, 22 Aug. 1785, Kinnaird, *Spain in the Mississippi Valley*, 2:138–39. On Bouligny, see Din, *Francisco Bouligny*; Din, *Louisiana in 1776*, 11–28.

2. Stoddard, *Sketches of Louisiana*, 273.

3. Anonymous ("Le Peuple des Illinois") to Galvez, 1780, McDermott, "Myth of the 'Imbecile Governor,'" 368–72; Valiniere to Miró, 23 Feb. 1788, Kinnaird, *Spain in the Mississippi Valley*, 2:242–44; Trudeau to Vallé, 4 Mar. 1795, Vallé Papers, box 2, MHS.

4. *Stevens v. City of Cannon Beach*, 317 Ore. 131, 854 P.2d 449 (1993), cert. denied, 114 S. Ct. 1332 (1994); U.C.C. § 2-208(2); Bederman, "Curious Resurrection of Custom"; Rose, "Comedy of the Commons," 739–49.

5. Arnold, "Early English Law of Obligations," 508. See also Millon, "Positivism," 704–6; Reid, "Principles of Vengeance," 34.

6. The best records in the remaining towns are for New Madrid. The New Madrid Colonial Archives contain lists of trials apparently compiled by the last commandant in 1804 for the benefit of incoming American officials. The lists include five criminal trials for the years 1791 through 1794, eight criminal trials still to be adjudicated from 1803 and 1804, twenty-three civil trials already adjudicated in the year 1804, and a list of seventeen criminal trials that has been so badly damaged that the years the trials took place can no longer be determined. New Madrid Colonial Archives, box 15, doc. 1412, MHS.

7. Kinnaird, *Spain in the Mississippi Valley*, 1:196. The total population was 605; the 273 black slaves and 120 white women figure in barely any of that year's cases.

8. Cf. Konig, *Law and Society*, xi–xii.

9. Langum, *Law and Community*, 123.

10. New Madrid Colonial Archives, box 10, docs. 1005, 1005A (Oct. 1801), MHS.

11. Ste. Geneviève Colonial Archives, Litigation 25 (June–Oct. 1794), MHS.

12. New Madrid Colonial Archives, box 15, doc. 1410 (Mar.–Apr. 1799), MHS.

13. Moses Austin against Robert Greer (Feb.–Mar. 1799), Washington County Court Collection, box 1, MHS. Such norms were generally accepted by the community of merchants, which did not include the slave whose future was in question, who no doubt would not have characterized the issue as purely one of commercial law.

14. New Madrid Colonial Archives, box 13, doc. 1365, MHS.

15. See, e.g., New Madrid Colonial Archives, box 13, doc. 1358, MHS.

16. Roubieu claimed in response that he only "struck her with the back of his fingertips, lightly and with restraint, on her head-kerchief; this could not have killed the weakest fly." After angry petitions back and forth, the case settled; Constance moved in with her sister. Dubreuil against Roubieu (Feb.–Nov. 1786), Litigation Collection, MHS.

17. Peyroux to François Vallé, 11 June 1792, Vallé Papers, box 1, MHS. Certain specialists may note a familiar ring to this dispute; the residents of Ste. Geneviève never spoke of transaction costs, but they would have agreed that the assignment of liability makes a difference. Cf. Coase, "Problem of Social Cost."

18. "Proceso entre Dn. Carlos Sanguinet y Dn. Santiago Clamorgan" (Feb.–Mar. 1787), Poepping Collection, MHS. After a few petitions back and forth, the case settled.

19. Vachard against Labadie (June 1785), Litigation Collection, MHS.

20. AGI, Cuba, leg. 118, doc. 609.

21. In at least one instance, custom was also used to ascertain the intent of contracting parties, in much the same way it is used in American law today. In 1801, Hugh Wallace defended against François Duquette's petition to collect on a note by pointing out that the scrivener had written 1900 rather than 1800 as the year payment was due. Wallace explained that he was fully prepared to pay Duquette one hundred years later. Lt. Gov. Charles Delassus ordered Wallace to pay Duquette immediately, on the ground that "it is not customary to enter into transactions like this one for a term of one hundred years." Delassus also sentenced Wallace to eight days in prison for making an argument so clearly in bad faith. Duquette against Wallace (Jan.–Mar. 1801), Emmons Collection, box 1, MHS.

22. Pourée against Chouteau (14–16 Nov. 1782), Chouteau Papers, box 1, MHS. A slightly different translation of this case has been published in *Missouri Historical Society Collections* as "The Case of Pourée against Chouteau." The arbitrators' decision poses a difficult problem of translation, because the phrase quoted in the text—"suivant conventions reciproques"—can be rendered as "following mutual understandings," "conventions," "agreements," or "contracts," each of which has a slightly different meaning, and those differences are crucial

to the point being made. Even in English, the words "understandings" and "conventions" have two different sets of meanings; they can refer to actual contracts among particular people, or they can refer to an unarticulated (and often unknown) congruence of belief or desire. Finally, the arbitrators did not preface this phrase with any possessive pronoun, which leaves open the possibility that the "conventions reciproques" actually belong to the arbitrators, or even to the community at large, rather than simply to Pourée and Chouteau. I have opted for the translation that preserves as much of the ambiguity of the French original as possible, in each of these ways.

23. William Cowen against James Ferrell (24 Sept. 1800), Vallé Papers, box 3, MHS.

24. The employees' response, dated 30 June 1780, is in the Chouteau Papers, box 1, MHS. The original petition of Labadie and Chouteau has been lost. The arbitrators' decision, dated 31 July 1780, is in the Soulard Papers, box 1, MHS. For a similar case, see Ste. Geneviève Colonial Archives, Litigation 205 (Apr.–Dec. 1798), MHS.

CHAPTER 4: COMMON FIELDS

1. Innes, *Labor in a New Land*, 127–28; D. G. Allen, *In English Ways*, 30–38; Lockridge, *A New England Town*, 82; Powell, *Puritan Village*, 94–97; Macphail, "Land Hunger and Closed-Field Husbandry," 157–62; Field, "Evolution of Individual Property Rights"; *Colonial Laws of New York*, 1:21; McIlvaine, *Minutes of the Council and General Court*, 517. On the similarities among the commons in various places in northern Europe, see Kerridge, *Common Fields of England*, 101–27; Friedmann, "Fencing, Herding, and Tethering in Denmark."

2. Bloch, *French Rural History*, 35–48, 167–89; Rosenthal, *Fruits of Revolution*, 15–17, 96–98; Vassberg, *Land and Society in Castile*, 26–56; Vassberg, "Spanish Background," 12–23.

3. Ebright, *Land Grants and Lawsuits*, 24–26; Westphall, *Mercedes Reales*, 10–11; Ortiz, *Roots of Resistance*.

4. The transfer of French agricultural practices to the Illinois country is traced in extraordinarily learned detail in Ekberg, *French Roots*, 6–110. On the St. Louis area in particular, see Peterson, *Colonial St. Louis*, 12–23; Green, "Material Culture of a Pre-Enclosure Village," 22–28.

5. Testimony of Baptiste Rivière, *Hunt's Minutes*, 2:102. *Hunt's Minutes* is a three-volume typescript of testimony taken by Theodore Hunt, the Recorder of Land Titles in St. Louis, in the summer of 1825. It is at the Missouri Historical Society.

6. Testimony of Auguste Chouteau, *Hunt's Minutes*, 2:6.

7. Houck, *Spanish Regime in Missouri*, 1:17.

8. Ekberg, *Colonial Ste. Genevieve*, 129; Testimony of Louis Barada, *Hunt's Minutes*, 3:80–81.

9. Schroeder, "Environmental Setting," 34–36.

10. Bradbury, *Travels in the Interior of America*, 271.

11. "Tracts within the Commonfield of Ste. Geneviève from the high land to the Missisipi," Hunt Collection, MHS.

12. Ebright, *Land Grants and Lawsuits*, 90–91.

13. See, e.g., Concession to François Roy (1797), Parker-Russell Collection, box 1, MHS.

14. Petitions for Land in New Common Field, Ste. Geneviève (1797), Ste. Geneviève Collection, box 1, MHS.

15. See, e.g., St. Louis Colonial Archives, box 1, folder 1, doc. 2B (1771), box 2, folder 1, doc. 119 (1773), MHS.

16. See, e.g., St. Louis Colonial Archives, box 9, folder 4, doc. 956 (1803), box 19, folder 4, doc. 2165 (1770), MHS.

17. Leyba to Galvez, 16 Nov. 1778, Kinnaird, *Spain in the Mississippi Valley*, 1:312–13.

18. Din and Nasatir, *Imperial Osages*, 386–87.

19. Foley, *Genesis of Missouri*, 162–63.

20. The classic exposition of this point is Hardin, "Tragedy of the Commons." Earlier discussions can be found in Olson, *Logic of Collective Action*, 5–52; and Gordon, "Common-Property Resource."

21. McKeon, ed., *Basic Works of Aristotle* (*Politics* 2:3), 1148.

22. Aquinas, *Summa Theologica* (2a2ae, Q. 66, art. 2), 1471.

23. McDermott, *Western Journals of Washington Irving*, 78.

24. Schultz, *Travels on an Inland Voyage*, 2:55.

25. Brackenridge, *Views of Louisiana*, 113, 127.

26. Frederick Bates to Richard Bates, 17 Dec. 1807, Marshall, *Life and Papers of Frederick Bates*, 1:243.

27. For an evocation of the effect these distances could have on everyday life, see Faragher, *Daniel Boone*, 49–50.

28. AGI, Cuba, leg. 214, doc. 4, leg. 2365, doc. 345.

29. "Defence de Ruine le Bois du Communne, 4 Juin 1804," Emmons Collection, box 1, MHS.

30. Houck, *Spanish Regime in Missouri*, 2:249.

31. Testimony of Baptiste Rivière, *Hunt's Minutes*, 2:105; Testimony of Réné Dodier, *Hunt's Minutes*, 2:100.

32. Agreement among the owners of the Barriere des Noyers Fields, 26 July 1806, St. Louis History Collection, box 1, MHS.

33. O. Bell, *Cote Sans Dessein*, 24–25.

34. Cf. McEvoy, *Fisherman's Problem*, 94–95.

35. Cf. Rose, "Comedy of the Commons." For recent suggestions that other types of property—wild animals and water, respectively—may be collectively owned by the people of a state but not by the state's government, see *Hughes v. Oklahoma*, 441 U.S. 322, 327–36 (1979); *Sporhase v. Nebraska ex rel.*

Douglas, 458 U.S. 941, 945–54 (1982). A similar idea, that the government holds certain property as trustee for the people, has long been a part of American law under the "public trust" doctrine. Selvin, *Tender and Delicate Business*.

36. Ebright, *Land Grants and Lawsuits*, 87–88, 113–14.

37. Claims of Seth and Jeremiah Millington (deriving title from Charles Tayon), *Hunt's Minutes*, 1:230; Claim of Antoine Bricot dit Lamarche, *Hunt's Minutes*, 1:148.

38. Claim of Joseph Durent's representatives, *Hunt's Minutes*, 3:2; see also Claims of William Bizette's representatives, Veuve Hebert's representatives, Veuve Dodier's representatives, and Joseph Mainville Duchine's representatives, *Hunt's Minutes*, 3:111–12; Claim of Louis Bompart's representatives, *Hunt's Minutes*, 2:122.

39. Testimony of Baptiste Rivière, *Hunt's Minutes*, 2:51.

40. AGI, Cuba, leg. 201, doc. 1146.

41. AGI, Cuba, leg. 199, doc. 532 (emphasis added). Cf. *Illinois Central R.R. Co. v. Illinois*, 146 U.S. 387, 452–59 (1892).

42. Petitions, 18 and 20 Feb. 1804, St. Charles Collection, box 1, MHS.

43. "Convention de M. Mackay à l'égard des habitans de St. Charles," Emmons Collection, box 1, MHS. See also "Convention de M. Ch.ls Tayon à l'égard des habitans de St. Charles," Emmons Collection, box 1, MHS.

44. "Reglement des Cloture," 6 Jan. 1802, Emmons Collection, box 1, MHS.

45. Ste. Geneviève Colonial Archives, box 4A, doc. 28 (St. Louis), doc. 27 (Ste. Geneviève). The owners of the strips on either end of a common field would seem to have had a much larger fencing burden than the owners of strips in the middle. I have not come across any reference to this inequity, or any indication of whether the owner of a strip on the end was actually responsible for fencing the entire length of the strip.

46. Ste. Geneviève Colonial Archives, box 4A, doc. 30, MHS.

47. "Copie de la deliberation Pour la Comunne de St. Charles," 18 Jan. 1801, Emmons Collection, box 1, MHS.

48. Cf. Kiralfy, "Humble Jumble."

49. McDermott, "Myth of the 'Imbecile Governor.'"

50. Cf. Dahlman, *Open Field System*, 115–25.

51. Several historians of European agriculture have suggested this possibility. It is persuasively rejected, for the English case, in D. N. McCloskey, "Open Fields of England," 26–27.

52. D. N. McCloskey, "English Open Fields"; D. N. McCloskey, "Persistence of English Common Fields."

53. Kanter, *Commitment and Community*, 94–99; see Weisbrod, *Boundaries of Utopia*, 43–44.

54. Bouvard, *Intentional Community Movement*, 23.

55. Quoted in Zablocki, *Alienation and Charisma*, 107.

56. Michelman, "Formal and Associational Aims."

57. Lazarus, "Debunking Environmental Feudalism," 1768–73.

CHAPTER 5: TRANSITION

1. Stoddard, *Sketches of Louisiana*, v, 226.

2. English, *Pioneer Lawyer*, 21.

3. Lewis Bond to J. B. C. Lucas, 7 Oct. 1803, Lucas Papers, box 2, MHS.

4. J. B. C. Lucas to James Mountain, 3 Nov. 1803, Lucas Papers, box 2, MHS; J. B. C. Lucas to Peter Derbigny, 14 Jan. 1804, Lucas Papers, box 2, MHS.

5. Ephraim Kirby to Rufus Easton, 14 Aug. 1803, Easton Papers, box 1, MHS; DeWitt Clinton to Rufus Easton, 1 Sept. 1803, Easton Papers, box 1, MHS; Foley, *Genesis of Missouri*, 161.

6. 2 Stat. 245 (1803); 2 Stat. 283 (1804).

7. Rufus Easton to Thomas Jefferson, 27 Dec. 1803, Easton Papers, box 1, MHS.

8. Gideon Granger to Rufus Easton, 7 July 1804, Easton Papers, box 1, MHS.

9. Thompson J. Skinner to Thomas Jefferson, 9 Jan. 1804, Carter, *Territorial Papers*, 13:12.

10. Ph. Van Cortlandt to [Thomas Jefferson], 1 Feb. 1804, M418, RG 59, National Archives (hereafter cited as NA); Oliver Phelps to Thomas Jefferson, 11 Feb. 1804, M418, RG 59, NA; see also N. Williams to Thompson J. Skinner, 2 Jan. 1804, Carter, *Territorial Papers*, 13:13.

11. See Easton's law license, from Kaskaskia, Indiana Territory (a town in present-day Illinois, not far from St. Louis), 1 Oct. 1804, Easton Papers, box 1, MHS.

12. 2 Stat. 324; 2 Stat. 331 (1805).

13. Gideon Granger to Rufus Easton, 16 Mar. 1805, Easton Papers, box 1, MHS; Aaron Burr to Rufus Easton, 18 Mar. 1805, Easton Papers, box 1, MHS.

14. J. B. C. Lucas to Albert Gallatin, 9 Mar. 1805, Carter, *Territorial Papers*, 13:96–97; James Madison to J. B. C. Lucas, 22 Mar. 1805, Lucas Papers, box 2, MHS.

15. Cleland, "John B. C. Lucas, Physiocrat," 2, 146; Ellis, *Jeffersonian Crisis*, 164.

16. J. B. C. Lucas to Albert Gallatin, 9 Apr. 1805, Gallatin Collection, 1805 Correspondence 19, New-York Historical Society.

17. J. B. C. Lucas to James Madison, 4 May 1805, Carter, *Territorial Papers*, 13:123.

18. Sebin Lucas to John Lucas, 22 May 1805, Lucas Papers, box 2, MHS.

19. Albert Gallatin to J. B. C. Lucas, 9 May 1805, Lucas Papers, box 2, MHS. The case was most likely *Huidekoper's Lessee v. Douglass*, 7 U.S. 1 (1805), in which the Court had resolved a Pennsylvania land dispute in favor of settlers

from Holland. Had the federal courts' jurisdiction been limited in the manner contemplated by Gallatin, the dispute would have been in the Pennsylvania state courts rather than the federal courts, and the result might have been different. See Haskins and Johnson, *Foundations of Power*, 317–22, 591–96; G. E. White, *Marshall Court and Cultural Change*, 762–78.

20. J. B. C. Lucas to Albert Gallatin, 19 May 1805, Gallatin Collection, 1805 Correspondence 35, New-York Historical Society.

21. Tench Coxe to James Madison, n.d., 1805, Carter, *Territorial Papers*, 13:121–22.

22. J. B. McKean to Thomas Jefferson, 11 Apr. 1805, M418, RG 59, NA; William Shippen to Thomas Jefferson, 17 Apr. 1805, Carter, *Territorial Papers*, 13:116; Clement B. Penrose to Albert Gallatin, 18 May 1805, Carter, *Territorial Papers*, 13:129.

23. P. Smith to Robert Smith, 4 Apr. 1805, M418, RG 59, NA.

24. James L. Donaldson to Robert Smith, 5 Apr. 1805, Carter, *Territorial Papers*, 13:112–13.

25. Samuel Smith to Thomas Jefferson, 17 Apr. 1805, Carter, *Territorial Papers*, 13:115.

26. Albert Gallatin to James L. Donaldson, 8 May 1805, Carter, *Territorial Papers*, 13:124.

27. John Coburn to James Madison, 28 Feb. 1805, Carter, *Territorial Papers*, 13:91–92.

28. Caleb Wallace to James Madison, 22 Feb. 1805, Carter, *Territorial Papers*, 13:90.

29. Harry Innes to James Madison, 6 Mar. 1805, Carter, *Territorial Papers*, 13:96.

30. Samuel Hopkins to James Madison, 20 Mar. 1805, M418, RG 59, NA; see also Thomas Sandford to [James Madison], 4 May 1805, M418, RG 59, NA ("staunch republican"); Isaac Shelby to James Madison, 20 Mar. 1805, Carter, *Territorial Papers*, 13:108; John Graham to James Madison, 3 May 1805, M418, RG 59, NA.

31. John Coburn to Albert Gallatin, 9 June 1805, M418, RG 59, NA.

32. John Coburn to James Madison, 20 Aug. 1806, M418, RG 59, NA.

33. John Coburn to James Madison, 16 Sept. 1807, Carter, *Territorial Papers*, 14:147. Coburn was not one of the original three judges; the third (along with Lucas and Easton) was Return J. Meigs of Ohio, who served for only a short period.

34. Arnold, *Unequal Laws*, 165–66.

35. Eblen, *First and Second United States Empires*, 280–81.

36. Rufus Easton to Thomas Jefferson, 21 Feb. 1806, Easton Papers, box 1, MHS.

37. J. B. C. Lucas to Albert Gallatin, 18 Jan. 1825, Gallatin Collection, 1825 Correspondence 3, New-York Historical Society.

38. J. B. C. Lucas to John Calhoun, 18 Jan. 1825, M439, RG 59, NA.

39. Amos Stoddard to William C. C. Claiborne and James Wilkinson, 26 Mar. 1804, Stoddard Papers, box 1, MHS.

40. Frederick Bates to Richard Bates, 17 Dec. 1807, Marshall, *Life and Papers of Frederick Bates*, 1:238, 243.

41. William C. C. Claiborne to Lieut. Bowmar, 27 June 1804, Rowland, *Letter Books of Claiborne 1801–1816*, 2:223–24.

42. Peter Du Ponceau to J. B. C. Lucas, 7 Dec. 1803, Lucas Papers, box 2, MHS.

43. Frederick Bates to Meriwether Lewis, 28 Apr. 1807, Marshall, *Life and Papers of Frederick Bates*, 1:107.

44. John Watkins, Report to William C. C. Claiborne, 2 Feb. 1804, Robertson, *Louisiana under the Rule*, 2:317.

45. Baily, *Journal of a Tour*, 150.

46. Berquin-Duvallon, *Travels in Louisiana and the Floridas*, 55–56.

47. Bradbury, *Travels in the Interior of America*, 284.

48. Flint, *Recollections*, 208.

49. Albert Gallatin to Thomas Jefferson, 20 Aug. 1804, Adams, *Writings of Albert Gallatin*, 1:202.

50. Gouverneur Morris to unknown recipient, 19 Feb. 1804, Louisiana Purchase Transfer Collection, box 1, MHS.

51. William C. Carr to Mrs. Charles Carr, 21 June 1804, Carr Papers, box 1, MHS.

52. Stoddard, *Sketches of Louisiana*, 291.

53. Frederick Bates to Richard Bates, 17 Dec. 1807, Marshall, *Life and Papers of Frederick Bates*, 1:242–43.

54. Brackenridge, *Views of Louisiana*, 144.

55. Moses Austin to James Wilkinson, 22 July 1805, Barker, *Austin Papers*, 2:97.

56. Frederick Bates to Richard Bates, 17 Dec. 1807, Marshall, *Life and Papers of Frederick Bates*, 1:242–43.

57. Smith, *Virgin Land*.

58. Cole, "Law and Community in the New Nation," 171.

59. Langum, "Californios."

60. Kagan, "Prescott's Paradigm," 425–30.

61. Ferguson, *American Enlightenment*, 125.

62. Langum, *Law and Community*, 47, 69–70, 145–46.

63. J. B. C. Lucas to Thomas Jefferson, 10 Dec. 1805, Lucas Papers, box 2, MHS.

64. John Coburn to James Madison, 15 Aug. 1807, Robertson, *Louisiana under the Rule*, 2:358.

65. Amos Stoddard to secretary of war, 10 Mar. 1804, Stoddard Papers, box 1, MHS.

66. William Henry Harrison to Thomas Jefferson, 6 Nov. 1804, Hammond Collection, box 1, MHS.

67. Remonstrance, 4 Jan. 1805, *American State Papers, Miscellaneous*, 1:401.

68. Thomas Waters to Thomas Jefferson, 23 Aug. 1804, Carter, *Territorial Papers*, 13:38.

69. Remonstrance, 4 Jan. 1805, *American State Papers, Miscellaneous*, 1:403

70. John Coburn to James Madison, 15 Aug. 1807, Robertson, *Louisiana under the Rule*, 2:359.

71. Grand jury presentment, 1 Nov. 1805, Courts Collection, box 1, MHS.

72. Petition to Senate, 4 Nov. 1805, Gratiot Papers, box 1, MHS.

73. Grand jury protest, 1805, Courts Collection, box 1, MHS.

74. 2 Stat. 287–89 (1804).

75. Remonstrance, 4 Jan. 1805, *American State Papers, Miscellaneous*, 1:402.

76. Petition, 18 Dec. 1808, Carter, *Territorial Papers*, 14:245.

77. Moses Austin to Albert Gallatin, Aug. 1806, Barker, *Austin Papers*, 2:118, 120.

78. Thomas Waters to Jefferson, Carter, *Territorial Papers*, 13:39.

79. Petition on slavery, 4 Aug. 1804, Stoddard Papers, box 1, MHS.

80. Remonstrance, *American State Papers, Miscellaneous*, 1:403.

81. My understanding of this process bears the marks of R. White, *Middle Ground*, and Clifford, *Predicament of Culture*.

82. Carter, *Territorial Papers*, 13:545–46

83. Foley and Rice, *First Chouteaus*, 179.

84. "The Autobiography of Thomas L. Anderson," 4–5, Anderson Papers, Western Historical Manuscripts Collection (hereafter cited as WHM).

85. Arnold, *Unequal Laws*, 161–65.

86. Davis, "Community and Conflict."

87. 2 Stat. 287 (1804).

88. 2 Stat. 332 (1805).

89. Amos Stoddard to William C. C. Claiborne and James Wilkinson, 26 Mar. 1804, Stoddard Papers, box 1, MHS.

90. J. B. C. Lucas to unidentified recipient, 24 Mar. 1806, Lucas Papers, box 3, MHS.

91. Amos Stoddard to William C. C. Claiborne, 26 Mar. 1804, Stoddard Papers, box 1, MHS.

92. J. B. C. Lucas to unidentified recipient, 24 Mar. 1806, Lucas Papers, box 3, MHS.

93. William C. Carr to Albert Gallatin, 6 Sept. 1807, Missouri Register of Land Titles Collection, box 1, MHS.

94. J. B. C. Lucas to Thomas Jefferson, 10 Dec. 1805, Lucas Papers, box 2, MHS.

95. John Coburn to James Madison, 15 Aug. 1807, Robertson, *Louisiana under the Rule*, 2:358.

96. J. B. C. Lucas to unidentified recipient, 24 Mar. 1806, Lucas Papers, box 3, MHS.

97. *Laws of a Public and General Nature, up to the Year 1824*, 1:436.

98. Bakken, "Mexican and American Land Policy," 242; Bowden, *Spanish and Mexican Land Grants*; Westphall, *Mercedes Reales*, 237–68; G. E. Hall, *Four Leagues of Pecos*.

99. Hamilton Gamble to M. M. Marmaduke, 27 Mar. 1844, Gamble Papers, box 8, MHS.

100. "Reminiscences," n.d. (but after the Civil War), Treat Papers, Vol. 1, MHS.

101. *Delassus v. United States*, 34 U.S. 117 (1835); *Chouteau's Heirs v. United States*, 34 U.S. 137 (1835); *Soulard's Heirs v. United States*, 35 U.S. 100 (1836); *Strother v. Lucas*, 37 U.S. 410 (1838); *Stoddard v. Chambers*, 43 U.S. 284 (1844); *Barry v. Gamble*, 44 U.S. 32 (1845); *Mackay v. Dillon*, 45 U.S. 421 (1846); *Les Bois v. Bramell*, 45 U.S. 449 (1846); *Landes v. Brant*, 51 U.S. 348 (1850); *Chouteau v. Molony*, 57 U.S. 203 (1850); *Guitard v. Stoddard*, 57 U.S. 494 (1850); *Meegan v. Boyle*, 60 U.S. 130 (1856); *Massey v. Papin*, 65 U.S. 362 (1860); *Carondelet v. Saint Louis*, 66 U.S. 179 (1861); *Magwire v. Tyler*, 66 U.S. 195 (1861); *Glasgow v. Hortiz*, 66 U.S. 595 (1861); *Maguire v. Tyler*, 75 U.S. 650 (1868); *Dent v. Emmeger*, 81 U.S. 308 (1871); *Gibson v. Chouteau*, 80 U.S. 92 (1871); *Tyler v. Magwire*, 84 U.S. 253 (1872); *Mackay v. Easton*, 86 U.S. 619 (1873); *Carpenter v. Rannels*, 86 U.S. 138 (1873); *Morrison v. Jackson*, 92 U.S. 654 (1875); *Bryan v. Kennett*, 113 U.S. 179 (1885); *Glasgow v. Baker*, 128 U.S. 560 (1888).

102. Thomas, *It's Good to Tell You*, 217–19, 229–31; Gold, "Lead Mining."

CHAPTER 6: LAWYERS

1. W. A. Hall to Lydia Marmon, 6 Dec. 1841, Hall Papers, box 1, MHS.

2. *Laws of a Public and General Nature, up to the Year 1824*, 1:57–64.

3. For present-day Louisiana, see Dargo, *Jefferson's Louisiana*, 17, 123; Gaspard, "Rise of the Louisiana Bar," 187. For Washington, see Wunder, *Inferior Courts*, 122. For Montana, Wyoming, and Colorado, see Guice, *Rocky Mountain Bench*, 41–42. For California, see Fritz, *Federal Justice*, 11–16; Reid, *Law for the Elephant*, 17. Many of these early California lawyers came from Missouri, the home state of by far the greatest percentage of overland emigrants. Bakken, *Practicing Law*, 7; Bakken, "Industrialization," 127; Unruh, *Plains Across*, 341–42.

4. James Wilkinson to James Madison, 28 July 1805, Carter, *Territorial Papers*, 13:174.

5. Thomas Oliver to William C. Carr, 29 July 1805, Carr Papers, box 1, MHS.

6. John Bowman to John Bowman, 17 May 1810, Ste. Geneviève Collection, box 1, MHS.

7. J. B. C. Lucas to William Lucas, 10 Aug. 1817, Lucas, *Letters of Hon. J. B. C. Lucas*, 4.

8. Wade, *Urban Frontier*, 210.

9. Adler, *Yankee Merchants*, 67.

10. Edward Hempstead to Stephen Hempstead, 15 Aug. 1805, Hempstead Papers, box 2, MHS.

11. Charles D. Drake, "Autobiography," 510, Drake Papers, WHM.

12. J. Davis to Lewis Sawyer, 25 Sept. 1837, St. Louis History Collection, box 1, MHS.

13. James S. Cowan to John W. Ellis, 25 July 1847, Cowan Papers, WHM.

14. J. Davis to Frederick Gale, 24 Aug. 1837, A-F Frederick Gale, MHS.

15. William Lucas to J. B. C. Lucas, 17 Nov. 1824, Lucas Papers, box 11, MHS; see also William Lucas to J. B. C. Lucas, 19 Nov. 1823, Lucas Papers, box 11, MHS.

16. Gerlach, *Settlement Patterns*, 19; Reichard, "Origins of Urban Police," 29.

17. Foley and Rice, *First Chouteaus*, 179; "The Autobiography of Thomas L. Anderson," 4–5, Anderson Papers, WHM.

18. J. Davis to Frederick W. Gale, 31 July 1838, A-F Frederick Gale, MHS.

19. William Lucas to J. B. C. Lucas, 26 Sept. 1829, Lucas Papers, box 12, MHS.

20. W. A. Hall to Lydia Marmion, 6 Dec. 1841, Hall Papers, box 1, MHS.

21. Arnold, *Unequal Laws*, 198–99; Wade, *Urban Frontier*, 115; Batman, "California Political Frontier," 464–66.

22. W. A. Hall to Lydia Marmion, 6 Dec. 1841, Hall Papers, box 1, MHS.

23. James S. Cowan to John W. Ellis, 25 July 1847, Cowan Papers, WHM.

24. J. B. C. Lucas to unidentified son (he had a few), 12 Oct. 1815, Lucas Papers, box 6, MHS.

25. Gustorf, *Uncorrupted Heart*, 77–78; Babcock, *Forty Years of Pioneer Life*, 147; Flint, *Recollections*, 198–206.

26. Ferris Forman to Clark Hyatt, 1836, quoted in English, *Pioneer Lawyer*, 94.

27. J. Davis to Frederick W. Gale, 24 Aug. 1837, A-F Frederick Gale, MHS.

28. Hamilton Gamble to Archibald Stuart, 13 June 1842, Gamble Papers, box 7, MHS.

29. Robert and John Heath to Charles Lucas, 10 Sept. 1816, Lucas Papers, box 7, MHS.

30. O'Brien, *Legal Fraternity*, 88.

31. William Lucas to J. B. C. Lucas, 26 Sept. 1829, Lucas Papers, box 12, MHS.

32. This and the other business directories discussed are located at the Missouri Historical Society. The population estimate for 1821—4,723—is derived

by linear interpolation from the population figures reported by the 1820 and 1830 censuses, which were respectively 4,598 and 5,852. The number of lawyers in St. Louis in 1821 is reported to be 27 in Paxton, "Notes on St. Louis" (1821), 67.

33. The Massachusetts figure is for 1820 and is derived from information in Gawalt, *Promise of Power*, 14.

34. Curran and Carson, *Lawyer Statistical Report*, 25, 157.

35. Business directories survive for 1821, 1836, and then most years thereafter. There is no surviving directory for 1850. The index to the 1855 directory lists 172 lawyers but the directory itself lists 242. The 1860 index lists 261 lawyers; assuming the same rate of error provides a total of 367. Population figures for all years after 1821 are from Holt, "Shaping of St. Louis," 508. The population estimate for 1804 is derived by linear interpolation between the figures Holt gives for 1800 and 1810, which are respectively 1,039 and 1,400.

36. On Los Angeles, see Bakken, *Practicing Law*, 3; on Wisconsin, see Curti, *Making of an American Community*, 249.

37. Gawalt, *Promise of Power*, 14.

38. Limerick, *Legacy of Conquest*, 173.

39. Reid, *Law for the Elephant*; see also Reid, *Policing the Elephant*; Reid, "Layers of Western Legal History."

40. H. M. Brackenridge to J. B. C. Lucas, 4 June 1816, Lucas Papers, box 7, MHS.

41. Rufus Easton (at the time in "Washington City") to J. B. C. Lucas, 15 Mar. 1816, Lucas Papers, box 6, MHS.

42. James S. Cowan to John W. Ellis, 25 July 1847, Cowan Papers, WHM.

43. "Autobiography," 475, Drake Papers, WHM.

44. Perly Wallis to "all whom it may concern," 27 Oct. 1812, Lucas Papers, box 5, MHS; A. H. to J. B. C. Lucas, 28 Oct. 1812, Lucas Papers, box 5, MHS; Rufus Easton to William Sprigg, 13 Apr. 1813, Lucas Papers, box 5, MHS.

45. David Ritchie to Hamilton Gamble, 5 Nov. 1847, Gamble Papers, box 8, MHS.

46. Cain, *Lincoln's Attorney General*, 1–5.

47. *Laws of a Public and General Nature, up to the Year 1824*, 1:49. Beginning in 1830, a license from the state supreme court authorized a lawyer to practice in any court in the state. *Laws of a Public and General Nature, between the Years 1824 and 1836*, 2:206.

48. Friedman, *History of American Law*, 316.

49. Frederick Bates to Richard Bates, 17 Dec. 1807, Marshall, *Life and Papers of Frederick Bates*, 2:246–47.

50. Silas Bent to J. B. C. Lucas, 28 July 1817, Lucas Papers, box 8, MHS.

51. Chambers, *Old Bullion Benton*, 63.

52. Virginia license (May 1817), Tennessee license (June 1817), Gamble Papers, box 1, MHS.

53. Goodrich and Gentzler, "'I Well Remember,'" 1, 7, 13.

54. Larkin, *Reshaping of Everyday Life*, 9–10.

55. S. H. Hempstead to William Hempstead, 8 July 1835, Hempstead Papers, box 1, MHS.

56. William Lucas to J. B. C. Lucas, 22 July 1817, 9 Nov. 1817, and 25 Nov. 1817, Lucas Papers, box 8, MHS; William Lucas to J. B. C. Lucas, 13 Jan. 1818, Lucas Papers, box 9, MHS. Rufus Easton had attended the same school two decades earlier; his student notebook is with the Easton Papers, MHS.

57. J. Davis to Frederick W. Gale, 24 Aug. 1837, A-F Frederick Gale, MHS.

58. William Augustus Linn to Elizabeth A. R. Linn, 14 Oct. 1845, Linn Papers, box 1, MHS.

59. McIntosh, *Appeal of Civil Law*, 54. In other times and places in North America, suits on contracts have likewise been found to dominate the civil caseload. See, e.g., Offutt, *Of "Good Laws" and "Good Men,"* 93–94.

60. "Record of Suits Employed In, 1818–19," Gamble Papers, box 1, MHS. On Gamble's later career, see Rosin, "Hamilton Rowan Gamble: Governor."

61. Jennings, *Pioneer Merchant of St. Louis*, 39–42; Melom, "Economic Development of St. Louis," 31–55.

62. Phelan, "Boosterism in St. Louis," 88; Primm, *Lion of the Valley*, 139; "The Autobiography of Thomas L. Anderson," 9, Anderson Papers, WHM.

63. *O'Fallon v. Elliott*, 1 Mo. 364, 365 (1823).

64. *Revised Statutes for the State of Missouri*, 409–10.

65. See, e.g., *King v. Bailey*, 6 Mo. 575 (1840); *Shepherd v. Trigg*, 7 Mo. 151 (1841); Morris, *Southern Slavery and the Law*, 121–31.

66. Samuel G. Mason to William Lucas, 7 June 1837, Lucas Papers, box 14, MHS.

67. "The Autobiography of Thomas L. Anderson," 9–10, Anderson Papers, WHM. For a similar conclusion with respect to antebellum South Carolina, see Russell, "Antebellum Courthouse," 352–55.

68. John Keirle to Hamilton Gamble, 1 June 1836, Gamble Papers, box 5, MHS.

69. Miller & Burke to Archibald Gamble, 22 Feb. 1834, Gamble Papers, box 5, MHS; see also Montelius & Fuller to Hamilton Gamble, 15 July 1833, Gamble Papers, box 5, MHS.

70. Davis & Krum to [illegible, in New York], 14 Nov. 1835, Davis Papers, vol. 2, MHS.

71. Yeatman, Pittman & Co. to B. F. Hagerman, 2 May 1853, Hagerman-Hayden Papers, folder 1, WHM; E. K. Mordivant to B. F. Hagerman, 15 Aug. 1855, Hagerman-Hayden Papers, folder 2, WHM; Wm. Goodrich & Co. to B. F. Hagerman, 18 Dec. 1854, Hagerman-Hayden Papers, folder 1, WHM.

72. For Los Angeles, see Bakken, *Practicing Law*, 51; for Chippewa County, Wisconsin, see Laurent, *Business of a Trial Court*, 155; for the Mississippi

Territory, see Hamilton, *Anglo-American Law on the Frontier*, 119; for Tennessee, see Calhoun, *Professional Lives in America*, 80–85.

73. "Record of Suits Employed In, 1818–19," Gamble Papers, box 1, MHS; Kaufman, *Dred Scott's Advocate*, 121–24.

74. J. B. Wallace to Abiel Leonard, 1 Apr. 1843, Leonard Papers, folder 174, WHM; A. Miller to Hamilton Gamble, 6 Apr. 1830, Gamble Papers, box 4, MHS; "Record of Suits Employed In, 1818–19," Gamble Papers, box 1, MHS.

75. Partnership agreement, Rufus Easton and Charles Lucas, 15 Apr. 1814, Lucas Papers, box 5, MHS.

76. Edward Hempstead to David Barton, 10 Sept. 1812, Hempstead Papers, box 2, MHS.

77. Partnership agreement, John Scott and Beverley Allen, 10 Oct. 1821, Sturgeon Papers, box 1, MHS.

78. Beverley Allen to Hamilton Gamble, 5 Mar. 1836, Gamble Papers, box 6, MHS.

79. William Lucas to J. B. C. Lucas, 27 Aug. 1832, Lucas Papers, box 13, MHS.

80. H. S. Geyer to Hamilton Gamble, 4 Oct. 1829, Gamble Papers, box 3, MHS.

81. Robert Hood to Hamilton Gamble, 1 Oct. 1829, Gamble Papers, box 3, MHS.

82. Edward Charless to Hamilton Gamble, 17 Nov. 1823, Gamble Papers, box 2, MHS.

83. Williams & Curtis advertisement, 1 Feb. 1847, St. Louis History Collection, box 2, MHS.

84. "The Autobiography of Thomas L. Anderson," 7, Anderson Papers, WHM.

85. G. E. White, *Marshall Court and Cultural Change*, 163 n.29; *Statistical Abstract of the United States 1994*, 488; *Historical Statistics of the United States*, 211.

86. Account Book, 1849, folder marked "Business 1849 Nov.–Dec.," Leonard Papers, WHM.

87. "Autobiography," 511, Drake Papers, WHM.

88. J. L. Collins to Wilson P. Hunt, 7 Nov. 1837, Lucas Papers, box 14, MHS.

89. Quoted in Primm, *Economic Policy*, 11.

90. "The Autobiography of Thomas L. Anderson," 8–9, Anderson Papers, WHM.

91. "Autobiography," 511, Drake Papers, WHM.

92. Account Book, 1849, Leonard Papers, WHM. This chart includes only income Leonard explicitly denoted as legal fees. He also earned income from the sale of land, and in a few instances entered payments received without indicating the source. If any of these latter payments were for legal services, the chart understates Leonard's income as a lawyer.

93. W. G. Wells to Hamilton Gamble, Jan. 1843, Gamble Papers, box 8, MHS.

94. "The Autobiography of Charles Gibson," Gibson Papers, box 1, MHS.

95. "The Autobiography of Thomas L. Anderson," 8–9, Anderson Papers, WHM.

96. Melvin L. Gray to Isaac Sturgeon, 15 Dec. 1902, Sturgeon Papers, box 3, MHS; Minutes of bar meeting, 8 Dec. 1836, Gamble Papers, box 6, MHS; Hamilton Gamble to M. M. Marmaduke, 27 Mar. 1844, Gamble Papers, box 8, MHS; Charles Drake to Hamilton Gamble, 11 Apr. 1851, Gamble Papers, box 8, MHS.

97. William Russell to Joseph McMinn, 24 Nov. 1816, Lucas Papers, box 7, MHS; J. B. C. Lucas to A. J. Dallas, 1 Dec. 1816, Lucas Papers, box 7, MHS. Dallas is best remembered today as the first of the reporters of Supreme Court decisions and as the secretary of the treasury in the last years of Madison's second administration. Joyce, "Rise of the Supreme Court Reporter," 1291, 1295–1306.

98. Darby, *Personal Recollections*, 80.

99. "'I Well Remember,'" 13 n.24, 20.

100. This list was compiled from the first sixty-five volumes of the *United States Reports*. It includes only those lawyers who were physically present in Washington to argue. (In many other instances, St. Louis lawyers submitted written briefs but are not listed as having presented oral argument.) Because counsel are normally listed only by last name in the reports, I have, with rare exception, not included cases originating in places other than Missouri, so as not to include by mistake a lawyer with the same name as a St. Louis lawyer. (The exceptions are where I was reasonably certain that a St. Louis lawyer is the person listed.) As a result, some St. Louis lawyers who argued cases not arising in Missouri are almost certainly omitted from the chart. The chart may in fact seriously understate the frequency with which Missouri lawyers appeared in the Supreme Court, because many of the cases omitted are from nearby less-populated places such as Arkansas, Iowa, Kansas, and southern Illinois, and it would not have been unreasonable for litigants from such places to hire a lawyer from St. Louis. I have also omitted cases arising in Missouri in which counsel cannot be identified from business directories or correspondence as residing in St. Louis. These omissions may likewise cause the number of lawyers listed to be too low. The number of lawyers given in the text is thus the lower bound of the possible range of the number of local lawyers who argued cases in the Supreme Court, rather than an estimate of the actual number who argued in the Supreme Court. The list does not include the many cases argued by Thomas Hart Benton, who was a St. Louis lawyer but who was present in Washington as one of Missouri's senators for most of the period. The years in parentheses represent the Court terms during which the cases were argued. In some cases, including most famously *Dred Scott v. Sandford*, opinions were published the following year. The heavy weighting of the cases toward the end of the period simply reflects the

increase in the rate at which Missouri cases were appealed to the Supreme Court, a rise most likely attributable to Missouri's increasing population and the increasing ease of travel between Missouri and Washington.

101. See, for example, *Strother v. Lucas*, 31 U.S. 763 (1832), in which Daniel Strother was represented by Roger Taney and Thomas Hart Benton, while J. B. C. Lucas was represented by William Wirt.

102. Receipt for *New York Observer*, Gamble Papers, box 6, MHS.

103. Bloomfield, *American Lawyers*, 32–58; Bakken, *Practicing Law*, 124–32.

104. Daniel Ashby, "Daniel Ashby, One of the Pioneers of Missouri," 40, undated typescript, Ashby Papers, MHS.

105. Quoted in Primm, *Economic Policy*, 11.

106. Quoted in Larsen, *Federal Justice in Western Missouri*, 13.

CHAPTER 7: WRITTEN LAW

1. *Laws of a Public and General Nature, up to the Year 1824*, 1:15–19; Pease, *Laws of the Northwest Territory*, 13–21 (subsequent page numbers in the note are from these two volumes, respectively). Other statutes copied from the Northwest Territory include one on justices' courts, 20–27, copied from a 1799 statute, 389–401; one on revenue, 34–41, modified from a 1799 statute, 478; one on the militia, 42–46, copied from a 1788 statute, 1–4; one on recording land titles, 46–48, copied from a 1795 statute, 197–201; one on constables, 51–53, copied from a 1799 statute, 402–4; one on defalcation, 54–55, copied from a 1795 statute, 149–51; one on probate courts, 57–58, copied from a 1788 statute, 9–10; one on other courts, 58–64, copied from a 1795 statute, 154–60; one on oaths of office, 64, copied from a 1788 statute, 12; and one on sheriffs, 65, copied from a 1788 statute, 8.

2. Trexler, *Slavery in Missouri, 1804–1865*, 59, n.10.

3. J. G. Harris, "Early Missouri Trial Courts"; *Laws of a Public and General Nature, up to the Year 1824*, 1:20–27, 1:58–64; Carter, *Territorial Papers*, 13:545–46.

4. This conclusion is drawn from leafing through early court records, in the Missouri Supreme Court Minute Books, vols. 1–3, MHS (which contain the minutes of the General Court, the predecessor to the Missouri Supreme Court in the sense that it was the highest court in the territory); the St. Louis Circuit Court Records, box 1, MHS (which primarily contain the records of the Court of Common Pleas); and the earliest records of the Missouri Supreme Court, Missouri State Archives.

5. "Record of Suits Employed In, 1818–19," Gamble Papers, box 1, MHS; Peyton R. Hayden, Law Note Book, 1835–42, Hagerman-Hayden Papers, WHM.

6. Tachau, *Federal Courts in the Early Republic*, 14–15; Hamilton, *Anglo-American Law on the Frontier*, 121; Brown, "Bar on a Frontier," 155; Blume, "Civil

Procedure," 209. For a summary of the debate, see Bakken, *Law on the Rocky Mountain Frontier*, 9–16.

7. Law Note Book (ca. 1845), Hardin Papers, file 5, WHM; Hayden, Law Note Book. Hagerman-Hayden Papers, WHM. The earliest published opinions of the Missouri Supreme Court, from 1821, are full of citations to English treatises and cases from England and other American jurisdictions.

8. J. H. Birch to Abiel Leonard, 29 Aug. 1833, Leonard Papers, folder 69, WHM.

9. Brown, "Frontier Justice," 152.

10. English, *Pioneer Lawyer*, 125; "List of My Law Books" (1838), Leonard Papers, folder marked "Business 1838 Dec.," WHM.

11. Thomas M. Campbell to Abiel Leonard, 8 Feb. 1846, Leonard Papers, folder 207, WHM; H. Everett to Abiel Leonard, 30 Aug. 1851, Leonard Papers, folder 300, WHM.

12. Haywood, *Cowtown Lawyers*, 62; Reid, *Law for the Elephant*, 273; Hamilton, *Anglo-American Law on the Frontier*, 136–38; Guice, *Rocky Mountain Bench*, 25–26; M. H. Harris, "Frontier Lawyer's Library"; Brown, "Frontier Justice," 139–51.

13. Ellickson, *Order Without Law*; Weyrauch and Bell, "Autonomous Lawmaking."

14. See, e.g., Bernstein, "Merchant Law."

15. J. B. C. Lucas to Thomas Jefferson, 10 Dec. 1805, Lucas Papers, box 2; J. B. C. Lucas to unidentified recipient, 24 Mar. 1806, Lucas Papers, box 3, MHS; see generally Foley, *Genesis of Missouri*, 162–69.

16. See, e.g., Gilmore, *Ages of American Law*; Chroust, *Rise of the Legal Profession*; Pound, *Spirit of the Common Law*.

17. See, e.g., Sellers, *Market Revolution*, 49–51; Mann, *Neighbors and Strangers*, 36; Hindus, *Prison and Plantation*, 86.

18. Langum, *Law and Community*, 138.

19. Nelson, *Americanization of the Common Law*.

20. Mann, *Neighbors and Strangers*, 101–36; Horwitz, *Transformation of American Law*, 145–55.

21. Reid, "In Accordance with Usage," 335.

22. Melom, "Economic Development of St. Louis," 35.

23. *Gordon v. State*, 4 Mo. 375, 376 (1836).

24. *Downing v. State*, 4 Mo. 572, 576 (1837).

25. *Woodson & Trigg v. McClelland*, 4 Mo. 495, 504 (1837).

26. *Bates v. Hinton*, 4 Mo. 78, 79 (1835).

27. *State v. Fry*, 4 Mo. 120 (1835).

28. *Helm v. Wilson*, 4 Mo. 41 (1835).

29. See, e.g., Blackstone, *Commentaries on the Laws of England*, 1:17; R. G. McCloskey, *Works of James Wilson*, 1:362; Sullivan, *History of Land Titles*, 14.

30. Dunne, *Missouri Supreme Court*, 7.

31. *Laws of a Public and General Nature, up to the Year 1824*, 1:125, 394.

32. *Laws of a Public and General Nature, up to the Year 1824*, 1:436; Brown, *British Statutes in American Law*, 25–26, 42–43.

33. Mo. Laws, 15th Sess., 73 (1849); van Ee, *David Dudley Field*, 21–45; Cook, *American Codification Movement*, 187–94; Millar, *Civil Procedure of the Trial Court*, 52–55; Hepburn, *Historical Development of Code Pleading*, 92–113.

34. Mo. Laws, 16th Sess., 45 (1850); K. L. Hall, "Judiciary on Trial."

35. Mo. Laws, 15th Sess., 67 (1849); Chused, "Married Women's Property Law."

36. R. Moore, "Ray of Hope, Extinguished," 4.

37. Finkelman, *Imperfect Union*; Schafer, *Slavery, Civil Law*, 263–88.

38. *Scott v. Emerson*, 15 Mo. 576, 586 (1852).

39. Fehrenbacher, *The Dred Scott Case*.

40. Bakken, *Law in Frontier California*, 3, 112. Bakken notes that the law in action often diverged from the law in books, but that too was almost certainly characteristic of every other state. The interesting question is whether different sorts of divergences occurred in different places, so that one could speak meaningfully of state-specific legal development at the level of actual practice, but to my knowledge that question has never been explicitly studied.

41. Missouri Supreme Court Minute Books, vol. 1, MHS.

42. Primm, *Economic Policy*, 11.

43. J. Davis to Frederick W. Gale, 31 July 1838, A-F Frederick Gale, MHS.

44. "Autobiography," 511, Drake Papers, WHM.

45. Flint, *Recollections*, 185.

46. McCurdy, *Stump, Bar, and Pulpit*.

47. Edward Bates, Diary, 29 Jan. 1847, Bates Family Papers, vol. 8, MHS.

48. William Lucas to J. B. C. Lucas, 26 May 1823, Lucas Papers, box 11, MHS.

49. See Adler, "Streetwalkers, Degraded Outcasts"; Adler, "Vagging the Demons."

50. "The Autobiography of Charles Gibson," 23, Gibson Papers, box 1, MHS.

51. J. Davis to Frederick W. Gale, 31 July 1838, A-F Frederick Gale, MHS.

52. Cf. Starr, *Social Transformation of American Medicine*, 9–28, 142–44.

53. Thelen, *Paths of Resistance*, 182–89.

54. McCandless, *History of Missouri*, 35.

CHAPTER 8: PRIVATE LAND

1. 2 Stat. 289 (1804).

2. *American State Papers, Public Lands*, 2:549; March, *History of Missouri*, 1:233.

3. Carter, *Territorial Papers*, 13:426–27.

4. 2 Stat. 391 (1806).

5. *Glasgow v. Baker*, 128 U.S. 560, 575–77 (1888); *Glasgow v. Hortiz*, 66 U.S. 595, 599–602 (1861); Williams, *History, Abstracts of Title, Evidences of Location*.

6. 2 Stat. 748–50 (1812) (emphasis added).

7. Ebright, *Land Grants and Lawsuits*, 216.

8. Petition of Inhabitants of St. Charles (n.d.), St. Charles Collection, MHS; Carter, *Territorial Papers*, 15:451–52, 242.

9. *Laws of a Public and General Nature, up to the Year 1824*, 1:184–86.

10. *Laws of a Public and General Nature, up to the Year 1824*, 1:320–21.

11. *Laws of the State of Missouri: Revised and Digested,* 1:211.

12. *Hunt's Minutes*, 3:92.

13. Cf. Hartog, *Public Property and Private Power*, 13; *Vidal v. The Mayor, Aldermen, and Citizens of Philadelphia*, 43 U.S. 127, 129 (1844).

14. *Hunt's Minutes,* 3:92.

15. *Laws of a Public and General Nature, between the Years 1824 and 1836*, 2:296–97, 488–89.

16. *Laws of the State of Missouri, Passed*, 35.

17. Davis, "Community and Conflict."

18. *Laws of a Public and General Nature, between the Years 1824 and 1836*, 2:501.

19. *Missouri Republican*, 31 Mar. 1835, 3, col. 1.

20. "An Ordinance for the Sale of the St. Louis Commons," 26 Jan. 1836.

21. St. Louis Commons Claim Book, Mesker Collection, MHS; Sandweiss, "Construction and Community," 49–55.

22. *City of St. Louis v. Morton*, 6 Mo. 476 (1840).

23. *St. Louis City Register*, 58:1 (Feb. 1854), MHS.

24. *Carondelet v. Saint Louis,* 66 U.S. 179 (1861). For the same phenomenon across the river in East St. Louis, Illinois, a city by then encompassing what had once been the commons in the old French village of Cahokia, see *Haps v. Hewitt*, 97 Ill. 499, 503 (1881).

25. Carter, *Territorial Papers*, 15:242.

26. Carter, *Territorial Papers*, 15:452.

27. *Missouri Gazette,* 25 Sept. 1818, St. Charles Collection, MHS.

28. Petition of inhabitants of St. Charles (n.d.), St. Charles Collection, MHS. I am inferring that this petition was presented to Congress in 1819 because the 1818 letter to the editor of the *Missouri Gazette* mentions that a petition containing identical language is "intended to be submitted to Congress at the next session."

29. *Missouri Republican*, 23 July 1835, 2, col. 6.

30. Thompson, *Making of the Working Class*, 218. See also J. L. Hammond and B. Hammond, *Village Labourer 1760–1832*, 73–81. This is an issue over which

there is still some controversy. For more nuanced statements of the same point, with the benefit of more recent studies of individual communities, see Neeson, *Commoners*; Yelling, *Common Field and Enclosure*, 214–32; R. C. Allen, "Efficiency and Distributional Consequences."

31. Brackenridge, *Views of Louisiana*, 140.

CONCLUSION

1. D. G. Allen, *In English Ways*; Fischer, *Albion's Seed*; Reid, *Law for the Elephant*; Reid, *Policing the Elephant*.

Bibliography

ARCHIVES

Missouri Historical Society (St. Louis)

A-F Frederick Gale
Amoureux-Bolduc Collection
Archivo General de Indias
Ashby Papers
Bates Family Papers
Berthold Collection
Boone Collection
Carr Papers
Census Collection
Chouteau Papers
Courts Collection
Davis Papers
Delassus Papers
Easton Papers
Emmons Collection
Gamble Papers
Gibson Papers
Governors Collection
Gratiot Papers
Guibord Collection
Hall Papers
Hammond Collection
Hempstead Papers
Hunt Collection
Hunt's Minutes
Laclède Papers

Linn Papers
Litigation Collection
Long Papers
Louisiana Purchase Transfer Collection
Lucas Papers
Mesker Collection
Missouri Register of Land Titles Collection
Missouri Supreme Court Minute Books
New Madrid Colonial Archives
Parker-Russell Collection
Pettus Collection
Poepping Collection
Semsrott Collection
Soulard Papers
St. Charles Collection
St. Charles Colonial Archives
St. Louis Circuit Court Records
St. Louis City Register
St. Louis Colonial Archives
St. Louis History Collection
Ste. Geneviève Collection
Ste. Geneviève Colonial Archives
Stoddard Papers
Sturgeon Papers
Treat Papers
Vallé Papers
Washington County Court Collection

Missouri State Archives (Jefferson City)
Missouri Supreme Court

National Archives
"Letters of Application and Recommendation during the Administration of Thomas Jefferson, 1801–1809," Microfilm Publication M418, RG 59
"Letters of Application and Recommendation during the Administration of John Quincy Adams, 1825–1829," Microfilm Publication M439, RG 59

New-York Historical Society (New York)
Gallatin Collection

Western Historical Manuscripts Collection, University of Missouri (Columbia)
Anderson Papers
Cowan Papers
Drake Papers

Hagerman-Hayden Papers
Hardin Papers
Leonard Papers

BOOKS AND ARTICLES

Adams, Henry, ed. *The Writings of Albert Gallatin*. Philadelphia: J. B. Lippincott, 1879.

Adler, Jeffrey S. "Streetwalkers, Degraded Outcasts, and Good-for-Nothing Huzzies: Women and the Dangerous Class in Antebellum St. Louis." *Journal of Social History* 25 (1992): 737–55.

———. "Vagging the Demons and Scoundrels: Vagrancy and the Growth of St. Louis, 1830–1861." *Journal of Urban History* 13 (1986): 3–30.

———. *Yankee Merchants and the Making of the Urban West: The Rise and Fall of Antebellum St. Louis*. Cambridge: Cambridge University Press, 1991.

Allen, David Grayson. *In English Ways: The Movement of Societies and the Transferal of English Local Law and Custom to Massachusetts Bay in the Seventeenth Century*. Chapel Hill: University of North Carolina Press, 1981.

Allen, Robert C. "The Efficiency and Distributional Consequences of Eighteenth Century Enclosures." *Economic Journal* 92 (1982): 937–53.

American State Papers, Miscellaneous. Washington, D.C.: Gales & Seaton, 1834.

American State Papers, Public Lands. Washington, D.C.: Gales & Seaton, 1832.

Aquinas, Thomas. *Summa Theologica*. Christian Classics, 1948.

Arena, C. Richard. "Land Settlement Policies and Practices in Spanish Louisiana." In *The Spanish in the Mississippi Valley 1762–1804*, edited by John Francis McDermott. Urbana: University of Illinois Press, 1974.

Arnold, Morris S. "Toward an Ideology of the Early English Law of Obligations." *Law and History Review* 5 (1987): 505–21.

———. *Unequal Laws unto a Savage Race: European Legal Traditions in Arkansas, 1686–1836*. Fayetteville: University of Arkansas Press, 1985.

Baade, Hans W. "The Law of Slavery in Spanish Luisiana 1769–1803." In *Louisiana's Legal Heritage*, edited by Edward F. Haas. Pensacola, Fla.: Perdido Bay Press, 1983.

———. "Marriage Contracts in French and Spanish Louisiana: A Study in 'Notarial' Jurisprudence." *Tulane Law Review* 53 (1978): 1–92.

Babcock, Rufus, ed. *Forty Years of Pioneer Life: Memoir of John Mason Peck D.D.* Philadelphia: American Baptist Publication Society, 1864.

Baily, Francis. *Journal of a Tour in Unsettled Parts of North America in 1796 and 1797*. 1856. Reprint, edited by Jack D. L. Holmes, Carbondale: Southern Illinois University Press, 1969.

Bakken, Gordon Morris. *The Development of Law in Frontier California: Civil Law and Society, 1850–1890*. Westport: Greenwood Press, 1985.

———. *The Development of Law on the Rocky Mountain Frontier: Civil Law and Society, 1850–1912*. Westport: Greenwood Press, 1983.

———. "Industrialization and the Nineteenth-Century California Bar." In *The New High Priests: Lawyers in Post–Civil War America*, edited by Gerard W. Gawalt. Westport: Greenwood Press, 1984.

———. "Mexican and American Land Policy: A Conflict of Cultures." *Southern California Quarterly* 75 (1993): 237–62.

———. *Practicing Law in Frontier California*. Lincoln: University of Nebraska Press, 1991.

Balesi, Charles J. *The Time of the French in the Heart of North America 1673–1818*. Chicago: Alliance Française Chicago, 1992.

Barker, Eugene C., ed. *The Austin Papers*. Washington, D.C.: Government Printing Office, 1924.

Batman, Richard Dale. "The California Political Frontier: Democratic or Bureaucratic?" *Journal of the West* 7 (1968): 461–70.

Beckwith, Paul. *Creoles of St. Louis*. St. Louis: Nixon-Jones Printing Co., 1893.

Bederman, David J. "The Curious Resurrection of Custom: Beach Access and Judicial Takings." *Columbia Law Review* 96 (1996): 1375–1455.

Bell, David A. *Lawyers and Citizens: The Making of a Political Elite in Old Regime France*. New York: Oxford University Press, 1994.

Bell, Ovid. *Cote Sans Dessein: A History*. Fulton, Missouri: Ovid Bell, 1930.

Belting, Natalia Maree. *Kaskaskia under the French Regime*. Urbana: University of Illinois Press, 1948.

Bender, Thomas. *Community and Social Change in America*. Baltimore: Johns Hopkins University Press, 1982.

Berlanstein, Lenard R. "Lawyers in Pre-Revolutionary France." In *Lawyers in Early Modern Europe and America*, edited by Wilfred Prest. New York: Holmes & Meier, 1981.

Bernstein, Lisa. "Merchant Law in a Merchant Court: Rethinking the Code's Search for Immanent Business Norms." *University of Pennsylvania Law Review* 144 (1996): 1765–1821.

Berquin-Duvallon. *Travels in Louisiana and the Floridas, in the Year 1802*. New York: I. Riley, 1806.

Blackstone, William. *Commentaries on the Laws of England*. 9th ed., London, 1783. Reprint, New York: Garland, 1978.

Bloch, Marc. *French Rural History*. Translated by Janet Sondheimer. Berkeley and Los Angeles: University of California Press, 1966.

Bloomfield, Maxwell. *American Lawyers in a Changing Society, 1776–1876*. Cambridge: Harvard University Press, 1976.

Blume, William Wirt. "Civil Procedure on the American Frontier: A Study of a Court of Common Pleas of the Northwest and Indiana Territories (1796–1805)." *Michigan Law Review* 56 (1957): 161–224.

Boag, Peter G. *Environment and Experience: Settlement Culture in Nineteenth-Century Oregon*. Berkeley and Los Angeles: University of California Press, 1992.

Boswell, John. *Same-Sex Unions in Premodern Europe*. New York: Villard, 1994.

Bouvard, Marguerite. *The Intentional Community Movement: Building a New Moral World*. Port Washington, N.Y.: Kennikat Press, 1975.

Bowden, J. J. *Spanish and Mexican Land Grants in the Chihuahuan Acquisition*. El Paso: Texas Western Press, 1971.

Boyle, Susan C. "Did She Generally Decide? Women in Ste. Genevieve, 1750–1805." *William and Mary Quarterly* 44 (1987): 775–89.

Brackenridge, Henry Marie. *Views of Louisiana*. Pittsburgh: Cramer, Spear, 1814.

Bradbury, John. *Travels in the Interior of America, in the Years 1809, 1810, and 1811*. 2d ed. Liverpool: Sherwood, Neely, and Jones, 1819.

Briggs, Charles L., and John R. Van Ness, eds. *Land, Water, and Culture: New Perspectives on Hispanic Land Grants*. Albuquerque: University of New Mexico Press, 1987.

Briggs, Winstanley. "Le Pays des Illinois." *William and MaryQuarterly* 47 (1990): 30–56.

Brown, Elizabeth Gaspar. "The Bar on a Frontier: Wayne County, 1796–1836." *American Journal of Legal History* 14 (1970): 136–56.

———. *British Statutes in American Law 1776–1836*. New York: Da Capo Press, 1974.

———. "Frontier Justice: Wayne County 1796–1836." *American Journal of Legal History* 16 (1972): 126–53.

Burkholder, Mark A. "Honest Judges Leave Destitute Heirs: The Price of Integrity in Eighteenth-Century Spain." In *Virtue, Corruption, and Self-Interest: Political Values in the Eighteenth Century*, edited by Richard K. Matthews. Bethlehem, Pa.: Lehigh University Press, 1994.

Burkholder, Mark A., and Lyman L. Johnson. *Colonial Latin America*. New York: Oxford University Press, 1990.

Burns, Francis P. "The Spanish Land Laws of Louisiana." *Louisiana Historical Quarterly* 11 (1928): 557–81.

Cain, Marvin R. *Lincoln's Attorney General: Edward Bates of Missouri*. Columbia: University of Missouri Press, 1965.

Calhoun, Daniel H. *Professional Lives in America: Structure and Aspiration 1750–1850*. Cambridge: Harvard University Press, 1965.

Carter, Clarence Edwin, ed. *The Territorial Papers of the United States*. Washington, D.C.: Government Printing Office, 1934–75.

"The Case of Pourée against Chouteau." *Missouri Historical Society Collections* 2(6) (1906): 68–81.

Chambers, William Nisbet. *Old Bullion Benton: Senator from the New West*. Boston: Little, Brown, 1956.

Chapman, Carl H. *The Origin of the Osage Indian Tribe*. New York: Garland, 1974.

Chapman, Carl H., and Eleanor F. Chapman. *Indians and Archaeology of Missouri*. Rev. ed. Columbia: University of Missouri Press, 1983.

Chroust, Anton-Hermann. *The Rise of the Legal Profession in America*. Norman: University of Oklahoma Press, 1965.

Chused, Richard H. "Married Women's Property Law: 1800–1850." *Georgetown Law Journal* 71 (1983): 1359–1425.

Cleary, Patricia. "Contested Terrain: Environmental Agendas and Settlement Choices in Colonial St. Louis." In *Common Fields: An Environmental History of St. Louis*, edited by Andrew Hurley. St. Louis: Missouri Historical Society Press, 1997.

Cleland, Hugh G. "John B. C. Lucas, Physiocrat on the Frontier." *Western Pennsylvania Historical Magazine* 36 (1953): 1–15, 87–100, 141–68.

Clifford, James. *The Predicament of Culture: Twentieth-Century Ethnography, Literature, and Art*. Cambridge: Harvard University Press, 1988.

Coase, Ronald. "The Problem of Social Cost." *Journal of Law and Economics* 3 (1960): 1–44.

Cole, Richard P. "Law and Community in the New Nation: Three Visions for Michigan, 1788–1831." *Southern California Interdisciplinary Law Journal* 4 (1995): 161–252.

The Colonial Laws of New York. Albany: J. B. Lyon, 1894.

Cook, Charles M. *The American Codification Movement: A Study of Antebellum Legal Reform*. Westport: Greenwood Press, 1981.

Cronon, William, George Miles, and Jay Gitlin, eds. *Under an Open Sky: Rethinking America's Western Past*. New York: W. W. Norton, 1992.

Crouch, Dora P., Daniel J. Garr, and Axel I. Mundigo. *Spanish City Planning in North America*. Cambridge: MIT Press, 1982.

Curran, Barbara A., and Clara N. Carson. *The Lawyer Statistical Report: The U.S. Legal Profession in the 1990s*. Chicago: American Bar Foundation, 1994.

Curti, Merle. *The Making of an American Community*. Palo Alto: Stanford University Press, 1959.

Cutter, Charles R. *The Legal Culture of Northern New Spain, 1700–1810*. Albuquerque: University of New Mexico Press, 1995.

Dahlman, Carl J. *The Open Field System and Beyond*. Cambridge: Cambridge University Press, 1980.

Darby, John F. *Personal Recollections*. St. Louis: G. I. Jones & Co., 1880.

Dargo, George. *Jefferson's Louisiana: Politics and the Clash of Legal Traditions*. Cambridge: Harvard University Press, 1975.

Davis, Ronald L. F. "Community and Conflict in Pioneer Saint Louis, Missouri." *Western Historical Quarterly* 10 (1979): 337–55.

de Finiels, Nicolas. *An Account of Upper Louisiana*. 1803. Edited by Carl J. Ekberg and William E. Foley, translated by Carl J. Ekberg. Columbia: University of Missouri Press, 1989.

Dickinson, John A. "New France: Law, Courts, and the *Coutume de Paris*, 1608–1760." *Manitoba Law Journal* 23 (1996): 32–54.

Din, Gilbert C. *Francisco Bouligny: A Bourbon Soldier in Spanish Louisiana*. Baton Rouge: Louisiana State University Press, 1993.

———. "The Immigration Policy of Governor Esteban Miró in Spanish Louisiana." *Southwestern Historical Quarterly* 73 (1969): 155–75.

———. "Spain's Immigration Policy in Louisiana and the American Penetration, 1792–1803." *Southwestern Historical Quarterly* 76 (1973): 255–76.

Din, Gilbert C., ed. *Louisiana in 1776: A Memoria of Francisco Bouligny*. New Orleans: J. D. L. Holmes, 1977.

Din, Gilbert C., and John E. Harkins. *The New Orleans Cabildo: Colonial Louisiana's First City Government*. Baton Rouge: Louisiana State University Press, 1996.

Din, Gilbert C., and A. P. Nasatir. *The Imperial Osages: Spanish-Indian Diplomacy in the Mississippi Valley*. Norman: University of Oklahoma Press, 1983.

Dunne, Gerald T. *The Missouri Supreme Court: From Dred Scott to Nancy Cruzan*. Columbia: University of Missouri Press, 1993.

Eblen, Jack Ericson. *The First and Second United States Empires: Governors and Territorial Government, 1784–1912*. Pittsburgh: University of Pittsburgh Press, 1968.

Ebright, Malcolm. "Frontier Land Litigation in Colonial New Mexico: A Determinant of Spanish Custom and Law." *Western Legal History* 8 (1995): 199–226.

———. "Introduction." In *Spanish and Mexican Land Grants and the Law*, edited by Malcolm Ebright. Manhattan, Ks.: Sunflower University Press, 1989.

———. *Land Grants and Lawsuits in Northern New Mexico*. Albuquerque: University of New Mexico Press, 1994.

———. "New Mexican Land Grants: The Legal Background." In *Land, Water, and Culture: New Perspectives on Hispanic Land Grants*, edited by Charles L. Briggs and John R. Van Ness. Albuquerque: University of New Mexico Press, 1987.

Ebright, Malcolm, ed. *Spanish and Mexican Land Grants and the Law*. Manhattan, Ks.: Sunflower University Press, 1989.

Ekberg, Carl J. *Colonial Ste. Genevieve: An Adventure on the Mississippi Frontier*. Gerald, Mo.: Patrice Press, 1985.

———. *French Roots in the Illinois Country: The Mississippi Frontier in Colonial Times*. Urbana: University of Illinois Press, 1998.

Ellickson, Robert C. *Order Without Law: How Neighbors Settle Disputes*. Cambridge: Harvard University Press, 1991.

Ellis, Richard E. *The Jeffersonian Crisis: Courts and Politics in the Young Republic*. New York: W. W. Norton & Co., 1974.

English, William Francis. *The Pioneer Lawyer and Jurist in Missouri*. Columbia: University of Missouri Press, 1947.

Faragher, John Mack. *Daniel Boone: The Life and Legend of an American Pioneer*. New York: Henry Holt & Co., 1992.

Fehrenbacher, Don E. *The* Dred Scott *Case: Its Significance in American Law and Politics*. New York: Oxford University Press, 1978.

Ferguson, Robert A. *The American Enlightenment, 1750–1820*. Cambridge: Harvard University Press, 1997.

Field, Barry C. "The Evolution of Individual Property Rights in Massachusetts Agriculture, 17th–19th Centuries." *Northeastern Journal of Agriculture and Resource Economics* 14 (1985): 97–109.

Finkelman, Paul. *An Imperfect Union: Slavery, Federalism, and Comity*. Chapel Hill: University of North Carolina Press, 1981.

Fischer, David Hackett. *Albion's Seed: Four British Folkways in America*. New York: Oxford University Press, 1989.

Flint, Timothy. *Recollections of the Last Ten Years*. Boston: Cummings, Hilliard, & Co., 1826.

Foley, William E. *The Genesis of Missouri: From Wilderness Outpost to Statehood*. Columbia: University of Missouri Press, 1989.

Foley, William E., and C. David Rice. *The First Chouteaus: River Barons of Early St. Louis*. Urbana: University of Illinois Press, 1983.

Foner, Laura. "The Free People of Color in Louisiana and St. Domingue: A Comparative Portrait of Two Three-Caste Slave Societies." *Journal of Social History* 3 (1970): 406–30.

Friedman, Lawrence M. *A History of American Law*. 2d ed. New York: Simon & Schuster, 1985.

Friedman, Lawrence M., and Robert V. Percival. *The Roots of Justice: Crime and Punishment in Alameda County, California, 1870–1910*. Chapel Hill: University of North Carolina Press, 1981.

Friedmann, Karen J. "Fencing, Herding, and Tethering in Denmark, from Open-Field Agriculture to Enclosure." *Agricultural History* 58 (1984): 584–97.

Fritz, Christian. *Federal Justice in California: The Court of Ogden Hoffman, 1851–1891*. Lincoln: University of Nebraska Press, 1991.

Galenson, David W., ed. *Markets in History: Economic Studies of the Past*. Cambridge: Cambridge University Press, 1989.

Gaspard, Elizabeth. "The Rise of the Louisiana Bar: The Early Period, 1813–1839." *Louisiana History* 28 (1987): 183–97.

Gawalt, Gerard W., ed. *The New High Priests: Lawyers in Post–Civil War America*. Westport: Greenwood Press, 1984.

———. *The Promise of Power: The Emergence of the Legal Profession in Massachusetts 1760–1840*. Westport: Greenwood Press, 1979.

Gerlach, Russel L. *Settlement Patterns in Missouri*. Columbia: University of Missouri Press, 1986.

Gilbert, Judith A. "Esther and Her Sisters: Free Women of Color as Property Owners in Colonial St. Louis, 1765–1803." *Gateway Heritage* 17, no. 1 (1996): 14–23.

Gilmore, Grant. *The Ages of American Law*. New Haven: Yale University Press, 1977.

Gitlin, Jay. "On the Boundaries of Empire: Connecting the West to Its Imperial Past." In *Under an Open Sky: Rethinking America's Western Past*, edited by William Cronon, George Miles, and Jay Gitlin. New York: W. W. Norton, 1992.

Gold, Gerald L. "Lead Mining and the Survival and Demise of French in Rural Missouri." In *French America: Mobility, Identity, and Minority Experience Across the Continent*, edited by Dean R. Louder and Eric Waddell, translated by Franklin Philip. Baton Rouge: Louisiana State University Press, 1993.

Goodrich, James W., and Lynn Wolf Gentzler, eds. "'I Well Remember': David Holmes Conrad's Recollections of St. Louis, 1819–1823." *Missouri Historical Review* 90 (1995): 1–37, 129–65.

Gordon, H. Scott. "The Economic Theory of a Common-Property Resource: The Fishery." *Journal of Political Economy* 62 (1954): 124–42.

Guice, John D. W. *The Rocky Mountain Bench*. New Haven: Yale University Press, 1972.

Gustorf, Fred, ed. *The Uncorrupted Heart: Journal and Letters of Frederick Julius Gustorf, 1800–1845*. Translated by Fred Gustorf and Gisela Gustorf. Columbia: University of Missouri Press, 1969.

Haas, Edward F., ed. *Louisiana's Legal Heritage*. Pensacola, Fla.: Perdido Bay Press, 1983.

Hackett, Charles W., et al., eds. *New Spain and the Anglo-American West*. Lancaster: Lancaster Press, 1932.

Hall, G. Emlen. *Four Leagues of Pecos: A Legal History of the Pecos Grant, 1800–1933*. Albuquerque: University of New Mexico Press, 1984.

Hall, Kermit L. "The Judiciary on Trial: State Constitutional Reform and the Rise of an Elected Judiciary, 1846–1860." *The Historian* 45 (1983): 337–54.

Hamilton, William Baskerville. *Anglo-American Law on the Frontier: Thomas Rodney and His Territorial Cases*. Durham: Duke University Press, 1953.

Hammond, J. L., and Barbara Hammond. *The Village Labourer 1760–1832*. 4th ed. London: Longmans, Green, and Co., 1932.

Hardin, Garrett. "The Tragedy of the Commons." *Science* 162 (1968): 1243–48.

Haring, C. H. *The Spanish Empire in North America*. New York: Harcourt, Brace & World, 1947.

Harris, Michael H. "The Frontier Lawyer's Library: Southern Indiana, 1800–1850, as a Test Case." *American Journal of Legal History* 16 (1972): 239–51.

Hartog, Hendrik. *Public Property and Private Power: The Corporation of the City of New York in American Law, 1730–1870.* Ithaca: Cornell University Press, 1989.

Haskins, George Lee, and Herbert A. Johnson. *Foundations of Power: John Marshall, 1801–15.* New York: Macmillan, 1981.

Haywood, C. Robert. *Cowtown Lawyers: Dodge City and Its Attorneys, 1876–1888.* Norman: University of Oklahoma Press, 1988.

Hepburn, Charles M. *The Historical Development of Code Pleading.* Cincinnati: W. H. Anderson & Co., 1897.

Hindus, Michael Stephen. *Prison and Plantation: Crime, Justice, and Authority in Massachusetts and South Carolina, 1767–1878.* Chapel Hill: University of North Carolina Press, 1980.

Historical Statistics of the United States. Washington, D.C.: U.S. Department of Commerce, 1975.

Horwitz, Morton J. *The Transformation of American Law, 1780–1860.* Cambridge: Harvard University Press, 1977.

Houck, Louis, ed. *The Spanish Regime in Missouri.* Chicago: R. R. Donnelley & Sons, 1909.

Hurley, Andrew, ed. *Common Fields: An Environmental History of St. Louis.* St. Louis: Missouri Historical Society Press, 1997.

Hutchins, Thomas. *An Historical Narrative and Topographical Description of Louisiana and West-Florida.* Philadelphia: Robert Aitken, 1784.

Ingersoll, Thomas N. "Free Blacks in a Slave Society: New Orleans, 1718–1812." *William and Mary Quarterly* 48 (1991): 173–200.

Innes, Stephen. *Labor in a New Land: Economy and Society in Seventeenth-Century Springfield.* Princeton: Princeton University Press, 1983.

Jennings, Marietta. *A Pioneer Merchant of St. Louis 1810–1820: The Business Career of Christian Wilt.* New York: Columbia University Press, 1939.

Joyce, Craig. "The Rise of the Supreme Court Reporter: An Institutional Perspective on Marshall Court Ascendancy." *Michigan Law Review* 83 (1985): 1291–1391.

Kagan, Richard L. *Lawsuits and Litigants in Castile 1500–1700.* Chapel Hill: University of North Carolina Press, 1981.

———. "Prescott's Paradigm: American Historical Scholarship and the Decline of Spain." *American Historical Review* 101 (1996): 423–46.

Kanter, Rosabeth Moss. *Commitment and Community: Communes and Utopias in Sociological Perspective.* Cambridge: Harvard University Press, 1972.

Kaufman, Kenneth C. *Dred Scott's Advocate: A Biography of Roswell M. Field.* Columbia: University of Missouri Press, 1996.

Kerr, Derek N. *Petty Felony, Slave Defiance, and Frontier Villainy: Crime and Criminal Justice in Spanish Louisiana, 1770–1803.* New York: Garland, 1993.

Kerridge, Eric. *The Common Fields of England.* Manchester: Manchester University Press, 1992.

Kinnaird, Lawrence. "American Penetration into Spanish Louisiana." In *New Spain and the Anglo-American West*, edited by Charles W. Hackett et al. Lancaster: Lancaster Press, 1932.

Kinnaird, Lawrence, ed. *Spain in the Mississippi Valley, 1765–1794*. Washington, D.C.: Government Printing Office, 1946.

Kiralfy, Albert. "The Humble Jumble: Legal Redress under the Open-Field System." *Journal of Legal History* 10 (1989): 23–28.

Konig, David Thomas. *Law and Society in Puritan Massachusetts*. Chapel Hill: University of North Carolina Press, 1979.

Korn, Bertram Wallace. *The Early Jews of New Orleans*. Waltham, Mass.: American Jewish Historical Society, 1969.

Langum, David J. "Californios and the Image of Indolence." *Western Historical Quarterly* 9 (1978): 181–96.

———. "The Introduction of Conciliation into Modern Spanish Law and Its Practice in the Spanish-American Borderlands." In *Studies in Roman Law and Legal History in Honour of Ramon D'Abadal i de Vinyals on the Occasion of the Centenary*, edited by Manuel J. Peláez. Barcelona, 1989.

———. *Law and Community on the Mexican California Frontier: Anglo-American Expatriates and the Clash of Legal Traditions, 1821–1846*. Norman: University of Oklahoma Press, 1987.

———. "The Legal System of Spanish California: A Preliminary Study." *Western Legal History* 7 (1994): 1–23.

Larkin, Jack. *The Reshaping of Everyday Life, 1790–1840*. New York: Harper & Row, 1988.

Larsen, Lawrence H. *Federal Justice in Western Missouri*. Columbia: University of Missouri Press, 1994.

Laurent, Francis W. *The Business of a Trial Court*. Madison: University of Wisconsin Press, 1959.

Laws of a Public and General Nature of the District of Louisiana, of the Territory of Louisiana, of the Territory of Missouri, and of the State of Missouri, up to the Year 1824. Jefferson City: W. Lusk & Son, 1842.

Laws of a Public and General Nature of the State of Missouri, Passed between the Years 1824 and 1836, Not Published in the Digest of 1825, Nor in the Digest of 1835. Jefferson City: W. Lusk, 1842.

Laws of the State of Missouri, Passed at the First Session of the Ninth General Assembly. 2d ed. Jefferson City: Calvin Gunn, 1841.

Laws of the State of Missouri: Revised and Digested by Authority of the General Assembly. St. Louis: E. Charless, 1825.

Lazarus, Richard J. "Debunking Environmental Feudalism: Promoting the Individual Through the Collective Pursuit of Environmental Quality." *Iowa Law Review* 77 (1992): 1739–74.

Levasseur, Alain A. "The Major Periods of Louisiana Legal History." *Loyola Law Review* 41 (1996): 585–628.

Lewis, David Rich. *Neither Wolf Nor Dog: American Indians, Environment, and Agrarian Change*. New York: Oxford University Press, 1994.

Limerick, Patricia Nelson. *The Legacy of Conquest: The Unbroken Past of the American West*. New York: W. W. Norton, 1987.

Lockridge, Kenneth A. *A New England Town: The First Hundred Years*. New York, Norton, 1970.

Louder, Dean R., and Eric Waddell, eds. *French America: Mobility, Identity, and Minority Experience across the Continent*. Translated by Franklin Philip. Baton Rouge: Louisiana State University Press, 1993.

Lucas, John B. C., ed. *Letters of Hon. J. B. C. Lucas from 1815 to 1836*. St. Louis: John B. C. Lucas, 1905.

Lukes, Steven. *Individualism*. Oxford: Basil Blackwell, 1973.

Lyon, E. Wilson. *Louisiana in French Diplomacy 1759–1804*. Norman: University of Oklahoma Press, 1934.

Magnaghi, Russell M. "The Role of Indian Slavery in Colonial St. Louis." *Bulletin of the Missouri Historical Society* 31 (1975): 264–72.

Mann, Bruce H. *Neighbors and Strangers: Law and Community in Early Connecticut*. Chapel Hill: University of North Carolina Press, 1987.

March, David D. *The History of Missouri*. New York: Lewis Historical Publishing Co., 1967.

Marshall, Thomas Maitland, ed. *The Life and Papers of Frederick Bates*. St. Louis: Missouri Historical Society, 1926.

Matthews, Richard K., ed. *Virtue, Corruption, and Self-Interest: Political Values in the Eighteenth Century*. Bethlehem, Pa.: Lehigh University Press, 1994.

McCandless, Perry. *A History of Missouri, vol. 2: 1820 to 1860*. Columbia: University of Missouri Press, 1972.

McCloskey, Donald N. "English Open Fields as Behavior towards Risk." *Research in Economic History* 1 (1976): 124–70.

———. "The Open Fields of England: Rent, Risk, and the Rate of Interest, 1300–1815." In *Markets in History: Economic Studies of the Past*, edited by David W. Galenson. Cambridge: Cambridge University Press, 1989.

———. "The Persistence of English Common Fields." In *European Peasants and Their Markets: Essays in Agrarian Economic History*, edited by William N. Parker and Eric L. Jones. Princeton: Princeton University Press, 1975.

McCloskey, Robert Green, ed. *The Works of James Wilson*. Cambridge: Harvard University Press, 1967.

McCurdy, Frances Lea. *Stump, Bar, and Pulpit: Speechmaking on the Missouri Frontier*. Columbia: University of Missouri Press, 1969.

McDermott, John Francis. *A Glossary of Mississippi Valley French, 1673–1850*. St. Louis, 1941.

———. "The Myth of the 'Imbecile Governor': Captain Fernando de Leyba and the Defense of St. Louis in 1780." In *The Spanish in the Mississippi Valley*

1762–1804, edited by John Francis McDermott. Urbana: University of Illinois Press, 1974.

———. "Myths and Realities Concerning the Founding of St. Louis." In *The French in the Mississippi Valley*, edited by John Francis McDermott. Urbana: University of Illinois Press, 1965.

———. *Private Libraries in Creole St. Louis*. Baltimore: Johns Hopkins Press, 1938.

McDermott, John Francis, ed. *The Early Histories of St. Louis*. St. Louis: St. Louis Historical Documents Foundation, 1952.

———. *The French in the Mississippi Valley*. Urbana: University of Illinois Press, 1965.

———. *The Spanish in the Mississippi Valley 1762–1804*. Urbana: University of Illinois Press, 1974.

———. *The Western Journals of Washington Irving*. Norman: University of Oklahoma Press, 1944.

McEvoy, Arthur F. *The Fisherman's Problem: Ecology and Law in the California Fisheries, 1850–1980*. Cambridge: Cambridge University Press, 1986.

McIlvaine, H. R., ed. *Minutes of the Council and General Court of Colonial Virginia*. Richmond: Colonial Press, 1924.

McIntosh, Wayne V. *The Appeal of Civil Law: A Political-Economic Analysis of Litigation*. Urbana: University of Illinois Press, 1990.

McKeon, Richard, ed. *The Basic Works of Aristotle*. New York: Random House, 1941.

McKnight, Joseph W. "Law Books on the Hispanic Frontier." *Journal of the West* 27 (1988): 74–84.

McLaren, John, Hamar Foster, and Chet Orloff, eds. *Law for the Elephant, Law for the Beaver: Essays in the History of the North American West*. Regina: Canadian Plains Research Center, 1992.

Merryman, John Henry. *The Civil Law Tradition*. 2d ed. Palo Alto: Stanford University Press, 1985.

Meyer, Michael C. *Water in the Hispanic Southwest: A Social and Legal History, 1550–1850*. Tucson: University of Arizona Press, 1984.

Michelman, Frank I. "Formal and Associational Aims in Procedural Due Process." In *Nomos XVIII: Due Process*, edited by J. Roland Pennock and John W. Chapman. New York: New York University Press, 1977.

Millar, Robert Wyness. *Civil Procedure of the Trial Court in Historical Perspective*. New York: National Conference of Judicial Councils, 1952.

Millon, David. "Positivism in the Historiography of the Common Law." *Wisconsin Law Review* 1989 (1989): 669–714.

Moore, John Preston. *Revolt in Louisiana: The Spanish Occupation, 1766–1770*. Baton Rouge: Louisiana State University Press, 1976.

Moore, Robert, Jr. "A Ray of Hope, Extinguished: St. Louis Slave Suits for Freedom." *Gateway Heritage* 14, no. 3 (1993–94): 4–15.

Morris, Thomas D. *Southern Slavery and the Law, 1619–1860*. Chapel Hill: University of North Carolina Press, 1996.

Musick, James B. *St. Louis as a Fortified Town*. St. Louis: R. F. Miller, 1941.

Nasatir, Abraham P. "Anglo-Spanish Rivalry on the Upper Missouri." *Mississippi Valley Historical Review* 16 (1929): 359–82, 507–28.

———. *Borderland in Retreat: From Spanish Louisiana to the Far Southwest*. Albuquerque: University of New Mexico Press, 1976.

Nasatir, A. P., ed. *Before Lewis and Clark: Documents Illustrating the History of the Missouri 1785–1804*. St. Louis: St. Louis Historical Documents Foundation, 1952.

Neeson, J. M. *Commoners: Common Right, Enclosure and Social Change in England, 1700–1820*. Cambridge: Cambridge University Press, 1993.

Nelson, William E. *Americanization of the Common Law*. Cambridge: Harvard University Press, 1974.

Nicollet, Joseph N. "Sketch of the Early History of St. Louis." 1842. In *The Early Histories of St. Louis*, edited by John Francis McDermott. St. Louis: St. Louis Historical Documents Foundation, 1952.

O'Brien, Gail Williams. *The Legal Fraternity and the Making of a New South Community, 1848–1882*. Athens: University of Georgia Press, 1986.

Offutt, William M., Jr. *Of "Good Laws" and "Good Men": Law and Society in the Delaware Valley, 1680–1710*. Urbana: University of Illinois Press, 1995.

Olson, Mancur. *The Logic of Collective Action*. Cambridge: Harvard University Press, 1965.

"Ordinances of Don Alexander O'Reilly." *Louisiana Law Journal* 1, no. 2 (1841): 1–65.

Ortiz, Roxanne Dunbar. *Roots of Resistance: Land Tenure in New Mexico, 1680–1980*. Los Angeles: UCLA Chicano Studies Research Center and American Indian Studies Center, 1980.

Parker, William N., and Eric L. Jones, eds. *European Peasants and Their Markets: Essays in Agrarian Economic History*. Princeton: Princeton University Press, 1975.

Paxton, John A. "Notes on St. Louis." 1821. In *The Early Histories of St. Louis*, edited by John Francis McDermott. St. Louis: St. Louis Historical Documents Foundation, 1952.

Pease, Theodore Calvin, ed. *The Laws of the Northwest Territory 1788–1800*. Springfield: Illinois State Historical Library, 1925.

Peláez, Manuel J., ed. *Studies in Roman Law and Legal History in Honour of Ramon D'Abadal i de Vinyals on the Occasion of the Centenary*. Barcelona, 1989.

Penick, James Lal, Jr. *The New Madrid Earthquakes*. Rev. ed. Columbia: University of Missouri Press, 1981.

Pennock, J. Roland, and John W. Chapman, eds. *Nomos XVIII: Due Process*. New York: New York University Press, 1977.

Peterson, Charles E. *Colonial St. Louis: Building a Creole Capital.* 2d ed. Tucson: Patrice Press, 1993.

Pittman, Philip. *The Present State of the European Settlements on the Mississippi.* London: J. Nourse, 1770.

Pound, Roscoe. *The Spirit of the Common Law.* Boston: MarshallJones Co., 1921.

Powell, Sumner Chilton. *Puritan Village: The Formation of a New England Town.* Middletown, Conn.: Wesleyan University Press, 1963.

Prest, Wilfred, ed. *Lawyers in Early Modern Europe and America.* New York: Holmes & Meier, 1981.

Primm, James Neal. *Economic Policy in the Development of a Western State: Missouri, 1820–1860.* Cambridge: Harvard University Press, 1954.

———. *Lion of the Valley: St. Louis, Missouri.* 2d ed. Boulder: Pruett Publishing Co., 1990.

Ramirez, Bibiano Torres. *Alejandro O'Reilly en las Indias.* Sevilla: Escuela de Estudios Hispanos-Americanos, 1969.

Reid, John Phillip. "In Accordance with Usage: The Authority of Custom, the Stamp Act Debate, and the Coming of the American Revolution." *Fordham Law Review* 45 (1976): 335–68.

———. *Law for the Elephant: Property and Social Behavior on the Overland Trail.* San Marino, Calif.: Huntington Library, 1980.

———. "The Layers of Western Legal History." In *Law for the Elephant, Law for the Beaver: Essays in the History of the North American West*, edited by John McLaren, Hamar Foster, and Chet Orloff. Regina: Canadian Plains Research Center, 1992.

———. *Policing the Elephant: Crime, Punishment, and Social Behavior on the Overland Trail.* San Marino, Calif.: Huntington Library, 1997.

———. "Principles of Vengeance: Fur Trappers, Indians, and Retaliation for Homicide in the Transboundary North American West." *Western Historical Quarterly* 24 (1993): 21–43.

The Revised Statutes for the State of Missouri, Revised and Digested by the Eighth General Assembly during the Years One Thousand Eight Hundred and Thirty-Four, and One Thousand Eight Hundred and Thirty-Five. St. Louis: Argus Office, 1835.

Richardson, Lemont K. "Private Land Claims in Missouri." *Missouri Historical Review* 50 (1956): 132–44, 271–86, 387–99.

Robertson, James Alexander, ed. *Louisiana under the Rule of Spain, France, and the United States.* Cleveland: A. H. Clark Co., 1911.

Rollings, Willard H. *The Osage: An Ethnohistorical Study of Hegemony on the Prairie-Plains.* Columbia: University of Missouri Press, 1992.

Rose, Carol. "The Comedy of the Commons: Custom, Commerce, and Inherently Public Property." *University of Chicago Law Review* 53 (1986): 711–81.

Rosenthal, Jean-Laurent. *The Fruits of Revolution: Property Rights, Litigation, and French Agriculture, 1700–1860.* Cambridge: Cambridge University Press, 1992.

Rowland, Dunbar, ed. *Official Letter Books of W. C. C. Claiborne 1801–1816*. Jackson, Miss.: State Department of Archives and History, 1917.

Russell, Thomas D. "The Antebellum Courthouse as Creditors' Domain: Trial-Court Activity in South Carolina and the Concomitance of Lending and Litigation." *American Journal of Legal History* 40 (1996): 331–64.

Schafer, Judith Kelleher. *Slavery, Civil Law, and the Supreme Court of Louisiana*. Baton Rouge: Louisiana State University Press, 1994.

Scharf, J. Thomas. *History of Saint Louis City and County from the Earliest Periods to the Present Day*. Philadelphia: L. H. Everts & Co., 1883.

Schroeder, Walter. "The Environmental Setting of the St. Louis Region." In *Common Fields: An Environmental History of St. Louis*, edited by Andrew Hurley. St. Louis: Missouri Historical Society Press, 1997.

Schultz, Christian. *Travels on an Inland Voyage*. New York: Isaac Riley, 1810.

Sellers, Charles. *The Market Revolution: Jacksonian America, 1815–1846*. Oxford: Oxford University Press, 1991.

Selvin, Molly. *This Tender and Delicate Business: The Public Trust Doctrine in American Law and Economic Policy*. New York: Garland, 1987.

Smith, Henry Nash. *Virgin Land: The American West as Symbol and Myth*. Cambridge: Harvard University Press, 1950.

Starr, Paul. *The Social Transformation of American Medicine*. New York: Basic Books, 1982.

Statistical Abstract of the United States 1994. Washington, D.C.: U.S. Department of Commerce, 1994.

Stoddard, Amos. *Sketches, Historical and Descriptive, of Louisiana*. Philadelphia: Mathew Carey, 1812.

Stout, David B., Erminie Wheeler-Voegelin, and Emily J. Blasingham. *Sac, Fox and Iowa Indians, vol. 2: Indians of E. Missouri, W. Illinois, and S. Wisconsin from the Proto-Historic Period to 1804*. New York: Garland, 1974.

Sullivan, James. *The History of Land Titles in Massachusetts*. Boston: I. Thomas and E. T. Andrews, 1801.

Tachau, Mary K. Bonsteel. *Federal Courts in the Early Republic: Kentucky 1789–1816*. Princeton: Princeton University Press, 1978.

Tanner, Norman P., ed. *Decrees of the Ecumenical Councils*. Washington: Georgetown University Press, 1990.

Texada, David Ker. *Alejandro O'Reilly and the New Orleans Rebels*. Lafayette: University of Southwestern Louisiana, 1970.

Thelen, David. *Paths of Resistance: Tradition and Dignity in Industrializing Missouri*. New York: Oxford University Press, 1986.

Thomas, Rosemary Hyde. *It's Good to Tell You: French Folktales from Missouri*. Columbia: University of Missouri Press, 1981.

Thompson, E. P. *The Making of the English Working Class*. New York: Vintage Books, 1963.

Thorne, Tanis C. *The Many Hands of My Relations: French and Indians on the Lower Missouri*. Columbia: University of Missouri Press, 1996.

Trexler, Harrison Anthony. *Slavery in Missouri, 1804–1865*. Baltimore: Johns Hopkins University Press, 1914.

Unruh, John D. *The Plains Across: The Overland Emigrants and the Trans-Mississippi West, 1840–60*. Paperback ed., Urbana: University of Illinois Press, 1982.

Usner, Daniel H., Jr. *Indians, Settlers, and Slaves in a Frontier Exchange Economy: The Lower Mississippi Valley Before 1783*. Chapel Hill: University of North Carolina Press, 1992.

van Ee, Daun. *David Dudley Field and the Reconstruction of the Law*. New York: Garland, 1986.

Van Kleffens, E. N. *Hispanic Law until the End of the Middle Ages*. Edinburgh: Edinburgh University Press, 1968.

Vassberg, David E. *Land and Society in Golden Age Castile*. Cambridge: Cambridge University Press, 1984.

———. "The Spanish Background: Problems Concerning Ownership, Usurpations, and Defense of Common Lands in 16th Century Castile." In *Spanish and Mexican Land Grants and the Law*, edited by Malcolm Ebright. Manhattan, Ks.: Sunflower University Press, 1989.

Violette, Eugene Morrow. "Spanish Land Claims in Missouri." *Washington University Studies* 8, no. 2 (1920–21): 167–200.

Wade, Richard C. *The Urban Frontier: The Rise of Western Cities, 1790–1830*. Cambridge: Harvard University Press, 1959.

Wallach, Kate. *Bibliographic History of Louisiana Civil Law Sources, Roman, French, and Spanish*. Baton Rouge: Louisiana State Law Institute, 1955.

Walton, Clifford Stevens. *The Civil Law in Spain and Spanish-America*. Washington, D.C.: W. H. Lowdermilk & Co., 1900.

Weber, David J. *The Spanish Frontier in North America*. New Haven: Yale University Press, 1992.

Weisbrod, Carol. *The Boundaries of Utopia*. New York: Pantheon, 1980.

Westphall, Victor. *Mercedes Reales: Hispanic Land Grants of the Upper Rio Grande Region*. Albuquerque: University of New Mexico Press, 1983.

Weyrauch, Walter Otto, and Maureen Anne Bell. "Autonomous Lawmaking: The Case of the 'Gypsies.'" *Yale Law Journal* 103 (1993): 323–99.

Whitaker, Arthur Preston. *The Mississippi Question 1795–1803: A Study in Trade, Politics, and Diplomacy*. New York: C. Appleton-Century Co., 1934.

White, G. Edward. *The Marshall Court and Cultural Change, 1815–35*. New York: Macmillan, 1988.

White, Richard. *Land Use, Environment, and Social Change: The Shaping of Island County, Washington*. Seattle: University of Washington Press, 1980.

———. *The Middle Ground: Indians, Empires, and Republics in the Great Lakes Region, 1650–1815*. Cambridge: Cambridge University Press, 1991.

Williams, Henry W. *History, Abstracts of Title, Evidences of Location, etc., Relating to the Common Field Lots of the South Grand Prairie and Cul de Sac of the Grand Prairie and an Argument in Support of Cozens' Surveys*. St. Louis: Republican, 1854.

Worster, Donald. *Nature's Economy: A History of Ecological Ideas*. 2d ed. Cambridge: Cambridge University Press, 1994.

Wunder, John R. *Inferior Courts, Superior Justice: A History of the Justices of the Peace on the Northwest Frontier, 1853–1889*. Westport: Greenwood Press, 1979.

Yelling, J. A. *Common Field and Enclosure in England 1450–1850*. London: Macmillan, 1977.

Zablocki, Benjamin. *Alienation and Charisma: A Study of Contemporary American Communes*. New York: Free Press, 1980.

THESES AND DISSERTATIONS

Briggs, Winstanley. "The Forgotten Colony: *Le Pays des Illinois*." Ph.D. diss., University of Chicago, 1985.

Gould, Lois Virginia Meacham. "In Full Enjoyment of Their Liberty: The Free Women of Color of the Gulf Ports of New Orleans, Mobile, and Pensacola, 1769–1860." Ph.D. diss., Emory University, 1991.

Green, Mary Susan. "The Material Culture of a Pre-Enclosure Village in Upper Louisiana: Open Fields, Houses, and Cabinetry in Colonial Ste. Genevieve, 1750–1804." M.A. thesis, University of Missouri, 1983.

Hanger, Kimberly S. "Personas de Varias Clases y Colores: Free People of Color in Spanish New Orleans, 1769–1803." Ph.D. diss., University of Florida, 1991.

Harris, James Griffith. "The Background and Development of Early Missouri Trial Courts." Ph.D. diss., University of Missouri, 1949.

Holt, Glen E. "The Shaping of St. Louis 1763–1860." Ph.D. diss., University of Chicago, 1975.

Macphail, William A. B. "Land Hunger and Closed-Field Husbandry on the New England Frontier, 1630–1665: The First Generation of Settlement in Watertown, Massachusetts." Ph.D. diss., Brown University, 1972.

Melom, Halvor Gordon. "The Economic Development of St. Louis, 1803–1846." Ph.D. diss., University of Missouri, 1947.

Phelan, Doris Ann. "Boosterism in St. Louis, 1810–1860." Ph.D. diss., St. Louis University, 1970.

Reichard, Maximilian Ivan. "The Origins of Urban Police: Freedom and Order in Antebellum St. Louis." Ph.D. diss., Washington University, 1975.

Rosin, Wilbert Henry. "Hamilton Rowan Gamble: Missouri's Civil War Governor." Ph.D. diss., University of Missouri, 1960.

Sandweiss, Eric Todd. "Construction and Community in South St. Louis, 1850–1910." Ph.D. diss., University of California, Berkeley, 1991.

Vogel, Rachel F. "Social Life in St. Louis, 1764–1804." M.A. thesis, Washington University, 1921.

NEWSPAPERS

Missouri Gazette
Missouri Republican

CASES

Barry v. Gamble, 44 U.S. 32 (1845)
Bates v. Hinton, 4 Mo. 78 (1835)
Bryan v. Kennett, 113 U.S. 179 (1885)
Carondelet v. Saint Louis, 66 U.S. 179 (1861)
Carpenter v. Rannels, 86 U.S. 138 (1873)
Chouteau v. Molony, 57 U.S. 203 (1850)
Chouteau's Heirs v. United States, 34 U.S. 137 (1835)
City of St. Louis v. Morton, 6 Mo. 476 (1840)
Delassus v. United States, 34 U.S. 117 (1835)
Dent v. Emmeger, 81 U.S. 308 (1871)
Downing v. State, 4 Mo. 572 (1837)
Gibson v. Chouteau, 80 U.S. 92 (1871)
Glasgow v. Baker, 128 U.S. 560 (1888)
Glasgow v. Hortiz, 66 U.S. 595 (1861)
Gordon v. State, 4 Mo. 375 (1836)
Guitard v. Stoddard, 57 U.S. 494 (1850)
Haps v. Hewitt, 97 Ill. 499 (1881)
Helm v. Wilson, 4 Mo. 41 (1835)
Hughes v. Oklahoma, 441 U.S. 322 (1979)
Huidekoper's Lessee v. Douglass, 7 U.S. 1 (1805)
Illinois Central R.R. Co. v. Illinois, 146 U.S. 387 (1892)
King v. Bailey, 6 Mo. 575 (1840)
Landes v. Brant, 51 U.S. 348 (1850)
Les Bois v. Bramell, 45 U.S. 449 (1846)
Mackay v. Dillon, 45 U.S. 421 (1846)
Mackay v. Easton, 86 U.S. 619 (1873)
Maguire v. Tyler, 75 U.S. 650 (1868)
Magwire v. Tyler, 66 U.S. 195 (1861)
Massey v. Papin, 65 U.S. 362 (1860)
Meegan v. Boyle, 60 U.S. 130 (1856)
Morrison v. Jackson, 92 U.S. 654 (1875)
O'Fallon v. Elliott, 1 Mo. 364 (1823)
Riddick v. Walsh, 15 Mo. 519 (1852)

Scott v. Emerson, 15 Mo. 576 (1852)
Shepherd v. Trigg, 7 Mo. 151 (1841)
Soulard's Heirs v. United States, 35 U.S. 100 (1836)
Sporhase v. Nebraska ex rel. Douglas, 458 U.S. 941 (1982)
State v. Fry, 4 Mo. 120 (1835)
Stevens v. City of Cannon Beach, 317 Ore. 131, 854 P.2d 449 (1993), cert. denied, 114 S. Ct. 1332 (1994)
Stoddard v. Chambers, 43 U.S. 284 (1844)
Strother v. Lucas, 31 U.S. 763 (1832)
Strother v. Lucas, 37 U.S. 410 (1838)
Tyler v. Magwire, 84 U.S. 253 (1872)
Vidal v. The Mayor, Aldermen, and Citizens of Philadelphia, 43 U.S. 127 (1844)
Woodson & Trigg v. McClelland, 4 Mo. 495 (1837)

Index